THE ECONOMICS OF AGING

THE ECONOMICS OF AGING

Fourth Edition

JAMES H. SCHULZ
Florence Heller Graduate School
Brandeis University

AUBURN HOUSE
New York • Westport, Connecticut • London

Library of Congress Cataloging-in-Publication Data

Schulz, James H.
  The economics of aging / James H. Schulz.—4th ed.
  p. cm.
  Bibliography: p.
  Includes index.
  ISBN 0-86569-174-6
  1. Old age pensions—United States. 2. Retirement income—United
States. 2. Aged—United States—Economic conditions. I. Title.
HD7105.35U6S38 1988
330.973'0927'088—dc19   88-993

Library of Congress Catalog Card Number: 88-993
ISBN: 0-86569-174-6

First published in 1988

Auburn House, 88 Post Road West, Westport, CT 06881
An imprint of Greenwood Publishing Group, Inc.

Printed in the United States of America

The paper used in this book complies with the
Permanent Paper Standard issued by the National
Information Standards Organization (Z39.48-1984).

10 9 8 7 6 5 4 3 2

CONTENTS

CHAPTER 5
Social Security: Old Age and Survivors' Benefits · 121

CHAPTER 6
Social Security Financing: Who Pays?
Who Should Pay? · 155

PREFACE

"It was the best of times, it was the worst of times . . . ," wrote Charles Dickens in *A Tale of Two Cities*. This comment describing late eighteenth century Europe quite aptly sums up the situation with regard to the economics of aging in the United States today. In a sense, things have never been better; in another sense, things have never been worse.

If you are interested or concerned about the quality of life in old age, then you cannot avoid confronting some major questions related to who will pay and how we will pay for those "golden years." This is a book about those questions, including the following:

- Will social security be there when I need it?
- Will my retirement income be adequate?
- How do I judge the quality of the pension plans covering me?
- What options do I have to deal with skyrocketing medical costs?
- When should I retire: never, as early as possible, or when everybody else does?
- How serious will be the problem of inflation as I grow older?

But this is not a book designed solely to help individuals with their retirement planning. Many of the answers to our personal questions about the economics of aging depend on evolving policies and practices of business and government. Much of the book, therefore, looks at those past and present practices—the creation of what some call "the welfare state." We review the development of both public and private pensions, medical insurance, employment assistance, and aid to the "truly needy."

What does the future hold for the American welfare state and for those growing old in it? This book (or any other book) cannot provide all the answers. But it does provide its readers with an understanding of most basic underlying factors affecting the issues we must confront as a nation in the years to come. Any student of aging—be he or she studying for a degree, teaching, running a business, or working in government for the people—will be confronted continuously in the years to come up with some tough questions. There will be questions related to the so-called "economic burden" of the elderly, the relationship between entitlements and the federal deficit, jobs for the old vs. jobs for the young, the need to ration medical care, and the prospects for intergenerational conflict.

The questions, as I have expressed them above, are the fuel for media headlines and political rhetoric. You will not find much of that polemic language in these pages. Yet the book as a whole has much to say about the burning political issues of today and tomorrow. What it tries to do is to open up to both economists and noneconomists alike the now-burgeoning storehouse of social science knowledge and research related to these topics. I have tried to minimize economic jargon and the more technical aspects of the existing literature, while at the same time bringing the reader close to the cutting edge of our knowledge to date. The overwhelmingly favorable response to the previous three editions and the laudatory comments of so many prior readers indicate that the book walks that tightrope fairly well.

This new edition retains the organizational structure of the third, but the content of each chapter has been significantly changed to keep pace with the expanding wealth of knowledge in the area. Fortunately, the constraint on the length of the manuscript in prior editions was relaxed by the new publisher, allowing expansion of many parts of the book.

The success of past editions (and hopefully this new edition) owes much to those who have taken the time to review, critique, and suggest improvements in both organization and content of the book. The list of contributors over the years now numbers over 100 people. My heartfelt thanks to all of them and especially to Margaret Stubbs, who has assisted me in the production of all four versions.

This edition benefits from the review of various chapters by the following people: Stuart Altman, Merton C. Bernstein, Susan Grad, Hilda Kahne, Eric Kingson, Thomas Leavitt, Walter Leutz, Alicia Munnell, Robert Myers, Regina O'Grady-LeShane, Jane Ross, and Harold Sheppard. My sincere thanks to them.

The comments and help of my father-in-law, Clark Tibbitts, are sorely missed in this edition. Known to many as "the father of social gerontology," Clark died suddenly in October 1985 after a lifetime of dedicated work and inspiration promoting the welfare of people during the later years of their lives. As he did for many others, he was the person who got me, a young economics graduate student at Yale, interested in the then unfashionable topics (for an economist) of pensions and gerontology. Through his patient but demanding readings of my dissertation projecting aged income, he not only helped me improve my writing skills but also encouraged me to make data and analysis serve the public good rather than pander to the current popular vogues of my new academic discipline.

Clark Tibbitts wrote the introduction to the previous three editions. For the third edition I asked him not to focus on what I had written but rather to reflect on how the economics of aging had changed during *his* lifetime. As with all the tasks he undertook, he did not approach the job lightly. The resulting personal essay is a gem of insight and historic reflection. It is reproduced again as the introduction to this edition.

Clark Tibbitts retired at the age of 80, leaving the U.S. Administration on Aging after working 53 years in jobs related to aging. He left behind a big legacy. This book is only one small part of it. It is to his memory and inspiration that this book is dedicated.

West Newton, Massachusetts   JAMES H. SCHULZ
March 7, 1988

INTRODUCTION

by Clark Tibbitts

The appearance of three editions* of *The Economics of Aging* within a period of eight years testifies to the dynamic nature of the subject and to its cogency for students, practitioners, policymakers, and researchers in the field of gerontology and its underlying disciplines. The invitation to contribute an introduction to this new and extensively revised edition affords me the opportunity to reflect on some of the principal developments that have taken place in the field during the more than half century of my working life.

My first awareness of the economics of aging came to me during my adolescent years in Chicago. The United Charities of Chicago used to conduct an annual "tag day" to raise funds for needy older people in the Chicago area and help support the county home for the destitute. Hundreds of volunteers stationed on busy streets invited pedestrians to drop money into a hand-held container; contributors were awarded a stringed tag to be worn for the day, identifying them as "givers."

My initial professional experience with the economics of aging came during the Great Depression, when workers by the million were unemployed, as the saying went, "through no fault of their own"; when thousands of businesses and banks were failing; and when farms were being foreclosed in similar numbers. President Hoover attempted to assure the country that the return to prosperity was "just around the corner" and that there would soon be "a chicken in every pot." He backed his optimism with firm resolve, sending General Douglas MacArthur on horseback to break up the March of the Unemployed on the Washington Capitol.

Hoover's obstinancy helped elect Franklin Roosevelt to the

---

*Editor's note: As explained in the author's preface, this introduction is reproduced from the third edition and was written in 1985, just before Clark Tibbitts' death.

presidency. Taking office in March 1933, Roosevelt forthwith launched a constellation of alphabet agencies—NRA, FERA, PNA, WPA, FCA, HOLC, AAA, FmHA, PHA, and CCC—to give depressed Americans a New Deal. Every agency addressed the economics of aging in one way or another.

Restless to have a part in the precedent-breaking government actions, I joined the research unit of the Federal Emergency Relief Administration (FERA) and shortly thereafter the Public Health Service's National Health Inventory, funded by the Works Progress Administration (WPA). The two experiences revealed that one-fourth of all workers and one-half of *older* workers were unemployed and that chronic illness and difficulty in obtaining medical care were especially prevalent among older people, particularly those with low incomes.

I therefore reacted with enthusiasm to President Roosevelt's appointment of the Committee on Economic Security under the chairmanship of Frances Perkins. The committee drew up specifications for an old age insurance program (OASI), modified before it became operative to include survivors; a program of old age assistance (OAA) to provide income to the needy while the OASI program was building an operating reserve; and an unemployment compensation program for short-term financial assistance. As Professor Schulz discusses in his book, the objectives of the OASI program were both to remove older workers from the work force and to assist the states in providing income to the elderly needy during a period of dire economic vulnerability. The means-tested OAA program served millions not covered by OASI and was replaced by the supplemental security income program (SSI) in 1974.

I agreed with the late Professor Fred W. Cottrell's appraisal that enactment of his social security legislation represented the most radical extension of government into the private lives of citizens ever taken by the American government. The supplemental security income program (SSI), which superseded OAA in 1974, was also a dramatic and far-reaching development. The coverage it provides closes gaps left by the other financial aid programs and attempts to assure that no older person today will be without at least a modicum of income. Responsibility for management of SSI was assigned to the Social Security Administration to help remove the stigma attached to receipt of noncontributory assistance.

Social security was designed originally to provide only a modest floor of income. The assumption was that additional support required to sustain an adequate level of living would be available from earnings, personal savings, pensions, and gifts from adult children.

As this book explains in detail, the assumption proved to be quite erroneous; social security has achieved a much larger role than originally anticipated. The older population was increasing rapidly, doubling between 1900 and 1930 and again between 1930 and 1950. The transformation to a mechanized, industrial economy led many employers to divest themselves of older workers in favor of the plentiful supply of youth eager for jobs. Private pensions were few, and many adults were unable to support both young families and older parents as well. I was gratified, therefore, to witness the amendments that liberalized social security by broadening coverage, expanding protection, and raising benefit levels.

I was equally pleased with the later emergence of private pension plans that raised many retirement incomes above the basic social security levels. The emerging pension movement was advanced significantly during World War II, when employers used the promise of pensions to recruit urgently needed workers. Growth continued when the Supreme Court sanctioned (1948–49) organized labor's effort to include pensions—rationalized as deferred wages—in collective bargaining. Private pension systems now cover about half of all private wage and salary workers.

Enactment of legislation in 1965 for establishment of the Medicare-Medicaid programs represented to me a third major development in the economics of aging during the period. The Committee on Economic Security in 1935 omitted health insurance from its recommendations on the assumption that it could be obtained easily after the basic social security program had been put in place. Instead, organized medicine, the life insurance industry, and others opposed to further government intervention into affairs of the private sector delayed health insurance legislation for 30 years.

As I have observed it, one of the most compelling issues in the economics of aging over the century has been that of achieving a harmonious relationship between chronological age, employability, and pension eligibility. As noted above, employers have responded to our transformation into an industrial economy by replacing older workers with what they presumed to be healthier, stronger, physically and mentally more agile youth. At the beginning of this century, Sir William Osler, a Canadian physician, rationalized management's position when he stated that men past 40 were comparatively useless and those past 60 were absolutely useless. Both Theodore and Franklin Roosevelt disparaged the physical and intellectual performances of those who had survived the middle years. The social security eligibility age of 65, reflecting a compromise between reality and affordability, was adopted by employers as the age for compulsory retirement, with additional inducements for even earlier withdrawal.

Most of us teaching, doing research, and thinking about aging policy rebelled at the prejudice, inequity, and costs of this negative view of older people. Supported by Department of Labor and other studies of older worker performance, gerontologists saw compulsory retirement at age 65 or earlier to be wasteful of experienced manpower—manpower demonstrated to be careful, conscientious, loyal, and reliable.

A succession of national conferences on aging held strongly to this view. By 1967 older worker advocates were able to persuade the Congress to pass the Age Discrimination in Employment Act prohibiting discrimination in employment after age 40.

As I look back over the years, I am pleased by the variety of actions that have been taken to protect the income and employment of older persons. Federal and state income taxes provide for liberal personal exemptions; most states offer partial property tax exemptions for the elderly. Federal-state community programs offer food stamps, group and home-delivered meals, reduced local transportation fares, special housing (often subsidized), assistance with legal problems, and long-term care options.

In *The Economics of Aging* Professor Schulz has shown that the United States has gone far toward assuring older people opportunity to continue to enjoy the amenities and security of living the country seeks for all of its citizens. Government programs have laid the foundation, and the private sector has played a key complementary role. But, as I have emphasized in my writings over the years, these efforts have not so much substituted for the traditional activities of individuals and families as they have enhanced them and made them more viable. To my mind, confronting the challenges of aging in America, including the *economics* of aging, is truly a cooperative endeavor among various groups and institutions. And that is the way it should be in today's enlightened society.

Chapter 1

POPULATION AGING, DEPENDENCY, AND RETIREMENT

Not too many years ago it was relatively easy to write about the economic situation of the elderly population. All one needed to do was cite statistics that confirmed what most people knew from either personal experience or observation. In the past most of the elderly suffered from serious economic deprivation. Their incomes were inadequate, and inflation exacerbated the situation by reducing real incomes and eroding savings. Most people knew that the aged were one of the largest poverty groups in the country.

Today the situation is greatly improved, due in large part to our nation's very positive response to the past economic plight of the elderly. During the past few decades major breakthroughs have occurred in the development of private and public programs to deal with the economic problems of old age. For example:

1. Over the past 15 years, social security old-age benefits have been increased by almost 200 percent, significantly faster than inflation over the same period.
2. Private pension programs have spread throughout industry and have grown rapidly—with dramatic increases in benefit levels.
3. Medicare and Medicaid were legislated—currently providing over $100 billion a year in benefits to older persons.
4. Property tax relief laws have been legislated in all our states.
5. The state old age assistance programs have been abolished and a new Supplemental Security Income (SSI) program was

1

put in its place. SSI raised benefit levels in 24 states above previous levels—in some cases dramatically. In addition, a national food stamp program helps low-income people of all ages.

6. Social security, SSI, and the food stamp program are fully and automatically indexed for inflation.

Despite the economic problems that remain (which will be discussed later in this book), we must not lose sight of the important economic gains that have been made. Dramatic changes have occurred in the levels of income provided older persons, especially from public and private pensions. Consequently, there has been a significant improvement in the general economic status of this group—traditionally viewed as poverty-stricken. In fact, a study by Timothy Smeeding (1982) finds that if both money and in-kind income (defined on p. 42) are counted, few elderly currently fall below the official government "poverty level." In 1979, counting only money income, the poverty rate was 14.7 percent. However, Smeeding estimates that only about 5 percent fell below the poverty level, if in-kind benefits related to food, housing, and medical care are taken into account.

The methodology used to make these estimates is controversial, and hence not everyone agrees with the results. The Smeeding findings serve to dramatize, however, the undisputed progress that has been made in raising many from the ranks of the "most poor" to the ranks of the "near poor."[1]

So rapid and so great has been this improvement in the welfare of the aged that assessments of their condition have not kept pace with progress. Not only the general public but also many professionals concerned with the problems of the elderly have a serious misconception regarding the current economic situation of the aged. A study by Erdman Palmore (1977) reports that about one-half of the graduate students and faculty in the field of human development and aging at two prominent universities did not recognize as an *incorrect* statement the true-false quiz question: "The majority of old people have incomes below the poverty level (as defined by the federal government)." In contrast, these same students and faculty answered correctly about 90 percent of the other questions in the aging quiz covering 24 other areas of knowledge about older persons.

There is no doubt that many people are unaware of the rapidly improving economic status of the aged in America. Still fewer have

---

[1] Whether the progress is sufficient is a different question. In the next chapter we discuss, for example, the appropriateness of the official poverty index.

thought about its implications for policy on the aging. Given, for example, the projected shortfall of the social security system in meeting its long-term projected obligations (see Chapter 6), this news of a greatly improved economic situation for the aged is a development to be welcomed. As various ways of raising additional revenues for the system are considered, it is certainly heartening to hear that older people today are economically much better off than they were little more than a decade ago.

The decline in the seriousness of the elderly's economic problems means that the task of helping the aged may not need to be as high on the social agenda as in prior years. In fact, given the rising costs of providing for the aged, some people have begun to argue that we have already gone too far.

Aged Programs, the Federal Budget, and the Elderly

The significant, semi-hidden story in the . . . federal budget is that America's public resources are increasingly being mortgaged for the use of a single group within our country: the elderly.

The above quote is similar to many statements made in recent years. But it was voiced almost two decades ago by columnist David Broder (1973), writing in the *Washington Post*. Broder's article was one of the first assessments to raise questions about growing federal expenditures for the elderly.

In 1978, Health, Education and Welfare Secretary Joseph A. Califano, Jr. became the first cabinet secretary to publicize the problem of rising federal expenditures for the elderly. He estimated that $112 billion was paid out that year by federal programs assisting the elderly. And he projected that these expenditures would rise from 24 percent of the federal budget in 1978 to 40 percent in the early part of the 21st century (Califano, 1979).

A *Forbes* magazine article typifies the growing media attention being given to this issue. A feature article titled "The Old Folks" was headlined: "The myth is that they're sunk in poverty. The reality is that they're living well. The trouble is there are too many of them—God bless 'em" (Flint, 1980).

More recently, economist Barbara Boyle Torrey (1982), while employed in the federal government's Office of Management and Budget, summarized the issue in this way:

The traditional tradeoff between guns and butter may in the future be better characterized as a tradeoff between guns and canes.

The increase in the older population is likely to generate an increasingly powerful fiscal interest group, concentrating its attention on the federal government. The estimated outlay increases that could be expected in the future because of the increases in the older population are not insupportable. . . . It does, however, represent a clear shift in future priorities for the federal government that will need to be confronted.

When the Reagan administration commenced in 1981, the aged felt the effects of the first broad action taken to cut back expenditures for the elderly. President Reagan's budget request for 1983 called for $6.5 billion less expenditures for aged programs than would have occurred under pre-Reagan policies. Ultimately, $5.2 billion in cuts, over half in the Medicare programs, was legislated. In a review of both these spending decreases and the tax reductions occurring during this period, Storey (1983) concludes that the impacts varied greatly by level of income. The well-to-do aged received substantial tax cuts and escaped major benefit cuts; the middle-income aged were helped a little by tax cuts but were more affected by benefit cuts; and the low-income aged received no tax-cut benefits and bore the brunt of many of the largest spending cuts. "The net result of the policy changes made during the past 27 months [1981–83] has been to squeeze the resources available to the neediest among our Nation's elderly populations" (Storey, 1983).

According to political scientist Robert Binstock, the stereotypes that the aged are poor, frail, relatively impotent as a political force, and more deserving of help than some other groups in poverty have given way to a new set of axioms. The aged are increasingly perceived as relatively well off and a potent political force that will soon pose an unsustainable burden on the economy. "These new axioms regarding older persons have provided the foundation for the emergence of the aged as scapegoat in American society. That is, the aged are bearing the blame for a variety of economic and political frustrations" (Binstock, 1983).

 Have we collectively done enough for the elderly? Or have we, perhaps, done too much? To answer these questions we can no longer generalize about the economic situation of all the aged as one group. Instead, we must look at the multitude of programs for the elderly and analyze their impact on various subgroups of the elderly population. We must distinguish, for example, between the very old aged (the "vulnerable aged") and those just retiring, between widowed and married women, and between those families with two or more pensions and those with only social security.

In the chapters to follow we will survey the major economic changes that have occurred among various groups of the aged. But before we do this, it is important to discuss the changes in retirement expectations that have occurred in American society and the important demographic shifts that are now occurring.

The Right to Retire

As observed by Donahue, Orbach, and Pollak (1960), "retirement is a phenomenon of modern industrial society. . . . The older people of previous societies were not retired persons; there was no retirement role." A number of developments, however, changed this.

Even before public and private pension systems were widely established, large numbers of older persons were not in the labor force. As early as 1900, for example, almost one-third of all men age 65 and over were "retired," in large part because of health problems. Prior to the institution of **pension**[2] systems, however, older persons not in the labor force had to rely on their own (often meager) resources, help from relatives, or public and private charity. Over the years recognition spread that complete reliance on these sources of old age support was unsatisfactory. *Public pensions were, in part, a reaction to the need of more rational support mechanisms for older persons unable to work.*

Industrialization created a new problem. In contrast to the farm, where people could almost always "work" (even if it was at reduced levels), industry was characterized by a large amount of job insecurity. Recurrent **recessions** and **depressions** and shifts in employment opportunities created competition for the available jobs. *Thus, another motivation for establishing pensions was to encourage older workers to leave the work force and create jobs for younger workers.*

But probably most important of all, industrial growth—fueled by rapid technological change—resulted in vast increases in economic output. As we discuss at length in Chapter 3, economic growth provides an expanding option for greater leisure with a simultaneous increase in living standards. That is, the rapid economic growth of the 20th century made it possible to support more

---

[2] Many technical terms appearing in the text are defined or explained in a glossary at the back of the book. Terms in the glossary appear in boldface type the first time they enter the discussion in a major way and, in the case of very important terms, again at first appearance in subsequent chapters.

easily older people who could not (or did not wish to) work. Retirement became economically feasible.

Thus, we see the institutionalization of retirement arising as a result of and reaction to (1) the needs of large numbers of elderly unable to work, (2) short-run fluctuations in employment opportunities for both the young and the old, and (3) expanding national economic output over the long run. Pension programs were developed that "provided compensation based upon years of service rather than upon need per se. They were to emerge as an 'earned right' and were to become instrumental in defining a retirement status as appropriate for the older worker" (Friedman and Orbach, 1974).

Changing Expectations

As just indicated, until recently retirement meant dependency— on relatives, friends, private charity, or government welfare. Indications are that many elderly tended to accept a subsistence lifestyle as the best that could be expected in old age. Attitudinal surveys have found, for example, that despite their relatively low economic status, very high proportions of the elderly viewed their economic situation as satisfactory and not below their expectations.[3]

In earlier periods, studies did find that many people close to retirement viewed the approaching period negatively. According to Friedman and Orbach (1974), "the widespread opposition to retirement reported in studies during the 1940s and the early 1950s reflected an overwhelming concern over the consequences of serious deprivation associated with retirement." More recent studies, however, have found less negativism toward retirement as the economics of retirement have improved. Some researchers (for example, Shanas, 1977 and Atchley and Robinson, 1982) have found generally positive attitudes toward retirement both before and after retirement.

Thus, retirement expectations are changing. In part, this has resulted from increases in living standards at all ages. More importantly, the development of pension programs and the continuous improvement in their provisions have given the elderly

---

[3] See, for example, the report of Louis Harris and Associates listed in the "Suggested Readings" at the end of this chapter. For a conceptual framework that incorporates the notion of relative deprivation to help explain the perceived financial adequacy among the elderly, see Liang and Fairchild (1979).

increasing independence. For the first time, a comfortable standard of living is within the reach of many. And increasing pension benefits and pension coverage seem to stimulate demands for still higher retirement incomes.

Aging Populations

At the same time that retirement income expectations are changing, we are witnessing an aging of populations around the world. Demographers classify countries into "young," "mature," and "aged" populations according to the proportion of population age 65 and over. Cowgill and Holmes (1970) have suggested that countries with 4 to 6 percent aged should be classified as young, 7 to 9 percent as mature, and 10 percent or more as aged. Using this classification scheme, Myers (1982) finds for 1980 that 89 countries of the world were young, 10 were mature, and 27 were aged. Table 1–1 shows the number and percentage of aged persons for various regions of the world in 1980.

In the United States, persons age 65 or older represent about 11 to 12 percent of the population. This age group has increased more rapidly than the whole population. Yet, as Siegel (1976) points out, the growth of this age group during the 1960s and early 1970s was below its growth during the 1950s and the preceding decades. Given relatively stable mortality and net immigration rates, fluc-

Table 1–1 Population 65 Years and Over in Various Regions of the World, 1980

Region	Number (millions)	Percent
World	258	6
Developed	129	11
Developing	129	4
Africa	14	3
Latin America	15	4
Northern America	27	11
East Asia	67	6
South Asia	43	3
Europe	63	13
Oceania	2	8
USSR	27	10

Source: Based on data in George C. Myers, "The Aging of Populations." In Robert H. Binstock, Wing-Sun Chow, and J. H Schulz, *International Perspectives on Aging: Population and Policy Challenges* (New York: United Nations Fund for Population Activities, 1982), Tables 2 and 4.

tuations in population growth since the World War II have largely been due to fluctuations in the **fertility rate** (births per 1,000 women 15 to 44 years old). Figure 1–1 shows the changing fertility rate over the 1930–1981 period. Since the early 1970s, the rate has remained about the same. In 1986 the fertility rate was 1,840 births per 1,000.

Fertility is now at a historic low. If it remains near its present level, the U.S. Census Bureau projects a "graying" of the United States population with the following major characteristics:

1. The 65-and-over population will rise to between 18 and 23 percent of the total population by the year 2035.
2. The "very old" in their late 70s and 80s will become an increasingly larger fraction of the elderly population—rising from 38 to 47 percent.
3. Since women's life expectancy exceeds that of men by a growing number of years, the proportion of widows will rise; and they will face an ever longer widowhood. The sex ratio of the 65-and-over population showed 100 women for every 69 men in 1975; by the year 2000, the difference will grow to 6.5 million, or 100 women for every 65 men.
4. Given the "baby boom" of the 1940s and 1950s, the aged

Per 1,000
females 15–44

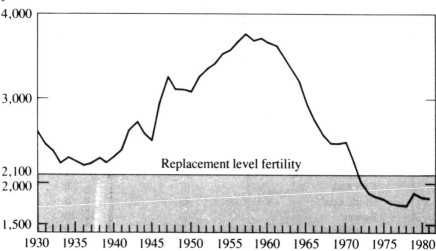

Figure 1-1   Total Fertility Rate, 1930-1981. Source: Based on U.S. Bureau of the Census, "Population Profile of the United States: 1981," *Current Population Reports*, Series P-20, No. 374 (Washington, D.C.: U.S. Government Printing Office, 1982), Table 5-1.

population will increase exceptionally rapidly around the year 2010.

5. The **median** age of the population will rise sharply—increasing from 29 in 1977 to about age 37 in the year 2020 (Figure 1–2).

The progressive aging of the population and the longer life expectancy of women create a new and growing problem. Older men are usually married and relatively few live alone. In contrast, almost two-thirds of older women are widowed, divorced, or single, and almost half of them live alone or with nonrelatives. As Sheppard (1978) points out:

Look at what's going to happen to a group of Older Americans that will affect dramatically our individual lives and our government's commitments more than ever before: the population 80 and older between 1977 and 2000. That age group will grow, not by 20 percent, but by 67 percent. . . . A smaller and smaller proportion of the very old who are in the greatest state of dependency will actually have any younger children who might otherwise be counted on to provide family based care. [Sheppard, 1978][4]

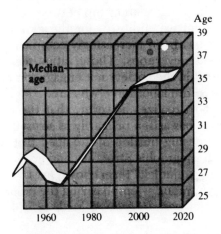

Figure 1-2   The Changing Median Age of the Population. Source: Reproduced from *National Journal, The Economics of Aging*, a National Journal Issues Book (Washington, D.C.: The Government Research Corporation, 1978). Used by permission.

---

[4]This important point, along with other issues concerned with the impact of demographic changes on the family, is given expanded treatment in excellent articles by Shanas and Hauser (1974) and Tibbitts (1977). Demographic developments are much more complex than our brief comments in this section might suggest. For a good discussion of the various issues see Cutler and Harootyan (1975) or Myers (1984).

Dependency Ratios

The increase in the number of the aged has caused concern among some policymakers. They worry about an increase in the number of nonworkers who must be economically supported by the working population.

Many people are concerned about the increased competition that may arise among age groups as each strives for a larger share of the nation's output. For example, improving retirement income by increasing social security often heads the list of demands by the aged segment of the population; in contrast, this is a relatively unimportant priority for younger workers.

Given the various mechanisms for retirement income provision—social security, public assistance, private insurance, private charity and/or personal savings—the fundamental economic fact remains that the part of national output consumed in any particular year by those *retired* is produced by the working population, regardless of the mix of mechanisms employed.[5] Some of society's total output is produced by elderly persons still in the labor force. But most of the aged (who consume about 10 percent of total output) do not participate in the production process.

To assess the changing relationship between consumption by the elderly, government expenditures for the elderly, and total economic output, it has been increasingly common to calculate what are called **dependency ratios.** These ratios seek to measure the number of persons in the society not engaged in producing output relative to those in the labor force who are.

It is important to realize, however, that the recent interest in dependency ratios has arisen primarily as a result of concern about the so-called increasing burden of the aged that might arise with changes in the demographic structure and economic support patterns. Hence, the prejudicial term chosen for these discussions has been "dependency ratios"—emphasizing the economically nonproductive potential of certain groups, such as children and retired persons.

The President's Commission on Pension Policy, a blue-ribbon panel appointed by President Carter, probably had the greatest impact in sounding the initial alarm:

After the turn of the century, an unprecedented shifting of older workers into retirement will begin to take place as the so-called

---

[5]While working, individuals "store up" claims to later output (produced after they stop working) by acquiring financial assets (saving) and by the accrual of pension credits.

"baby boom" generation grows older. Quite literally, this country's population will be coming of age.

As the population of the country matures severe strains will be placed on our already overburdened retirement income system. The inequities and inadequacies of the present retirement income system will become critical as more people retire and the active work force to support their retirement shrinks. [President's Commission on Pension Policy, 1981]

The Commission's focus on the retired population relative to the working population has also been the focus of policymakers, researchers, and the media who want to raise fears about a growing aged population. An article in the *New York Times*, for example, commented:

The "baby boom" generation, now 15 to 35 years old, will begin turning 65 in 2010, less than 30 years from now. At the same time, the productive working population of the country will be shrinking in relative size. In 2020 there will be only about three and a half working-age Americans for every person 65 or older, as against five today. [Weaver, 1981]

As pointed out by Cowgill (1981), "from a demographic standpoint such fears are not warranted. The analysis on which they are based is one-sided and misleading." Cowgill shows that most modernized countries of the world, all with relatively aged populations, have quite low dependency loads, much lower than developing nations (Figure 1–3). Historically, *total* dependency ratios in the United States have been declining, and projections show that they are likely to continue to decline in the future.

The definition of dependency ratio used by the President's Commission and stated in the last sentence of the *New York Times* article quoted above focuses only on dependents arising as old people retire from the work force. As Cowgill (and others) have pointed out, this is a very biased measure of the nonworking segment of the population. There are many other individuals who are not working: children, nonworking spouses, unemployed workers, and the severely disabled. Children have always constituted the major proportion of dependents in societies. While that burden has been sharply reduced in industrialized countries, children still represent a major dependency burden in developing countries (hence the results shown in Figure 1–3).

In a detailed analysis of dependency ratios, Crown and Schulz (1987) project "total dependency ratios" for the years 1950 through 2040. The ratio of all persons not in the labor force to those in the

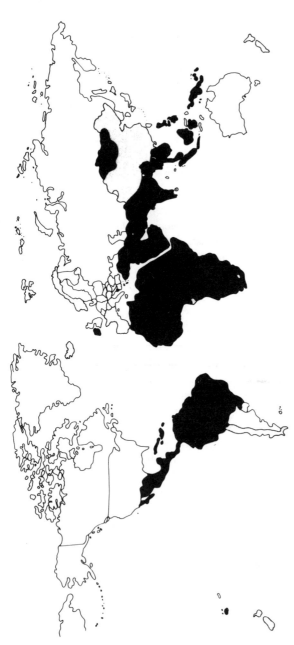

Map shows number of persons in each
country under age 15 and over age 64 (i.e.,
the "dependent" population) for every 100
persons age 15–64. Shaded areas indicate:

■ 80 or more persons

■ 70 to 79 persons

□ 60 to 69 persons

□ fewer than 60 persons

Figure 1-3   Dependency Around the World. Source: Donald O. Cowgill, "Can We Afford Our Aging Populations?" Paper prepared for Conference on Economics of Aging, Kansas City, April 3–5, 1981. Mimeo. Used by permission.

labor force *declines* from 1957 until the beginning of the 21st century. By the year 2050, when the total dependency ratio again peaks, *it will be lower* than what it was in the 1950s and 1960s.

Since projections of future labor force participation are difficult, all projections of future ratios are subject to large errors. The Crown/Schulz estimates—and others by Adamchak and Friedman (1983), Cowgill (1981), and DeVita (1981)—do serve to emphasize, however, that concerns about the economic burden of the aged based solely on *aged* dependency ratios may seriously overestimate the seriousness of the future problem.

The projected changes in the dependency ratio do indicate that we must continue to give attention to the changing numbers of *both* young and old. Thus, a related and perhaps more important question is the relative costs associated with young versus older dependents. Unfortunately, little information exists on the extent to which the reduced costs of fewer children might offset the rising costs of more retired persons. Robert Clark and Joseph Spengler (1978), using a broad measure of *public* support costs, find that government expenditures are three times greater for older dependents than for children. This is not surprising, since aside from education most expenditures for children are made directly by parents—not, as in the case of the aged, through public expenditure or transfer programs. A recent study by Crown and Schulz (1987) concludes that even taking account of the larger *private* expenditures of older persons (in contrast to children), "the future support burden will be less in the years 2030–50 than it was during 1950–70."

Even if the costs are less, the changing composition of the dependency ratio raises a number of major political questions. Parents directly pay for most of the expenditures on children (education in the early years is the big exception). In contrast, the elderly get about half their income through government programs supported by taxes.

Political scientist Robert Hudson (1978) argues that we can expect at least three political outcomes from these fiscal pressures: major new policy initiatives or appropriation for the aged beyond those provided for under existing legislation will meet with new and perhaps overwhelming resistance; agencies servicing the elderly will be subjected to more insistent demands for accountability; and, finally, the political influence of the aging and groups organized on their behalf may be put to a new and sterner test.

The Need for Individual and National Retirement Planning

Today, those who have not yet reached the retirement period of life can look forward to that period without many of the fears that worried so many in the past. A wide variety of institutional mechanisms are now available to help individuals provide for their economic needs. In fact, almost all individuals are *required* to make substantial provision for retirement by mandatory participation in social security and other pension programs.

With the emergence of retirement as a normative expectation and the development of a variety of institutional arrangements affecting the terms and conditions of retirement, the economics of aging takes on a different perspective. As we shall see in the chapters to follow, the level of retirement living has generally improved but is still subject to a large degree of variation and also to individual discretion. More importantly, however, the level and adequacy of retirement living are influenced by the many uncertainties and risks that are associated with the institutional mechanisms we have created. Savings opportunities completely secure from the risks of inflation are generally not available. Private pension coverage varies greatly among industries and occupations, and job change may mean the loss of some or all of these pension rights. The ultimate level of social security benefits can be severely reduced by the misfortunes of structural unemployment or illness and by the obligations of child care—all of which keep individuals out of the regular labor force for long periods.

People can and should begin to look forward to the challenges and opportunities of retirement. But there is still a major need for individuals to think about and plan for retirement. In this book we look at various economic aspects of that planning. The concurrent rise in (1) the level of benefits to the aged, (2) retirement expectations, and (3) the number of aged as a proportion of the population also creates a need for more national planning in the area of the economics of aging.

In the chapters to follow we will look at the retirement preparation problem, both from an individual and national standpoint. We begin with chapters concerned with the economic status of the current elderly and the special problems of older workers. We then discuss the nature and magnitude of the economic retirement preparation task. Finally, the concluding chapters of the book discuss pension and health programs and the major role they play in providing economic security in retirement.

Chapter 1 Highlights

What are the economic implications of "the graying of America"? Some of the important points made in this chapter are:

1. Dramatic improvements have occurred in the economic welfare of the aged.
2. At the same time, some public officials have begun to voice fears regarding the "economic burden" of the growing elderly population.
3. Our changing retirement patterns and expectations are, in part, a result of expanded opportunities for leisure resulting from economic growth. However, they are also a result of efforts to deal with recurrent unemployment in the American economy.
4. The American population is itself aging, primarily as a result of declining fertility.
5. Historically, *total* dependency ratios have been slowly declining and, contrary to often-voiced concerns, are likely to decline even further in future years.
6. Older people are now offered more meaningful choices in how they can spend their time in the later years. But with these choices comes the need for careful planning for the "golden years."

Suggested Readings

BINSTOCK, ROBERT H., WING-SUN CHOW, AND J. H. SCHULZ, EDS. *International Perspectives on Aging: Population and Policy Challenges*. Policy Development Studies No. 7. New York: United Nations Fund for Population Activities, 1982. One of the very few comprehensive overviews of aging in developing countries. See the article by George Myers on "The Aging of Populations."

CROWN, WILLIAM H. "Some Thoughts on Reformulating the Dependency Ratio," *The Gerontologist* 25 (1985):166–170. An excellent discussion of issues related to constructing dependency ratios.

ESPENSHADE, THOMAS J., AND WILLIAM J. SEROW, EDS. *The Economic Consequences of Slowing Population Growth*. New York: Academic Press, 1978. A discussion of all major aspects of the changing demographic profile and its economic implications.

HARRIS, LOUIS, AND ASSOCIATES. *The Myth and Reality of Aging in America*. Washington, D.C.: The National Council on the Aging, 1975. A report on a representative national sample of 4,254 persons 18 years and over conducted in 1974. Topics covered are (1) public attitudes toward old age, (2) the public's image of "most" people over 65, (3) perceived social and economic contributions of the aged, (4) preparation for old age, (5) being old, (6) access to facilities, (7) the media's portrayal of the aged, and (8) the politics of old age.

KINGSON, ERIC R., B. A. HIRSHORN, AND J. M. CORNMAN. *Ties That Bind—The*

Interdependence of Generations. Cabin John, Md.: Seven Locks Press, 1986. The interrelationships between demography, economics, and families with young and older persons are explored in this response to those preaching the message of intergenerational conflict.

RUSSELL, LOUIS B. *The Baby Boom Generation and the Economy*. Washington, D.C.: The Brookings Institution, 1982. This study examines economic developments, the housing market, and social security to determine whether the baby boom generation has been a major factor influencing the economy. One part of the study looks at projected expenditures for medical care and social security when the baby boom group reaches old age.

STOREY, JAMES R. *Older Americans in the Reagan Era—Impacts of Federal Policy Changes*. Washington, D.C.: The Urban Institute Press, 1983. This publication analyzes the course and consequences for older Americans of federal policy changes since 1980 and discusses proposals in the 1984 budget of the President.

WATTENBERG, BEN J. *The Birth Dearth*. New York: Pharos Books, 1987. "What happens when people in free countries don't have enough babies?" asks journalist Wattenberg. An overly pessimistic but thought-provoking view of population aging.

Chapter 2

THE ECONOMIC STATUS
OF THE AGED

The treatment of old people in America, many of whom have a hard life behind them, is remarkable. . . . [This is illustrated by] the terrifying extent to which old people are left in poverty and destitution. . . . It cannot possibly be the considered opinion of the majority of Americans that so many of those who in America are often called "senior citizens" should be left in misery, squalor and often forbidding loneliness, unattended though they are in need of care. The situation is overripe for a radical reform of the old age security system.

So wrote the well-known social commentator Gunnar Myrdal in his book *Challenge to Affluence* (1963). Myrdal was writing in the early 1960s. But as we noted in the preceding chapter, dramatic changes have occurred since then.

Contrast Myrdal's comment with a story that appeared in the *Washington Post* (19 August 1983):

A new Census Bureau study shows that the elderly in this country are much better off than previously believed and, in fact, are better off than the average American. . . .

The new figures are likely to become factors in the inter-generational politics that have developed around Social Security and Medicare. Both these programs for the elderly have been in trouble lately, and Congress has had to choose between tax increases for the young or benefit cuts for the old.

The article by Spencer Rich in the *Washington Post* goes on to describe how the per capita, after-tax income of the elderly was $6,300 in 1980 versus $5,964 for the population as a whole.

In this chapter we explain why the typical **money income** statistics usually reported do not give a full and accurate picture of the aged's economic status. We discuss a variety of factors, including family size and taxes, that should be taken into account.

Looking at the controversial Census Bureau findings reported by Rich and a number of other recent studies (discussed below), one can begin to see emerging a very important historical development. From a statistical point of view, *the elderly in this country are beginning to look a lot like the rest of the population:* some very rich, lots with adequate income, lots more with very modest incomes (often near poverty), and a significant minority still destitute. This is very different from the past when most were destitute.

Once we recognize that the similarities between the old and younger populations are increasing, we must also recognize the important and unique differences. While clearly most of those disadvantaged before old age remain disadvantaged, they are joined in old age by many for whom certain economic problems are unique:

- The elderly widow who finds her income but a small fraction of the income enjoyed when her husband was alive.
- The retired couple whose retirement cushion is wiped out when the electric power consortium in the state of Washington defaults on bonds sold to build nuclear power plants that are no longer economically viable.
- The engineer who, despite years of private pension coverage, never gains a vested pension (see Chapter 8).
- The retired executive who must sell off all his assets to pay for the institutional care needed for his wife with Alzheimer's disease.
- The retired teacher without social security whose state pension falls far behind needed purchasing power as a result of the double-digit inflation experienced in the late 1970s and early 1980s.
- The gas station mechanic who becomes unexpectedly disabled at the age of 50 and has nothing to supplement his meager social security disability pension.
- The appliance salesman living only on social security—who was never covered by a private pension and neglected ("could not afford") to contribute money into an Individual Retirement Account or some other personal investment program.

The list could go on and on. But the point of the list is not to elicit sympathy for the aged or to prove the need to do more. Rather, we seek to emphasize the heterogeneity of the aged and warn against those glib generalities: "the aged" are poor; or now, with greater frequency, "the aged" are well off.

Prior to the 1960s there were relatively few data available to analyze the economic situation of the aged population in the United States. This situation changed dramatically in the early 1960s as a result of the Social Security Administration's very comprehensive survey of the aged in 1962 (Epstein and Murray, 1967). Since then, a wide range of statistics has been published by the Social Security Administration, the Census Bureau, the Administration on Aging, the Department of Labor, and various private organizations. These data provide a variety of information on various aspects of the elderly's financial status.

Two important notes of caution are immediately in order, however. First, because it takes time to collect, check, analyze, and publish statistics, there is often a considerable lag in the availability of information. Throughout the chapter we present illustrative statistics—the latest that were available at the time of writing. Many readers, however, will want to seek the newer data available. Second, all statistical information is subject to great abuse; unless users are very careful, they may misinterpret or misuse the available data. The discussion below, therefore, also attempts to deal with two important questions: What are the most useful kinds of data for evaluating the economic status of the aged, and what are the major problems in interpreting the data available?

Aged Income

We begin our discussion of the elderly's economic status by looking at the income they receive. Income is not the only resource contributing to the economic welfare of the aged; later sections of this chapter will look at a number of other important factors (for example, assets). But as Mollie Orshansky has observed, "while money might not be everything, it is way ahead of whatever is in second place" (Irelan and Bond, 1976).

Income Distribution

Table 2–1 shows the distribution of money income for both aged families and unrelated individuals. In 1986, 15 percent of families with a head age 65 or older had money income of less than $10,000; about one-third had money income of less than $15,000. The income situation of unrelated individuals age 65 or older—most of

Table 2–1   Distribution of Total Money Income of the Aged in 1986

Total Money Income	Families	Unrelated Individuals
Less than $5,000	3%	22%
$5,000–9,999	12	40
$10,000–14,999	19	16
$15,000–19,999	17	9
$20,000–29,999	21	7
$30,000–49,999	18	4
$50,000 and over	10	1
Median Income	$19,932	$7,731
Total Percent	100%	100%

Source: U.S. Bureau of the Census, *Money Income and Poverty Status of Families and Persons in the United States: 1986,* Current Population Reports, P-60, No. 157 (Washington, D.C.: U.S. Government Printing Office, July 1987), Table 6.

whom live alone—was much different. Nearly two-thirds had income below $10,000, and 78 percent had income below $15,000.

Figure 2–1 compares the distribution of money income for *aged* families with the distribution of *nonaged* families. We see that in 1986 a much higher proportion of nonaged families had incomes over $30,000. At the lower end of the distribution, the proportion of elderly is much, much higher (except for the category "less than $5,000").

Not all the aged are covered by the data presented in Table 2–1. Only units where an aged person is *head* of the unit are included. If an aged person lives with his children or if the children live with their aged parent(s), should the two units be reported separately, or should the income be lumped together into one big family? It often makes a significant difference in the final results that are reported. There is a tendency to combine all the incomes of people living together. The result has been that a lot of aged poverty in the past has been hidden because the poorest aged—those who are unable to live by themselves—were submerged into the bigger and usually more prosperous family unit.

One might argue that if the aged are living with a family unit and the family unit is not itself poor, then the aged standard of living is not likely to be poor. Using this perspective, one can argue further that there is no problem in such cases and that if you statistically separate the aged out (perhaps to try to justify higher pension benefits), you are basing the analysis on an artificial situation. The opposing view, however, is that many of these people are not necessarily treated as members of the family. They

Ethel Shanas' studies?

I doubt this is true.

may be there by necessity, and often families do not permit them to share fully in the higher standard of living of the rest of the family. Or, even if the younger members of the family want them to share fully, many aged people are too independent to be willing to draw heavily upon the resources of the rest of the family. They would rather—even though they live within the family—live at a lower, perhaps subsistence, level.

Changes over Time

Historically, we know that as social security benefit levels have increased many aged persons have moved out of these families at the first opportunity and set up independent households. Statistically, as a result of these family units breaking up, new units headed by an aged person show up in the data. Since these new aged units almost always have very low income, the process tends to increase the reported incidence of poverty among the aged. We find, for example, that during certain periods the number of persons in poverty has declined among nonaged groups but has risen among the aged (partly as a result of the movement of the aged out of other families).

Thus, when the statistics show aged poverty increasing, it is not necessarily true that the situation is actually getting worse. In part, the statistics are a reflection of things getting better. As pension benefits go up, some of the poor aged who prefer independent living are able to break out of other family units and thus become identifiable statistical units. But, again, it can be argued that they were always poor, and all that has changed is their living arrangements.

Statistics from surveys by the Social Security Administration show the significant increase in elderly income that has occurred over the 1962 to 1984 period. Table 2–2 shows by sex and marital status the percentage increases in real income (that is, income increases after inflation has been accounted for). Over this period, nonmarried women experienced the largest increase in **median** income. Looking at data for a more restricted period (1970 to 1981), Chen (1984) finds that white women's income increased the most, while black men's income increased the least.

Sources of Income

Figure 2–2 shows the sources of income for the elderly. While social security is the major source (38 percent), asset income (28 percent) and earnings (16 percent) make large contributions. We

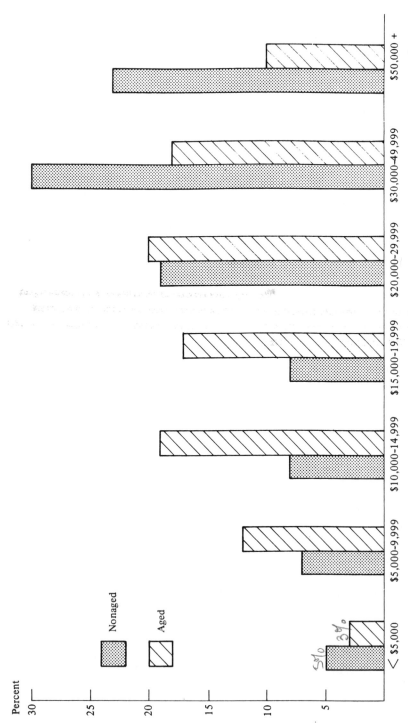

Figure 2-1   Comparison of Total Money Income, Aged and Nonaged Families, 1986. Source: U.S. Bureau of the Census, *Money Income and Poverty Status of Families and Persons in the United States: 1986,* Current Population Reports, P-60, No. 157 (Washington, D.C.: U.S. Government Printing Office, July 1987), Table 6.

Table 2-2 Rates of Increase in the Median Incomes of Aged Persons, 1962 versus 1986

	Median Income (1986 dollars)		Percentage Change
Marital Status	*1962*	*1986*	
All units	na	$10,960	na
Married couples	$10,430	18,890	81%
Nonmarried persons	4,100	7,180	75
Men	4,950	8,510	72
Women	3,680	6,870	87

Source: S. Grad, *Income of the Population 55 or Over, 1986* (Washington, D.C.: U.S. Social Security Administration, forthcoming), Table 12.

must remember, however, that various income sources are distributed unevenly among the subgroups of the aged population. Earnings go mostly to the nonretired; asset income goes mostly to a few high-income elderly. In a subsequent section we examine these differences more closely.

Over the years, as more people have retired (and at earlier ages), income from earnings has dropped steadily. Figure 2–3 shows the trend in income sources for couples over age 64 between 1968 and 1985. While the share from social security and employer-sponsored

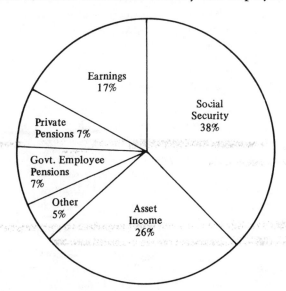

Figure 2-2 Sources of Aged Money Income. Source: S. Grad, *Income of the Population 55 or Over, 1986* (Washington, D.C.: U.S. Social Security Administration: forthcoming), Table 47.

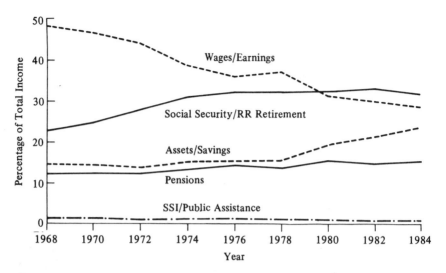

Figure 2-3   Income Sources for Couples over Age 64 Between 1968 and 1985. Source: U.S. Bureau of the Census, Current Population Survey, 1968-84, unpublished data. Reproduced from U.S. Senate Special Committee on Aging, *Developments in Aging:* 1985. Vol 3 (Washington D.C.: U.S. Government Printing Office, 1986).

pensions increased until the early 1980s, more recently there has been a small decline in these sources. This arises not from any decline or cutback in these programs. Rather, it is no doubt a reflection of high interests rates during the 1969–1972 period— pushing up the share of assets/savings.

An Important Statistical Warning

Almost all the statistics that have been presented in the prior sections were based on the government's Current Population Survey (CPS). The CPS is a household survey conducted by the U.S. Bureau of the Census. The survey is designed to gather monthly information on labor force participation and unemployment. At least once a year, however, information is obtained in the CPS on the kinds and amounts of income individuals and families receive.

Income information from surveys like the CPS are subject to substantial reporting errors by those interviewed. Respondents do not know, remember incorrectly, refuse to answer, or give false information out of anger or fear of government retribution. Such errors can produce substantial underestimates of income and can distort our view of the relative income positions of various socioeconomic groups. Thus, while the CPS data are relatively reliable for the great bulk of aged whose income is low, it is not for the small group of aged with extensive property, farm, or other self-employment income.

The Social Security Administration's Office of Research and Statistics has been researching this reporting problem for many years. It has published startling findings with regard to the seriousness of the problem (Radner, 1982). Errors were found to be very large, especially for the elderly. The study found that in 1977 the CPS underestimated the mean income of all family and single units by 11 percent. However, the incomes of family units headed by persons age 65 or older showed an increase, when adjusted for underreporting, of 41 percent! The extent of CPS underestimating was much larger for those with higher incomes and relatively small for those at the low-income levels. The major cause of error in the income estimates was underreporting of property income (interest, dividends, rent, royalties, and trust income) and to a lesser extent self-employment income (especially farm income). The study also made less precise estimates for the year 1979. The adjusted mean income numbers for this later year are equally surprising, as shown in Table 2–3.

The Social Security Administration's findings dramatically emphasize the need to be cautious in using and interpreting income statistics. Later in this chapter, when we look at asset statistics, the same caution applies—probably more so.

If only the above problems were the only ones involved in measuring the economic status of the elderly. Unfortunately, once we understand the underreporting limitations of the CPS data, our problems are only beginning.

The Aged Are Not a Homogeneous Group

The statistics given in the first part of this chapter unfortunately have other shortcomings: lumping all the aged population together

Table 2–3   Adjusted Mean Income for 1979

	Mean Income		
Age of Head	CPS	CPS Adjusted	% Change
14–24	$10,511	$10,300	− 2%
25–34	17,953	18,530	+ 3%
35–44	23,220	25,670	+ 10%
45–54	24,664	28,460	+ 13%
55–64	20,809	25,280	+ 18%
65 or older	**10,837**	**15,860**	+ 32%

Source: Daniel B. Radner, "Distribution of Family Income: Improved Estimates," *Social Security Bulletin* 45 (July 1982): 13–21.

seriously distorts the reality of the situation. It is common for writers and analysts to give only the mean or median income for all or large groups of the aged, but as we saw in Table 2–2, for example, there is a wide divergence in income among the aged. Similar distortions result from grouping all the aged together and generalizing about their social problems. Most people who study old age and the process of aging (gerontology) are familiar with this aggregation problem in the social and psychological areas. There is no such thing as the collective aged; the aged are as diverse as the population itself, and this is just as true for economic status as it is for other areas.

If one views the aged as one homogeneous group, there is a tendency to try to develop for them one appropriate economic policy—just as in other areas we have tried to develop one appropriate housing policy and one appropriate health policy. We have learned over the years that such attempts almost always fail in diverse groups.

Unfortunately, much of the data published on a regular basis do not show the significant differences existing among the elderly. Probably the most frequently used economic data on the elderly are from the National Census and the Current Population Survey. But these published tabulations are generally for all (or large groups) of the aged. The most useful type of data for analysis and evaluation are those that break down the aged population into smaller subgroups. Unfortunately, in order to look more closely at the heterogeneous nature of the economics of aging, we must often use older data.

The Retired Versus the Nonretired

The first step toward disaggregation of the data is very simple: Separate the aged into at least two broad categories—the retired and the nonretired. Unfortunately, most of the data sources do not or cannot provide such a breakdown. They "do not" because often it simply does not occur to those presenting the data that this is an important distinction. They "cannot" because in determining when a person is retired one must deal with difficult conceptual problems, and the questions asked in the survey providing the data do not always include the information necessary for judging whether a person is retired or not. Hence one typically sees data that group aged wage earners together with people without earnings. The earners, of course, tend to have much higher and more adequate incomes. When they are averaged together with the nonwage earners, the total mean and median income for "the aged" is increased. This makes the situation look much better than it actually is for retired people and much worse than it actually is for the employed.

If one wants to segregate the retired from the nonretired, one immediately runs into the problem of how to define retirement for statistical purposes. Many aged persons work to supplement their pension and other retirement income. Is a person who is working 20 hours a week to be counted as a retired person, or is he or she partially retired? If the latter, what does that mean? Thus, even if we divide the aged population on the basis of retirement, it is not clear whether there should be two categories or more than two. A three-category tabulation, for example, might be full-time workers, part-time and unemployed workers, and the fully retired. In general, most discussions of the economic status of the aged do not even attempt to deal with this problem when presenting data. This omission is unfortunate since (as we will show) this is such an important issue in evaluating the economic well-being of elderly people. In recent years the U.S. Bureau of the Census has begun publishing some data giving income by employment experience. Table 2–4 shows income by employment status in 1981. Note the

Table 2–4 1981 Money Income of Aged[a] Families and Unrelated Individuals, by Work Experience of Householder[b]

Work Experience Last Year	Median Income	Less than $5,000	$5,000– 14,999	$15,000 or more	Total Percent
Families					
Householder did not work	$11,632	16%	47%	37%	100
Worked part-time	14,729	12	40	48	100
26 weeks or less	12,825	19	40	41	100
Worked full-time	26,671	2	17	81	100
26 weeks or less	12,722	16	43	41	100
Unrelated individuals					
Householder did not work	4,948	51	42	7	100
Worked part-time	6,203	38	50	12	100
26 weeks or less	4,040	60	36	4	100
Worked full-time	12,476	14	45	41	100
26 weeks or less	5,425	46	45	9	100

Source: Based on data in U.S. Bureau of the Census, "Money Income of Households, Families, and Persons in the United States: 1981," *Consumer Income*. Current Population Reports, Series P-60, No. 137 (Washington, D.C.: U.S. Government Printing Office, 1983), Table 36.
[a]Age 65 or older.
[b]Householder is a Census Bureau definition for the person (or one of the persons) in whose name the home is owned or rented. If the unit is jointly owned, either husband or wife may be listed first.

dramatic differences between those working full time and the other groups.

Different Age Groups

Another major problem in analyzing data on the aged is that it often is not appropriate to group people together who differ in age by as much as 15 or 20 years. Most statistics on the economic status of aged people group all persons age 65 and over together. Again, conclusions drawn from such data will be misleading. To begin with, it is important to realize that the needs of people at the two extremes of the retirement period are often quite different.

Unfortunately, there is relatively little information on the changing consumption patterns of the elderly. However, a recent study (McConnel and Deljavan, 1983) of *retired* persons' expenditures in comparison to those of older people still working provides some interesting findings. On the average, the retired spend a significantly larger proportion of their budgets on shelter, food for home meals, and health care. However, as income increases, retired families commit a smaller proportion of additional income to necessities and a much larger proportion to gifts and charitable contributions.

Similar expenditure differences exist if one looks at those elderly age 65 to 74 in comparison to those age 75 or older. Table 2–5

Table 2–5   Shares of Total Expenditures by the Aged, 1984

	Age Group	
Item	*65–74*	*75 and over*
Total expenditures	$15,873	$11,196
Food at home	13.0%	13.6%
Food away from home	4.8	3.5
Housing	30.5	35.5
Transportation	19.2	13.0
Health care	8.4	13.3
Entertainment and reading	4.6	3.4
Personal insurance and pensions	4.9	2.1
Apparel	4.5	3.1
Other	10.1	12.5
Total	100.0%	100.0%

Source: Beth Harrison, "Spending Patterns of Older Persons Revealed in Expenditure Survey," *Monthly Labor Review,* Vol. 109 (October 1986), Table 2.

shows for each age group the proportion of total expenditures accounted for by different types of purchases.

If one wants to develop a budget for the aged, then, it is probably better to develop different budgets for at least two age groups (even though the range of ages chosen must be somewhat arbitrary). Not that you cannot find persons 85 and 90 years old who are as active and vigorous as someone 65 (or maybe 25). But on the average there seem to be enough distinctions for analytical purposes to warrant taking a range of ages into account in the presentation and analysis of economic data.

Another reason for separating the aged into various age groups is that the accustomed standard of living for the *very* old is usually quite different from that of the *newly* old. Each group grew up and worked over different periods of history. Each group's final earnings and the resulting levels of living prior to retirement are different. Given the lengths of time involved, these differences can be quite substantial. Thus, in evaluating the adequacy of income for aged people, one should allow for the fact that the *very* old themselves may have lower expectations about their standard of living than aged persons who retire a decade or two later.

There is, however, another factor that works in the opposite direction. Among the very old the incidence of exceptionally high expenditures for chronic illness and institutionalization rises dramatically. As Table 2–5 shows, expenditures on health care are nearly twice as great for the group of aged who are age 75 and over. And for those elderly persons who experience very serious medical problems, economic need can rise catastrophically.

Furthermore, the incomes of those who have recently retired are often much better than those who have been retired a long time—mainly because the former group's earnings are typically higher and pensions based upon them are consequently better. Also, the newer retirees are more likely to reap gains from the recent establishment of private pensions or improvements in old plans.

Table 2–6 shows the percent of aged in various age categories who had money incomes above and below the poverty level in 1983. The data indicate that persons over age 84 are nearly twice as likely to be below the poverty level (21.3 percent) as those age 65 to 74 (11 percent).

There is a final reason why one should be sensitive to age differences in assessing the economic status of the elderly. In recent years it has become increasingly unsatisfactory to talk of only those people 65 and older as being aged—given the rise of early retirement in the United States. We know that to arbitrarily

Table 2–6   How the Money Income of Various Elderly Age Groups Relates to the Poverty Level in 1983

Ratio of Income to the Poverty Level	Age Group		
	65–74	*75–84*	*85 and over*
Below the poverty level	11.9%	16.7%	21.3%
100 to 124% of the poverty level	6.7	10.6	12.7
125 to 149% of the poverty level	6.7	9.6	9.7

Source: G. Lawrence Atkins, "The Economic Status of the Oldest Old," *Milbank Memorial Fund Quarterly/Health and Society* 63 (1985), Table 2.

designate as old those who have reached a specific chronological age is a most inadequate way of approaching the problem of defining the aged. It takes no account of people's varying capacities for physical and mental activities and social involvement, among other things. We know that people age differently in terms of various characteristics.

The more serious economic problems of aging commonly arise from, or are aggravated by, the cessation of earnings following retirement. Thus it is important to study that part of the older population having the most economic problems—those families where there are no regular workers. Increasingly, this group includes people who are less than 65 years of age. If we look at persons younger than age 65, we can logically divide them into two groups: those younger than age 62 and those age 62 to 64. Age 62 seems to be an appropriate dividing point since this is the earliest age at which eligible persons can first receive social security old-age benefits (except for widows who can qualify at age 60).

Persons who retire before age 62 must rely on private pensions and/or their own assets and income from these assets. Data indicate that this group tends to be composed of both very high income people and very low income people—with very few in the middle (Kingson, 1979; Daymont and Andrisani, 1983). That is, we find among this very early retirement group those people who *have* to retire early even though they do not have enough money and those people who *can* retire very early because they have sufficient economic resources to live satisfactorily.

Those who retire reluctantly tend to be workers with health problems, difficulties obtaining and maintaining a job, and no pension to supplement social security. Those who retire voluntarily tend to be those with private pensions, those who worked for the government, those whose wives have pensions, and those who have mortgage-free houses (Morgan, 1980).

Thus, Karen Schwab's (1976) analysis of early labor force withdrawal found that most of the men leaving early reported health-imposed work limitations. Figure 2–4 shows the proportion of men age 58–63 no longer in the labor force in 1969. Of those with no work limitation, 63 percent had incomes over $5,000—in contrast to only 30 percent for the health-limited group.

A more recent study (Morgan, 1980) shows the importance of eligibility for a second pension to supplement social security. Persons with a private pension or a civil service pension from local, state, or federal government are much more likely to retire very early. Of course, ill health and a second pension are not mutually exclusive. Morgan finds that workers with two pensions and some degree of ill-health are the most likely to retire.

Shifting from those who retire before age 62 to those age 62–64, we focus on a group that is eligible for social security retirement benefits but at a reduced level. Ever since the early retirement provisions under social security were first introduced (in 1956 for women and 1961 for men), more than half of the men and women starting to receive social security old-age retirement benefits have opted for reduced benefits before age 65. (Table 5–5 in Chapter 5 shows the increasing proportion of beneficiaries electing early benefits.)

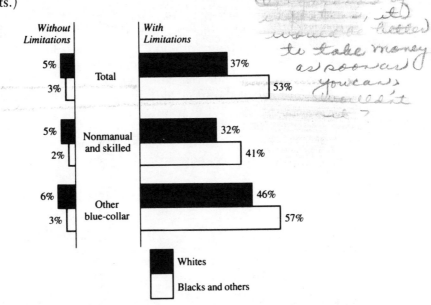

Figure 2-4   Percent of Men Aged 58-63 Out of the Labor Force in 1969, by Type of Longest Job, Health-Imposed Work Limitations, and Race. Source: Lola M. Irelan et al., *Almost 65: Baseline Data from the Retirement History Study*. Research Report No. 49 (Washington, D.C.: U.S. Social Security Administration, 1976).

Income by Age

Again, published economic data on the income of various age groupings of the elderly population are sparse. Table 2–7, however, presents data for 1986 that illustrate the income differences between age groups by looking at younger versus older units. The data in Table 2–7 might be interpreted as indicating the economic status of an older individual declines as he or she grows older. This is often not the case. Ross et al. (1987) show, for example, that the average incomes of cohorts of older persons, when in the same retirement and marital situation, did not decline over the 1950 to 1980 period. They find instead that incomes change significantly (usually drop) when aged units *move into retirement* and especially when someone *becomes widowed*—often increasing thereafter. This is consistent with the recent findings of Holden et al. (1987), a study of older persons in the 1970s, that the highest risk of becoming poor is during the period just after becoming widowed.

Black-White Differences

Differentiation of the aged population by various socioeconomic characteristics must also be made. One of the best studies of black-white differences is by Julian Abbott (1977), who analyzes data for persons aged 60 and older in March 1972. Abbott finds that only a small proportion of the elderly population depends on public assistance payments but that this proportion includes a much larger percentage of the black elderly (30 percent) than the white (7 percent). The reverse is true for the receipt of income from assets: 13 percent for blacks and 53 percent for whites. The two groups, however, are about equal in the proportion receiving income from earnings (44 percent).

Table 2–7 1986 Money Income of Aged Units (Married and Nonmarried), Age 55 and Older

Age	Median Income	Less than $5,000	$5,000–9,999	$10,000–14,999	$15,000 or More	Total Percent
55–61	$23,340	13%	11%	11%	66%	100[a]
62–64	18,190	13	15	14	58	100
65–69	14,540	13	22	17	49	100
70–74	12,430	15	26	17	42	100
75–79	9,570	18	34	18	31	100
80 and older	7,620	24	38	16	22	100

Source: Susan Grad, *Income of the Population 55 or Over, 1986* (Washington, D.C.: Social Security Administration, forthcoming).
[a]May not add to 100 percent due to rounding.

Figure 2–5 illustrates the similarities and differences in the shape of the income distribution curves for each racial group. Despite aggregate differences in money income, a sizable majority of individual black and white elderly units had similar incomes. Using a technical measure of the extent to which income distributions overlap, Abbott calculates an "index of integration" (i.e., overlap) equal to 0.74 and an "**index** of differentiation" equal to 0.26. These indices indicate that incomes for about three-fourths of black and white units were *not* different. Even within the lowest income groups, however, black and white units differed substantially in their sources of income. Abbott concludes, therefore, "that efforts to improve the income adequacy of the elderly will have different effects on the two races. Benefit increases in any of the retirement pensions would provide relatively less for blacks because of their lower rate of coverage and their lower lifetime earnings. . . . Blacks would benefit more from the improved, but means-tested, assistance programs and from the continued availability of jobs for those still able to work."

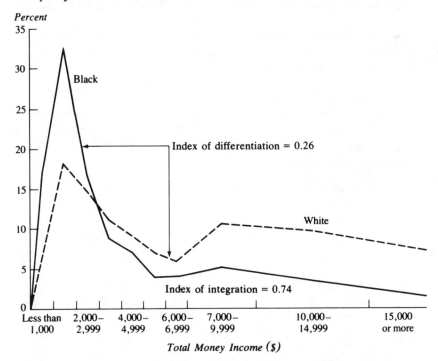

Figure 2-5 **Percentage Distribution of Black and White Elderly Units, by Total Money Income in 1971.** Source: Julian Abbott, "Socioeconomic Characteristics of the Elderly: Some Black-White Differences," *Social Security Bulletin* 40 (July 1977): 16–42.

More recent data showing black-white differences among the elderly are presented in Table 2–8. This table shows money income in 1985 for elderly persons living alone and/or married.

The plight of the minority aged has been characterized by some writers as one of "double jeopardy" or "multiple hazard" (Jackson, 1970). Data from a fairly large sample of middle-aged and aged blacks, Mexican Americans, and whites living in Los Angeles County provide insight on this issue. Dowd and Bengtson (1978) investigated differences across and within ethnic categories. Their analysis supported the double jeopardy characterization—especially with regard to income and self-assessed health.

Similar findings are also reported by Shanas (1977). Almost twice as high a proportion of the black aged, compared with whites, say they need medical and dental care but have delayed treatment—primarily because of financial problems. And the black elderly more often than whites reported that their financial situation was worse than it was when they were age 60.

There are some indications, however, that the situation is improving. In two reviews of the studies and data on this topic, Markides (1981 and 1983) concludes that while elderly members of ethnic minority groups continue to be economically disadvan-

Table 2–8 Distribution of 1985 Total Money Income for Aged Single-Person Economic Units, by Sex and Race

Income Class	White	Black
Women		
Less than $5,000	22%	53%
$5,000–9,999	43	36
$10,000–19,999	23	7
$20,000–49,999	11	4
$50,000 and over	1	—
Total	100	100
Men		
Less than $5,000	15%	37%
$5,000–9,999	36	39
$10,000–19,999	30	20
$20,000–49,999	17	4
$50,000 and over	2	—
Total	100	100

Source: Based on data in U.S. Bureau of the Census, *Money Income and Poverty Status of Households, Families, and Persons in the United States: 1985,* Current Population Reports, Series P-60, No. 156 (Washington, D.C.: U.S. Government Printing Office), Table 18.

taged, the data show a relative decline in the racial income gap in old age over time.

Dual Pensioners

We discuss in later chapters the fact that a high proportion of wage and salary workers in private industry are *not* covered by private **pensions.** The result is that many people reaching retirement age have to rely solely on social security pensions. Table 2–9 illustrates the income disparity between aged families with dual pensions and those receiving only social security. The median income of couples with dual pensions, for example, was much higher ($16,848) than of couples not receiving a second pension ($10,872).

In later chapters we will discuss further this divergency of economic status among one- and two-pension families. One major policy issue currently being discussed is the extent to which government policy promotes a growing "pension elite" (i.e., dual pensioners with high pension income) while at the same time large numbers of aged have, essentially, only their social security income to rely on.

The Impact of Taxation, Assests, and In-Kind Income

Thus far we have looked only at the distribution of money income among the aged. Three other factors have an important impact on the economic status of elderly people. First, there is the extent to which the income is actually available to meet current needs (what economists call *disposable income*); some of one's income usually goes to the government in taxes. Second, we need to assess the size, type, and distribution of assets held by older persons. And,

Table 2–9   Median Money Income of the Elderly by Income Source, 1984

Income Sources	Couples	Unrelated Individuals
Social security (no employer pension)[a]	$10,872	$5,568
Dual pensioners[b]	16,848	9,948
Earnings recipients[c]	22,776	12,972

Source: Author's tabulations of Survey of Income and Program Participation (SIPP).
[a]Total money income of people receiving social security but no income from earnings or an employer-sponsored pension.
[b]Total money income of people receiving both social security and an employer-sponsored pension.
[c]Total money income of people with some amount of earnings during the year.

finally, not all income is *money* income; sizable amounts of *in-kind* income are received by the elderly, improving their economic status.

Taxation

Most income distribution statistics look at the pretax distribution of income. Since taxes affect people differently, we would expect the after-tax distribution to be different. In 1980, for example, nonaged households in the United States paid taxes averaging about one-quarter of their yearly income to federal, state, and local governments.[1] In contrast, persons age 65 or older paid on average only 13 percent of their income in taxes (U.S. Bureau of the Census, 1983).

Until recently, these tax differences were largely a result of special provision in federal and state income tax laws. Before 1984 social security benefits were not subject to federal income tax. Starting in that year, half of benefits became taxable for individuals with very high income (in 1984 about 10 percent of beneficiaries).[2] Thus, nearly 40 percent of the elderly's income is still not subject to income tax as a result of this special treatment.

Another recent change in the federal income tax law eliminates the *double* "personal exemption" that persons age 65 and over could claim. However, the Tax Reform Act of 1986 raised the personal exemption for all individuals to $1,900 and allowed an addition to the "standard deduction" of $600 (for a couple) and $750 (single persons) for all persons age 65 or more (or blind), in addition to the $1,900 exemption. Persons over age 54 are still allowed to exclude from federal taxation profits of up to $125,000 resulting from the sale of one personal residence.

Property tax reductions are now granted in all states for elderly persons (Fairholm, 1978). The most common type of reduction is a "circuit breaker." Tax relief under this mechanism is tied to need, as defined by taxpayers' income levels in relation to their property tax liabilities. The amount of relief declines (or phases out) as taxpayer income rises, using a formula that avoids a sharp drop in relief at some arbitrary income level. For example, the Vermont circuit breaker comes into play when the property tax burden exceeds 7 percent of household income; for Minnesota it is 6 percent; for many states it is 3 to 5 percent. These and other provisions of the circuit breaker vary from state to state. Income

---

[1] Only income, payroll, and property taxes are included in this estimate.

[2] See p. 184 for a more detailed discussion of this provision.

ceilings or rebate limits are different; some laws do not cover renters.

Another common method of property tax relief is the "homestead exemption." Under this mechanism, a state excludes before the tax rate is applied a portion of the assessed value of a single-family home from total assessed value. A few states allow deferral of property taxes until after an elderly owner dies or sells his residence, and a few freeze the tax rate at the rate in force when the aged person reaches a certain age, usually 63 or 65.

Table 2–10 shows for 1983 that a small shift occurs downward in the distribution of aged income after taxes. For comparison purposes, statistics are also included for middle-age families; they show a similar drop. When grouped together as we have done, the shifts do not appear to be big. Remember, however, that for *particular individuals* the shifts can be quite large and are hidden for the most part by aggregation of the data.

Assets

In addition to current income, many of the aged own assets that provide housing, serve as a financial reserve for special or emergency needs, contribute directly to income through interest, dividends, and rents, and generally enhance the freedom with which they spend their available income. Most assets can be sold and thereby converted to money that can be used to buy goods and services. But one should distinguish between liquid assets and

Table 2–10 1983 Household Income Before and After Taxes,[a] "Householders"[b] Age 40–44 and Age 65 and Over

Before Tax Income	Age 40–44		Age 65 +	
	Before Taxes	After Taxes	Before Taxes	After Taxes
Less than $15,000	5%	6%	29%	32%
$15,000–29,999	21	23	33	34
$30,000–39,999	20	19	13	12
$40,000 or more	55	52	25	22
Total Percent[c]	100%	100%	100%	100%

Source: Based on data in U.S. Bureau of the Census, *After-Tax Money Income Estimates of Households: 1983*, Current Population Reports, Series P-23, No. 143 (Washington, D.C.: U.S. Government Printing Office, 1985), Table 1.
[a]Federal and state individual income taxes, FICA and federal retirement payroll taxes, and property taxes on owner-occupied housing.
[b]The person whose name is on the property deed or rental lease.
[c]May not total 100 due to rounding.

nonliquid assets. Fortunately, most published statistics on assets do make such a distinction.

Liquid assets are relatively easy to convert into goods and services or money (the most liquid of assets). These consist generally of cash, bank deposits, and corporate stocks and bonds. *Nonliquid assets* usually require more time to convert. The two major types of nonliquid assets are **equity** in housing and equity in a business.

Assets (or savings) are held by individuals because they perform a number of very useful economic functions. They are used as a precaution against unexpected happenings in the future. One puts money aside so that it can be drawn upon should the need arise. This saving might be viewed as self-insurance. Assets are also accumulated in anticipation of known or planned large expenditures in the future: because of a worsening illness one might anticipate going into a nursing home; or one might save in order to take a round-the-world retirement cruise. Still another reason for saving is to leave a legacy to one's children or to other people.

One of the most important reasons for saving is to smooth out the irregularities in the flow of income coming to an individual over his or her lifetime. People are becoming increasingly aware of the fact that (given current life expectancies) there is often a 10- to 30-year period of living in retirement after earnings from work have stopped. Thus, individuals must decide how to deal financially with this nonwork period of life and whether to provide through asset accumulation economic resources to supplement pension income.

Assets put aside as a precautionary measure or for anticipated major expenditures in old age are not available for meeting immediate needs. If you are worried, for example, about having high medical expenses that Medicare will not completely cover, if you expect that you might have to go into a nursing home, or if you anticipate that property taxes will increase dramatically in your city or town, you must accumulate additional assets to provide for such events. Thus, studies (e.g., Danziger et al., 1982–83; Mirer, 1980) show that contrary to predictions by economists based on the life-cycle hypothesis, the elderly as a group tend to save, not dissave. It is only among the very old that widespread dissaving by the elderly occurs.

Similarly, if you have nonliquid assets such as housing, as long as you are determined to keep that housing and not sell the property, that asset is not convertible into income to be used for day-to-day living. In effect, the asset is "locked in."

In fact, a high proportion of older people own a home or have an equity in it. About 80 percent of elderly couples live in an owned home, compared to about 40 percent of nonmarried elderly persons. The amount of mortgage debt on those homes is usually very low; in fact, about four-fifths of elderly homeowners own their homes free of any mortgage. Thus we find that many older persons have a sizable asset accumulation, but often most of it is not available for day-to-day living expenses. (See Table 2–11.)

Until recently in the United States there was no available financial mechanism that would permit people to sell the equity in their home, get back money over a period of time, and still be able to live in the house. In contrast, in France a home annuity plan called *viager* has been in existence for many years, and a story in the *Boston Globe* (3 December 1978) reports that there are over 400,000 currently in existence. A viager arrangement is negotiated by the homeowner with a buyer and results in the buyer paying an agreed-upon down payment and a monthly payment to the owner for the rest of the owner's life (in return for the property at death). The amounts paid are mutually agreed upon—with the age and health status of the owner taken into account. The arrangement, to a certain extent, represents a gamble on the part of both parties. The buyer, however, can go to an insurance company and take out an actuarial insurance plan to help offset the payments promised in the resulting legal agreement.

Since January 1, 1979, the Federal Home Loan Bank Board (FHLBB) in the United States has allowed federally chartered savings and loan associations to offer *reverse annuity mortgages*.

Table 2–11. Home Equity[a] of Elderly Households[b] in 1984

Equity	Percent
None	27
$1–19,999	8
$20,000–39,999	13
$40,000–59,999	13
$60,000–79,999	11
$80,000–99,999	7
$100,000–149,999	12
$150,000–199,999	5
$200,000 or more	5
Total Percent[c]	100

Source: Author's tabulations of Survey of Income and Program Participation (SIPP), Wave 4.
[a]Equity of elderly persons and, if married, their spouses. Equity of other household members is not included.
[b]Households with at least one elderly member.
[c]Does not add to 100 due to rounding.

Under this type mortgage, a homeowner may sell some equity in the house, receiving in return a fixed monthly sum based on a percentage of the current market value of the house. Reverse annuity mortgages are potentially available in all states, but each federal savings institution's program has to be approved by the FHLBB.

Thus far, the spread of this option has been very slow. As of January 1985, fewer than 400 reverse annuity mortgages had been issued throughout the entire United States (HUD, 1985). The slow acceptance is no doubt a result of unfamiliarity, the risks involved, and the small amount of income that often results. For the interested reader, Scholen and Chen (1980) give a good introduction to the complex set of issues that must be satisfactorily resolved before "unlocking home equity" becomes commonplace.

Table 2–12 shows the **net worth** of the aged in 1984. Net worth is the value of total assets less any debts owed by the individual or family. Looking at Table 2–12, we see that the net worth of many aged units is quite high when we add together financial assets, real estate (own home, rental property, vacations homes, and land holdings), any business holdings, and the value of motor vehicles. Forty-five percent of couples and about a quarter of the aged living alone have a net worth of $100,000 or more. At the same time, about another quarter of the aged living alone have a net worth under $5,000—with 10 percent of women and 13 percent of men in debt or without a positive asset balance.

Table 2–12   Distribution of Net Worth[a] for the Aged, 1984

Net Worth	Couples	Other Men	Other Women
Zero or negative	2%	13%	10%
$1–4,999	5	13	12
$5,000–9,999	3	5	5
$10,000–24,999	6	10	11
$25,000–49,999	13	16	18
$50,000–99,999	27	21	24
$100,000–249,999	31	16	18
$250,000–499,999	9	5	3
$500,000 or more	5	3	1
Total[b]	100%	100%	100%

Source: U.S. Bureau of the Census, *Household Wealth and Asset Ownership: 1984*, Current Population Reports, Series P-70, No. 7 (Washington, D.C.: U.S. Government Printing Office, 1986), Table 4.
[a]See explanation in text.
[b]Does not total 100 due to rounding.

As we saw from Table 2–11, many aged have large **equities** in their homes, which accounts for much of the high net worth we see in Table 2–12. When we look just at *financial* assets, a different picture emerges. Table 2–13 shows that large proportions of the elderly have little or no financial assets. One-fourth of unrelated aged men and women, for example, have no money in bank accounts nor hold stocks, bonds, or mutual funds. Over one-third of aged couples (both age 65 or over) have less than $15,000 in assets, with nearly one-quarter having less than $3,000.

Again, a note of caution is in order. As we discussed earlier in this chapter (p. 25), it is difficult to get accurate statistics on income and assets. Surveys to determine asset holdings of individuals have been undertaken very infrequently in the United States, and those attempted have been plagued by the problem that many people underreport their assets. Although surveys on the amounts and kinds of income also have underreporting problems, the amount of underreporting is greater when attempting to ascertain *assets*. In this regard, Juster, who is an expert on survey data, comments: "While my judgment is that we know remarkably little about saving in the aggregate, except for a few components of saving that are well-measured and well-understood, what we know at the macrolevel represents a solid concrete-and-steel edifice compared to what we know at the microlevel" (Juster, n.d.).

Table 2–13   Financial Assets[a] of the Elderly, 1984

Value of Assets	Married, Both Age 65 +	Couples, Only One Age 65 +	Unrelated Men, 65 +	Unrelated Women, 65 +
None	14%	19%	26%	25%
$1–2,999	9	10	15	19
$3,000–14,999	14	17	19	18
$15,000–29,999	11	10	12	13
$30,000–49,999	9	6	8	9
$50,000–74,999	9	11	11	9
$75,000–99,999	7	6	3	2
$100,000–149,999	10	7	2	3
$150,000–199,000	9	5	2	1
$200,000–249,999	3	3	*[b]	*[b]
$250,000 +	6	6	2	*[b]
Total Percent[c]	100%	100%	100%	100%

Source: Author's tabulation of Survey of Income and Program Participation (SIPP).
[a]Interest earning bank accounts, other interest earning assets, and stocks/bonds/mutual funds.
[b]Less than 1 percent.
[c]May not add to 100 percent due to rounding.

In-kind Income

In-kind income consists of goods and services available to the aged without expenditure of money or available at prices below their market value. For example, special housing programs for the elderly make apartments available at rates below the normal market price, a subsidy being paid by the government. The federal food stamp program issues coupons that can be used to purchase food in retail stores. Another large program provides "energy assistance" to the elderly. The largest in-kind programs, Medicare and Medicaid, provide the elderly with various health care services.

Timothy Smeeding (1982) estimates that in 1980 the total market value of the major food, housing, and medical care benefits for both the aged *and nonaged* was $72.5 billion. Table 2–14 shows that 85 percent of the aged receive none of the benefits from these services and that the energy assistance and food stamps assist the largest numbers of low-income elderly.

A major problem in estimating the impact of in-kind benefits on economic status is determining how best to value these benefits. As Schmundt, Smolensky, and Stiefel (1975) have noted, the value that the recipients themselves place on some in-kind goods may be substantially less than the market price.

Smeeding (1982) has estimated the value of major in-kind benefits using three alternative measures and finds that using different valuation techniques and different income definitions produces widely varying estimates. Table 2–15 shows that food and housing

Table 2–14 In-Kind Federal Benefits for Low-Income Households, 1984

	All Persons Age 65 or Over			
			Nonmarried	
Participation and Type of Program	*Total*	*Married Couples*	*Men*	*Women*
Percent participating in:				
None of the programs	85%	94%	84%	78%
One program	11	5	13	16
Two or more programs	4	1	3	6
Energy assistance	7	3	7	10
Food stamps	6	3	7	8
Public housing	4	1	4	6
Rental assistance	2	1	2	3

Source: U.S. Social Security Administration, *Income and Resources of the Population 65 and Over* (Washington, D.C.: U.S. Government Printing Office, 1986).

Table 2–15   Aged Poverty Rates Using Different
Valuation Techniques and Income Concepts, 1979

Valuation Technique	*(A)* Money Income Only	*(B)* A + Food and Housing Benefits	*(C)* B + Medical Care (excluding institutional care)	*(D)* B + Medical Care (including institutional care)
I[a]	14.7%	12.9%	5.2%	4.5%
II[b]	14.7	13.1	9.3	7.0
III[c]	14.7	13.7	10.8	10.8

Source: Timothy M. Smeeding, "Alternative Methods for Valuing Selected In-Kind Transfer Benefits and Measuring Their Effect on Poverty." Technical Paper 50 (Washington, D.C.: U.S. Bureau of the Census, 1982).
[a]The "market value" approach: the value is equal to the private market purchasing power of benefits received by individuals.
[b]The "recipient or cash equivalent value" approach: recipient value reflects the program beneficiary's own valuation of the benefit; it is most often measured by the amount of cash that would make the recipient just as well off as the in-kind transfer.
[c]The "poverty budget share" approach: assumes that, for the purposes of measuring poverty, the value of an in-kind benefit can be no more than that implied by observed consumption levels for people near the poverty level.

benefits for the aged reduce their poverty level slightly. If Medicare is taken into account, however, the poverty rate drops sharply.

Interfamily and Intrafamily Transfers

Another issue to be considered is the impact of transfers among various members of the family. While we know relatively little about the magnitude and nature of these transfers, available data indicate that it is an important means of support for a significant number of the elderly.

Numerous studies have documented the fact that the elderly in this country prefer to live apart from their children. For most older people, moving into a household with relatives remains an act of financial or social necessity rather than preference (see, for example, Soldo, 1981). Often, in an effort to enable an elderly person who is otherwise functioning well to remain in his or her home or apartment, relatives may provide economic assistance to supplement public transfers. However, the greatest transfers go to unmarried older people who for one reason or another have been forced to move in with relatives (Morgan, 1978).

Transfers within families take many forms, however, and go both ways (agewise). They include the provision of *emergency* money, loans, or services, regular support over relatively long periods, child care, gifts, food, and shelter. If one considers transfer at *all* ages, estimates by James Morgan at the University of Michigan indicate that "the family is by far the most important welfare or redistributional mechanism even in an advanced industrial country like the United States with extensive public and private income maintenance programs" (Morgan, 1983).

Focusing on the elderly, one study (Shuchman, 1983) has found that in 1980 only 13 percent of those elderly (age 60 and over) living alone received family transfers. However, the amount they received was substantial—on average, about $2,000. In contrast, over one-third of those who lived with others received family transfers. Unlike those recipients living independently, they received a relatively small amount—with the majority receiving less than $100.

The Adequacy of Income in Old Age

In 1976 a task force of government experts reviewed ways of measuring poverty more accurately. In their final report they emphasize the fact that assessing income adequacy necessitates standards that are *relative:*

> Poor persons living in the United States in the 1970s are rich in contrast to their counterparts in other times and places. They are not poor if by poor is meant the subsistence levels of living common in some other countries. Nor are most poor like their counterparts in this country fifty or one hundred years ago. This country is concerned about poverty, its causes and correlates. It is willing to relieve the poverty of some of the poor, and it wants to measure the effectiveness of its efforts to do so. None of this can be done without some idea of who is to be considered poor and who is not. [Poverty Studies Task Force, 1976]

In this section we look at various measures of adequacy in relation to the income of older persons. In early times, nations had little choice but to define basic needs in terms of survival. But for the more affluent nations of the world today, need becomes more relative and, hence, more difficult to measure.

The most common measure of poverty in America today is the government's poverty index. Developed in the early 1960s by the Social Security Administration, it gained prominence in President Johnson's declared War on Poverty. The index continues to be widely used today, despite the fact that the Nixon administration— very early in its first term—discouraged government agencies from using the index, arguing that because of conceptual and measurement problems it was a misleading and unreliable measure.

A succinct description of the Social Security Administration's poverty index was presented in 1967 testimony by Wilbur Cohen before the U.S. House Committee on Ways and Means (1967):

> *The starting point for the SSA poverty index is the amount of money needed to purchase the food for a minimum adequate diet as determined by the Department of Agriculture. The food budget is the lowest that could be devised to supply all essential nutrients using food readily purchasable in the U.S. market (with customary regional variations). The poverty line is then calculated at three times the food budget (slightly smaller proportions for one- and two-person families) on the assumption—derived from studies of consumers—that a family that has spent a larger proportion of its income on food will be living at a very inadequate level. The food budgets and the derivative poverty income cutoff points are estimated in detail for families of differing size and composition (62 separate family types) and a farm/nonfarm differential for each type. This variation of the poverty measure in relation to family size and age of members is its most important distinguishing characteristic.*
>
> *Because the level of living implied by the poverty index is lower than we think most people would regard as an appropriate measure of adequacy of income for retired persons or disabled workers and their families or widows and children, we have also developed a slightly higher index. We call this the low income index, and it is definitely low income.*

It is an interesting fact that in actual practice the low income index has rarely been used for policy evaluation purposes. Instead, the poverty index has almost exclusively dominated the discussions of how many nonaged and aged are in economic difficulty and what policies are needed to deal with these difficulties. It is important, therefore, to understand how the poverty index is calculated and its limitations.

Calculating the Poverty Index

Because of the wide use and importance of this poverty measure let us run through its construction step by step. First, as was indicated in Cohen's statement above, an amount of adequate food for the family unit is determined, and then the cost of that food at prevailing prices is ascertained by pricing foods in retail stores.

For about 30 years the Department of Agriculture has produced "food plans" that meet the nutritional standards set out by an organization called the National Research Council. While these plans meet nutritional standards, they also try to make the quantities and types of food chosen compatible with the general preferences of American families—preferences determined by food consumption studies. It is not simply a matter of giving poor people only beans to eat. General eating habits and preferences are taken into account.

Thus, in constructing a food plan, an attempt is made to respond to the fact that most people prefer meat to beans, although in terms of protein you can get more or at least as much protein from beans as you can from meat. The fact remains, however, that most of the protein in such plans is provided by the cheaper nonmeat products.

It is also important to note that the food plans were originally devised for *emergency periods only* and that no one is expected to have to live over a long period of time on these very minimal food amounts. This implies that these food diets could be detrimental to your health over an extended period.

Finally, the Department of Agriculture makes no pretense of assuming that all families can skillfully budget or that they are willing to eat the foods specified in the plans. The assumptions need not be made, given the purpose of the plans. They were developed simply as a device to provide social welfare agencies with a needs standard that was not completely subjective in determining how much money poor people need to avoid serious malnutrition.

The next step in developing the poverty measure is to construct food budgets for different types of families. The poverty index is based on family units with different combinations of the following characteristics: *(same as "equivalency scale?" eg. 54)*

1. Age of head over or under age 65
2. Size of family (2 to 7 or more)
3. Farm and nonfarm
4. Male and female head of household
5. Number or related children under age 18
6. "Unrelated" family units

The final step is to multiply the cost of the various food plans by three. As explained by the Social Security Administration:

The Agriculture Department evaluated family food consumption and dietary adequacy in a 1955 survey week and reported for all families of two or more—farm and nonfarm—an expenditure for food approximating one-third of money income after taxes. Two-person nonfarm families used about 27 percent of their income for food and families with three or more persons about 35 percent. A later study made in 1960–61 by the Bureau of Labor Statistics found for urban families that nearly a fourth of a family's income (after taxes) went for food. There is less variation by size of family than might have been anticipated, ranging between 22 percent and 28 percent. . . . The earlier relationship based upon the Department of Agriculture's study was adopted as the basis for defining poverty— that is, an income less than three times the cost of the economy food plan for families of three or more persons. [U.S. House Committee on Ways and Means, 1967]

Thus we see that the "three" used to calculate the poverty level is based upon a survey of the ratio of food consumption to other expenditures of *all* families in the United States. Averaging all families, the Agriculture Department came out with an estimate of three. The Bureau of Labor Statistics' estimate of four was ignored by the Social Security Administration for unstated reasons.

How Good a Measure?

The ratio of food to other expenditures is a key factor in constructing the poverty index. As we indicated above, a higher ratio based on Bureau of Labor Statistics data was not used when the index was first constructed. However, other data that have become available since 1955 also suggest that a higher ratio is appropriate. Tabulation of the 1965 Food Consumption Survey produced a 3.4:1 ratio. "More significantly, the Consumer Expenditure Surveys of 1960–61 and 1972–73 seem to indicate that the ratio exceeds 5:1" (Poverty Studies Task Force, 1976).

A related issue is the measurement of the minimum food requirements used to estimate food costs in the ratio. The current index uses a measure of adequate diet based on the Department of Agriculture's 1963 Economy Food Plan. In 1975 the Department of Agriculture replaced this food plan with a new Thrifty Food Plan. The Thrifty Food Plan reflects revised allowances for essential nutrients and newer data on family food selections.

Mollie Orshansky, who was a major participant in the development of the original government index, points out that the new food plan implies poverty income thresholds that are about 40 percent higher than current levels. Testifying before Congress in 1978, she estimated that "shifting to the more realistic update . . . would just about double the number of aged poor to include nearly a third of all persons 65 or older, and the number either poor or near poor would embrace approximately two in every five" (Orshansky, 1978).

Another problem involves not counting low-income persons as poor if they are institutionalized or living with relatives. In 1976 there were over a million "hidden poor" (mostly unmarried women) who were living with relatives because their low incomes did not permit independent living (Orshansky, 1978). A more recent estimate of the extent of this measurement problem is provided using statistics provided by Grad (1985). In 1984, 10 percent of 65 + aged units (couples and nonmarried persons) living with other family members were in families where the *total family income* was below poverty. If we look at *only the income of these aged units,* however, we find that not 10 but 34 percent of these aged have "own income" below the poverty level. Most of these poor aged are missed in the official poverty statistics.

Poverty Index Statistics

In 1986 the poverty index level for a two-person family with head age 65 or more was $6,630; the one-person level was 4,255.[3] In 1986 (the latest year for which data were available) there were 3.5 million aged (or 12.4 percent of all the aged) with *money* income below the poverty level. Figure 2–6 shows the sharp decline that has occurred in the rate of poverty over the 1959–1986 period. But Table 2–16 shows that there are wide differences in poverty rates among ethnic subgroups of the elderly. For example, while the poverty rate for the white aged was 14 percent in 1986, it was 31 percent for the black aged.

As we discussed previously, it is important to remember that the statistics discussed above are based on money income before paying taxes. If in-kind income is included, if taxes are taken out, and if other adjustments are made, a very different picture emerges. Earlier we reported the estimates by Smeeding (1982), based on adjustments for in-kind income. His estimates suggest that official poverty rate figures are too high. Another study by the Institute on Poverty at the University of Wisconsin-Madison takes the money income of the elderly and makes three different adjustments, focusing on the economic status of the elderly relative to the nonelderly (Danziger et al., 1984). The aged are more likely than their younger counterparts to own their own homes and other

---

[3]The corresponding levels for nonaged two-person and one-person families were $7,372 and $5,701, respectively.

Figure 2-6   Percent of Aged with Money Incomes Below the Poverty Level, 1959-1986. Source: Based on data in U.S. Bureau of the Census, *Consumer Income*, Current Population Reports, Series P-60, No. 105 (Washington, D.C.: U.S. Government Printing Office, 1987).

consumer durables (except cars). The study estimates the value of the contribution these durables made to family income (for example, the amount not spent for rent by owning a home). Since the aged have special tax advantages, they also adjust incomes for federal and state income tax and local property taxes. Finally, household size varies with age; households in the prime age groups (35–54) on average contain twice as many persons as those headed by someone age 65 or older. Since a four-person household, for example, requires more income than a two-person one to achieve the same living standard, some adjustment is needed.

Danziger et al. apply these adjustments to a national sample of families in 1973. In 1973 the average money income of the aged was only 49 percent of all other families. The Danziger estimates indicate, however, that the adjustments enumerated above raise the relative income of the aged to 90 percent of the rest of the population. If in-kind income were added in, the situation would be even better—significantly better. Reporting on the Danziger findings, the Institute on Poverty at the University of Wisconsin-

Table 2-16   Poverty Rates: 1959–1986[a]

	1959	1968	1977	1981	1986
All persons in U.S.	22%	13%	12%	14%	14%
All persons age 65 and over	35	25	14	15	12
White aged	33	23	12	13	11
Nonwhite aged	61	47	35	c	c
Black				39	31
Hispanic[b]				26	23

Source: Based on data in U.S. Bureau of the Census, Consumer Income, Current Population Reports, Series P-60 (Washington, D.C.: U.S. Government Printing Office, various years).
[a]The percentages in this table are rounded to the nearest percent and therefore differ slightly from published official government statistics.
[b]Persons of Hispanic origin may be of any race.
[c]Percent not available.

Madison (1983) concludes, "Thus it can be safely said that today the aged are *at least* as well off economically as the rest of us."

But remember: Quite a few people at all ages are economically disadvantaged. The University of Wisconsin study does not refute that fact. Rather, the study shows that the aged as a group are not—as in years past—an exceptionally or uniquely disadvantaged group. But the study also warns us about using the government poverty index. We can use poverty index statistics as an indicator of changes in the economic status of the low-income population. But they should be used with great caution and sensitivity to their many limitations.

Thus far we have talked only about how *the poverty index understates the economic status of the elderly*. Many people argue, however, that other measures are more appropriate for assessing the economic status of the *general* elderly population. As one major critic of the index has observed, "To tout a 'poverty line' based on a starvation diet and an outdated concept of a family's budget as an adequate measure of what is necessary to humanely survive is indefensible" (U.S. House Select Committee on Aging, 1978).

The Retired Couple's Budget

A second way of measuring the adequacy of aged income, used in past years, was the U.S. Bureau of Labor Statistics' Retired Couple's Budget (1966): "The retired couple is defined as a husband age 65 or over and his wife. They are self-supporting, living independently in their own home, in reasonably good health, able to take care of themselves."

Actually there are three budgets—indicative of three different levels of living. The illustrative family is assumed to have, for each budget level, *average inventories* of clothing, house furnishings, major durables, and other equipment. The budgets pertain only to *urban* families with the specified characteristics. No budgets are available for rural families. The budgets are not intended to represent a minimum or subsistence level of living but rather a level described by the Bureau of Labor Statistics as "modest but adequate."

The history of this budget is interesting. Originally, the Bureau of Labor Statistics had only one budget for a *nonaged* family of four persons, first developed in 1946–47. It was recognized quite early, however, that it was inappropriate to measure an older couple's needs in terms of the needs of a family of four. The younger family, for example, has extra expenses for clothing and educating children.

Reacting to the different living situations of different families, the Social Security Administration developed concurrently with the Bureau of Labor Statistics' budget effort a separate budget for retired couples. In 1959 the Bureau of Labor Statistics revised the older couple's budget. This budget was then up-dated every three or four years to take account of price changes. But more importantly, the budget was periodically adjusted in an attempt to account for general increases in the standard of living. Thus, for example, in the 1959 budget *five out of six* aged families were assumed to have home telephones (which were used for local calls only). By 1966 the budgets assumed that all older couples needed to have phones and that provision for some long-distance calls was appropriate.

How were the budget changes in living standards determined? Most were based on "consumer expenditure surveys" of families with different incomes. As average income increases, average expenditures for different goods change. As described by the Bureau of Labor Statistics, the amount chosen for the budget was "the point on the income scale where families stop buying 'more and more' and start buying either 'better and better' or something else less essential to them."

By means of this technique a majority of changes in the budget level reflect changes in the real standard of living of individuals (rather than just price changes). Thus the Bureau of Labor Statistics' budget standard was not locked into a mechanism similar to the Social Security Administration's three-times-the-food-budget assumption. Once again, however, the assumptions made were somewhat arbitrary. In the words of the Bureau of Labor Statistics:

"In general, the representative list of goods and services comprising the standard of budget reflects the collective judgment of families as to what is necessary and desirable to meet the conventional and social as well as the physical needs of families in the present decade."

In the autumn of 1971 the Bureau of Labor Statistics issued for the first time not one but three budget levels for an aged couple: a "lower," an "intermediate," and a "higher" budget. The development of alternative budgets was in part stimulated by the fact that some people were saying the Bureau of Labor Statistics' budget was too high for their purposes, while others were saying it was too low:

> *It has been evident that no single budget at one specified level would meet all of the important needs. Throughout the decade of the 1940s, for example, state public assistance agencies appealed to BLS [Bureau of Labor Statistics] to develop a budget for a lower living standard or to suggest ways in which the moderate budget could be scaled down. . . . On the other hand, representatives of voluntary social and welfare agencies providing services to families with a special problem . . . frequently requested budget estimates for a standard higher than moderate . . . in determining eligibility or establishing a scale of fees paid for the services provided. [U.S. Bureau of Labor Statistics, 1967]*

A major revision in the Retired Couple's Budget was made in 1969. The budget was then updated annually in succeeding years by adjusting various components of the budget by changes in the consumer price index. For the fall of 1981 the Bureau of Labor Statistics (1982) set the Retired Couple's Budget at $7,226 (low level), $10,226 (intermediate level), and $15,078 (high level). This is the last year for which the index is available. The Bureau of Labor Statistics has discontinued estimating the budget as a result of budgetary cutbacks.

Chen (1984) has calculated the proportion of retired couples with money incomes that fell below the low and intermediate budgets in various years:

Year	Below Low	Below Intermediate
1970	29%	49%
1975	21	42
1980	18	35

His estimates show a steady improvement over the 1970–1980 period. However, by 1980 there were still 2.3 million couples (35 percent) with incomes below the intermediate level.

Maintaining Living Standards

Today older workers are retiring at increasingly early ages (see Chapter 3). Following their departure from the labor force they are faced with the prospect of expenditure needs that do not decrease as much as many would like to believe. In the retirement period there are usually rising health expenditures, increased leisure activities, and increased need for supportive services. There is also a continuing need for the basic essentials of food and housing. Moreover, the retired quickly become aware of any rise in the living standards of nonretired families as these younger families share in the general, long-run economic growth of the country. Such increases no doubt generate a desire among many of the aged to "keep up."

It is this ability to keep up that we will focus on. In addition to the aged who find their income near or below the poverty level, there are other aged whose earnings during the working period allowed them to maintain a comfortable living standard but whose retirement incomes have dropped far below their preretirement levels.

This decline in living standards in retirement has become increasingly unacceptable in the United States. It is a generally accepted goal of retirement planning to provide enough income in retirement to prevent living standards from dropping significantly. Thus, the President's Commission on Pension Policy (1981) expressed the goals this way:

> *Individuals should be able to maintain their preretirement standard of living during retirement years. Retirees should not have to experience a sudden drop in their standard of living. These goals should be accomplished by using income from all sources, including benefits from retirement programs as well as from income derived from individual efforts.*

In later chapters we discuss in great detail the extent to which pensions replace preretirement earnings and the use of replacement rates to assess pension income adequacy. In anticipation of that discussion, a few statistics from a study by the Social Security Administration (Fox, 1982) are given here to show the magnitude of the problem. Of those couples who began receiving social security benefits in 1968–1976, about 90 percent received social security benefits below the amount necessary to maintain their preretirement living standard. For about 30–40 percent, social security benefits alone were so low that in the absence of other income, living standards would have dropped dramatically. About

40 percent of aged households also received public employee or private pension income. Close to half of these dual pension families or individuals had total pension incomes high enough to enjoy a living standard close to their preretirement situation.

Thus, many of the aged in the past have had incomes above the poverty level but have failed to achieve the adequacy levels specified by the older couple's budget. But even among the better-off elderly who met the BLS standard, there were many who found themselves faced with a sharp decline in income over their preretirement levels and a consequent decline in their living standards. (We will have much more to say about this problem in later chapters.)

Comparisons with the Nonaged

One often sees the median (or mean) income of the aged compared to the medians for other age groups. These crude comparisons are somewhat misleading, however. Elderly households are typically smaller than those of other age groups (except the very young); for example, households with a head age 34–54 are on the average twice as big. This means that elderly incomes are generally supporting fewer people, with more income potentially available to each person. Since we often want to compare the adequacy of aged income with other groups, we need to take account of these size differences.

One common adjustment for comparison purposes is to divide each family's income by the number of people in the household, thereby obtaining a "per capita" measure. Danziger et al. (1984) point out its weaknesses:

> The per capita measure is easy to understand and mathematically convenient but has little else to recommend it. Its use implies, for example, that people who marry spouses with no income or earnings potential are cutting their economic well-being in half. The per capita measure also ignores all economics of scale and specialization within households and is especially inappropriate for households that derive a large share of their full income in the form of leisure or production of home services.

There is an alternative approach to comparing different groups. One can develop an index that takes account of differences in family size and composition, health status, age, sex, and other relevant characteristics when determining the level of income necessary to achieve a given level of economic well-being. This measure is called an "equivalency scale."

The basic approach in calculating an equivalency scale is to develop an objective way of determining equivalent levels of consumption for families of varying composition. Historically, measures based on food-income relationships have been most common. As we saw previously, the current official poverty index embodies an equivalency scale based solely on food consumption needs.

Based on expenditures on all types of consumption goods and services, Danziger et al. (1984) have estimated an equivalency scale for a wide range of family types. Table 2–17 presents some of these estimates to illustrate some of the differences they found. For example, Danziger's estimates show that an elderly couple needs income that is about 64 percent of the income of a four-person family (age 35–54, children ages 12–17) to achieve a similar or equivalent level of well-being. And an older woman living alone needs about half the income of an aged couple to achieve a similar equivalency.

The principal advantage of this approach to comparing adequacy is its seeming objectivity. It can be calculated directly by direct measurements of actual consumer behavior of different groups. We must remember, however, that such measures do not take into account all of the factors that affect the consumption levels of families differing in size and stage in the life cycle. Moreover, as with other measures, underlying the calculations are certain assumptions that are essentially arbitrary—what consumption to measure, how to define different groups, how to interpret differences in savings rates, etc. Once again, therefore, we find that there is no agreement among experts on the best way to take account of family size differences when making comparative judgments about the economic well-being of various groups.

Table 2–17 Equivalence Scale

Consumer Unit Composition	Age of Head			
	35	35–54	54–64	65+
One person (female)	50	53	46	37
Two persons (man and wife)	77	80	73	64
Four persons (couple, two children):				
Age of children				
Under age 6	83	87	80	71
Ages 12–17	97	100	93	84
Ages 18 and over	101	105	97	89

Source: Based on data in Sheldon Danziger, J. Van der Gaag, E. Smolensky, and M. K. Taussig, "Implications of the Relative Economic Status of the Elderly for Transfer Policy." In H. J. Aaron and G. Burtless, eds., *Retirement and Economic Behavior* (Washington, D.C.: The Brookings Institution, 1984), Table 3.

The Impact of Inflation

Economic instability, causing unemployment and inflation, creates insecurity for families and individuals of all ages because of the uncertainty of when and how it will strike. For those actually affected, inflation or unemployment can have a major impact on their economic situation by changing the real value of their wealth or affecting their earning power.

The phenomenon of inflation is without doubt one of the least understood of economic occurrences.[4] Almost everyone feels *harmed* by inflation; yet the truth is that some people and institutions *gain* from inflation. One person's loss is typically somebody else's gain. The result is a redistribution of wealth and income that can be both quite drastic and quite haphazard.

Inflation is a general and widely diffused increase in the level of prices. In any period the prices of some goods are declining; for example, calculator and computer prices have fallen dramatically over the past 20 years. When there is inflation, however, the quantity of goods and services with rising prices far outnumbers those with declining prices.

The most commonly employed measure of inflation is the consumer price index (CPI). Until January 1978, the CPI measured changes in the prices of goods and services purchased by urban wage earners and clerical workers. In 1978, however, the Bureau of Labor Statistics began publication of a new version of the CPI for all urban consumers. This new **index** takes into account the expenditures not only of wage earners and clerical workers but also salaried professionals, technical and managerial workers, the self-employed, retirees, and the unemployed. This new index covers approximately 80 percent of the total noninstitutional civilian population—about twice the coverage of the old index.

The CPI is a weighted aggregative index with fixed weights; it seeks to represent the annual consumption patterns of various individuals. Consumption patterns are measured by the Survey of Consumer Expenditures. Based on this survey, a "market basket" of about 400 goods and services is randomly selected and weighted. Prices for the CPI market basket are then obtained monthly, mostly by personal visits to a representative sample of nearly 18,000 stores and service establishments.

The CPI has a major effect on most Americans. Through its

---

[4] We can go only briefly into the economics of inflation in this book. Readers interested in a relatively nontechnical but more extensive discussion on the issue should read Solow (1975).

widespread use as an escalator of wages, pensions, and welfare benefits, about 57 percent of the organized workers under contract have some of their earnings pegged to the CPI (Minarik, 1981). Moreover, virtually everyone is affected by its direct impact on aggregate economic policies instituted by the President, Congress, and the **Federal Reserve.**

While inflation affects people of all ages, we will restrict the discussion that follows to the older population. There are five principal ways older people can be affected adversely by inflation:

1. If they are net creditors, assets that do not adjust in value for inflation will depreciate in value, reducing the *net worth* of the individual or family.

2. If they are recipients of **transfer** (pensions, unemployment benefits, etc.) or other income, adjustments in these various income sources may lag behind inflation, reducing real income.

3. If they are employed, adjustments in earnings levels may lag behind inflation, reducing real wages.

4. If they are taxpayers, the real burden of federal and state income taxes may increase if the tax brackets specified in the laws are defined in *money* rather than *real* terms.

5. If inflation is concentrated among items such as food, which comprise a larger proportion of elderly persons' budgets, the older age group may be differentially affected—especially if indexes used to measure and adjust various sources of income do not correctly reflect aged buying patterns.

Wealth

With regard to the first item—the impact of inflation on the wealth position of the elderly—the evidence is most clear. As we indicated earlier in this chapter, substantial financial assets are held by some of the elderly; these assets are highly concentrated, in the possession of a relatively small number of the aged. On the other hand, tangible assets—such as homes, automobiles, and the like—are held by a large proportion of the aged population.

In general, the money value of tangible assets tends to increase with inflation, leaving the real value of this portion of the aged's wealth unaffected. The value of most *financial* assets does not adjust in any consistent fashion with changes in the general level of prices. Persons holding bonds, checking accounts, savings accounts, and insurance policies often find the real value of these assets falling with inflation; in contrast, persons with debts—such as an outstanding mortgage on a home—find the real value of these debts also falling (which is to their advantage).

A number of studies have investigated the effect of unanticipated inflation on the distribution of wealth among households. They have found that when households are grouped according to age of head, the largest decline in wealth occurs among families headed by elderly persons. In contrast, the largest increase in wealth occurs among those age 25 to 34 who tend to be net debtors. It is the minority of the aged with substantial nonadjusting financial assets who are most severely affected. That is, for those aged fortunate enough to have substantial savings, inflation is often a serious problem.

Transfer Income

With regard to the second item—lagging **transfer income**—again the impact is relatively clear, but in a way that will surprise some readers. Since persons living primarily on relatively fixed incomes are clearly hurt by rising prices and since the aged are so heavily dependent on pensions, the aged traditionally have been cited as the major group harmed by inflation. While this was a major problem for the aged in years past, recent developments have substantially moderated it. *The major source of retirement income, the social security program, now adjusts benefits automatically for inflation.*

As we discuss in later chapters, concern about rising pension costs caused Congress in 1983 to delay for six months the inflation adjustment due that year. Congress also passed legislation that, starting in 1985, the automatic benefit adjustment would be based on the increase in the CPI *or average earnings*, whichever is less. However, this latter provision is to go into effect *only* if the combined social security pension reserves fall to a specified low level, and "catch-up" benefit payments are to be made when the reserve situation improves.

Thus, we see that social security benefits are generally well protected against inflation. Unfortunately, many people do not realize this, including some older people currently receiving benefits. A survey by Peter D. Hart Research Associates (1979) for the National Commission on Social Security found that there was a significant lack of understanding about this aspect of social security. Over half of those interviewed did not think (or were not sure) that "social security benefits go up automatically to match the rise in the cost of living." Quite surprising was the fact that 24 percent of retirees receiving benefits thought the statement was not true.

The social security pension programs are not the only programs indexed for inflation. The federal Supplemental Security Income (SSI) and food stamp programs also adjust fully for inflation. Civil service and military pensions adjust almost fully. And many state and local pension plans are adjusted automatically; these increases, however, are typically limited to a 2 to 4 percent maximum per year.

The three major income sources that do not adjust automatically are veterans' pensions, private pension benefits, and most supplemental state payments under SSI. Also, the levels of allowable income determining eligibility for SSI, food stamps, and some Medicaid programs are not changed automatically.

Overall, then, we see that the bulk of aged income is currently adjusted for inflation with a relatively short lag. Those elderly who depend heavily on income from assets and/or private pension income are more vulnerable.

Earnings and Tax Brackets

Both of these items share the common characteristic of being very difficult to predict with regard to inflationary impact. While earnings generally increase over time, partly in response to inflation, earnings in particular firms or industries may lag behind inflation. Some of the aged still working will find this to be a problem, but in general few are affected because not many of the elderly continue to work full time and because not all who do are employed in firms where earnings lag behind inflation.

Similarly, many aged do not pay income taxes because their incomes are low and social security income is exempt from federal taxes for all but those with very high incomes. In the past, those who did faced two problems: Some of the added income to compensate for inflation was taxed away; moreover, it was taxed away under a progressive federal income tax structure at progressively higher marginal rates. Starting in 1985, however, the federal tax law operates to index the brackets for inflation, thereby eliminating the problem.

Expenditure Patterns and Cost-of-Living Indexes

During inflationary periods, the prices of various goods change by different amounts. Since the expenditure patterns of individuals and families differ, any particular pattern of inflationary price increases will have a varying impact, depending on the particular expenditure patterns of the individuals. For example, if food and housing prices go up faster than other goods and services and if the aged spend a larger share of their income on food and housing, the result is a larger increase in prices paid by the aged than the nonaged.

Thus, there is concern that the CPI used to measure inflation and adjust social security benefits does not accurately reflect the aged's buying patterns. Over the years certain organizations and individuals have advocated, for example, that a separate price index for the elderly be established. And in 1987 the U.S. Senate passed legislation to create such a special index, but the proposal was not agreed to by the House of Representatives.

Numerous studies over the years have investigated the need for such an index.[5] Rarely has there been such agreement among economists on a particular research question. *All studies have found that the differences between the CPI and a special aged index are likely to be very small.* Thus, Minarik (1981) concludes that "given the absence of solid evidence that . . . [a multiple price index system] would yield different indexing outcomes over the long haul, we should probably leave special group indices alone."

Instead of a special index for the aged, a better approach would be to improve the existing CPI. Measuring general price changes accurately is a very difficult task. The most serious problem is a general upward bias in the CPI. This is due primarily to a lag that occurs in the introduction of new products and quality improvements in old products into the index (see Gordon, 1981). With regard to quality change, for example, the CPI usually does not take into account improvements in product performance when prices of a product go up. Thus, the prices of motor oil, tires, light bulbs, appliances, and so forth, have increased, but the service life of many such products has also increased. And, thus, in an important sense not all the price increases are inflationary.

The Bureau of Labor Statistics does occasionally improve the index. Recently, for example, the bureau changed the way owner-occupied housing is handled. This item in the index had become particularly troublesome when interest rates, including mortgage rates for housing loans, rose to unprecedented levels over the 1969–1972 period. The old way of handling the item in the index did not distinguish between homeowners who took out mortgages some years ago at much lower rates and those who had purchased housing recently.

---

[5] Hollister and Palmer (1972), Torda (1972), Mirer (1974), King (1976), Borzilleri (1978), Michael (1979), DRI (1980), Minarik (1981), Barnes and Zedlewski (1981), Bridges and Packard (1981), and Boskin and Hurd (1982).

Many problems with the CPI remain. Given the amount of indexing that now occurs based on this index, it would seem appropriate for the government to undertake a major program for improving the index.

Chapter 2 Highlights

We have tried to show in this chapter that attempts to assess the economic status of the elderly as one group are not very meaningful. Mindful of this danger of overgeneralizing about the aged, let us now summarize some of the major observations presented in preceding sections:

1. The economic status of the elderly has changed dramatically in recent years, primarily as a result of rising social security, private pension, and government employees' pension income.
2. Great caution is in order in generalizing from available statistics on income and assets. Both underreporting and the lack of disaggregation cause serious problems.
3. The major source of elderly income is social security, but earnings still represent a large proportion of the total—going to the minority of aged still working.
4. Money incomes of the aged tend to be lower than those of younger persons. In 1986, 54 percent of the nonaged had money incomes over $30,000; only 28 percent of aged families had income this high.
5. However, expanding the analysis to include such factors as in-kind income, special tax provisions, and household size narrows the differences considerably. Some say there are no significant differences!
6. Poverty among the aged, as measured by the government's poverty index, is now much lower than in past years; when in-kind income is considered, poverty practically disappears using this measure. Large numbers of the elderly, however, remain clustered just above the poverty level, and many still experience a large drop in living standard when they retire (comparing pre- and postretirement income).
7. Economic deprivation still exists on a large scale among the elderly, especially if we take into account rising expectations.
8. Contrary to popular belief, the aged have a large measure of protection from inflation. Those heavily dependent on financial assets and private pensions are most vulnerable. *to problems of inflation*

Suggested Readings

BLINDER, ALAN S., IRVING KRISTOL, AND WILBUR J. COHEN. Three views on "The Level and Distribution of Economic Well-Being." In Martin Feldstein, ed., *The American Economy in Transition*. Chicago: The University of Chicago Press, 1980. Blinder's paper and the reaction comments by Kristol and Cohen provide an excellent overview to this chapter.

CLARK, ROBERT L., AND JOSEPH J. SPENGLER. *The Economics of Individual and Population Aging*. Cambridge, England: Cambridge University Press, 1980. A good review of the literature on most of the topics covered in this book. Chapter 4 is on the "economic status of the elderly."

HOLDEN, KAREN C., R. V. BURKHAUSER, AND D. A. MYERS. "Income Transitions of Older Stages of Life: The Dynamics of Poverty," *The Gerontologist* 26 (June 1986): 292–297. This study examines the risk of poverty among a sample of elderly couples and widows interviewed over a 10-year period. One of its many interesting findings is that a far larger percentage of the elderly are subject to the risk of poverty over their lifetime than is suggested by studies measuring poverty at a particular point in time.

MOON, MARILYN. *The Measurement of Economic Welfare—Its Application to the Aged Poor*. New York: Academic Press, 1977. A good theoretical discussion of nonmoney factors affecting economic welfare. The book also presents empirical measures for the aged.

MORGAN, JAMES N. "The Redistribution of Income by Families and Institutions and Emerging Help Patterns." In G. J. Duncan and J. N. Morgan, eds., *Five Thousand American Families—Patterns of Economic Progress*, Volume X. Ann Arbor, Michigan: Institute for Social Research, The University of Michigan, 1983. Given the dearth of information in this area, this article is a research goldmine of important findings.

"Perspectives on Measuring Hardship: Concepts, Dimensions, and Implications." *The Gerontologist* 26 (February 1986). A collection of symposium papers reviewing the concepts and politics of economic deprivation. See especially the papers by Robert H. Binstock and Fay L. Cook.

Poverty Studies Task Force. *The Measure of Poverty*. A report to Congress as Mandated by the Education Amendments of 1974. Washington, D.C.: U.S. Department of Health, Education, and Welfare, 1976. "Must reading" for those who want a sophisticated understanding of issues involved in measuring poverty and collecting needed data.

SMEEDING, T., M. O'HIGGINS, AND L. RAINWATER. *Poverty, Inequality, and the Distribution of Income in an International Context*. London: Wheatshear Press, 1988. The book provides an excellent comparative view of the elderly's economic status in Canada, Israel, Norway, Sweden, West Germany, the U.S.A., and the U.K. It includes comparisons between the retired and nonretired and between the aged and nonaged.

Social Security Bulletin. Washington, D.C.: U.S. Government Printing Office (monthly). This journal reports changes in social security and other similar legislation. It also publishes the results of research studies by the SSA (and SSA-sponsored research projects), various survey findings, and international social security developments.

U.S. Senate Special Committee on Aging. *Developments in Aging*. Washington, D.C.: U.S. Government Printing Office (annual). This yearly report by the committee reviews a wide range of developments in aging, including economic aspects. An appendix contains reports from federal departments and agencies with specific activities affecting the elderly.

Chapter 3

TO WORK OR NOT TO WORK

Everyone is in favor of keeping older people in the labor force except the unions, government, business, and older people.

So commented a participant at a recent conference on the roles of the elderly in society (Mothner, 1985). The observation astutely summarizes the paradox of current retirement policies in the United States. Everyone talks about permitting and even encouraging older people to work. Yet every year fewer and fewer do. And, in fact, public and private actions, as compared with words, have been instrumental over the years in biasing the work-retirement choice toward retirement.

The Work-Leisure Trade-off

Every individual during his or her lifetime makes important choices regarding the type and amount of work to be undertaken. The Institute for Social Research at the University of Michigan has found that people in the United States average 1,347 hours per year of *paid* work and 1,487 hours of *unpaid* work. Thus the individual chooses some combination of work in the labor force (paid and volunteer), unpaid work in the nonmarket sector, and leisure. Economists emphasize the trade-off between paid work and leisure. Work produces goods and services and results in the income necessary to buy the goods and services of others. Leisure, also useful and valuable, is unobligated, discretionary time spent in nonpaid activities. Thus, an individual can get more leisure but only at the expense of less money to buy goods and services.

Paid employment results in the country's economic output—

gross national product—as measured by **national income account-ing** techniques and reported regularly by government statistics. *Nonmarket work*—for example, homemaking or do-it-yourself home repairs—is not included by economists in the national income accounts but adds significantly to total output. Nordhaus and Tobin (1973) estimate that in 1965, for example, the value of nonmarket work was equal to nearly half of our (counted) gross national product. *Not working* translates into a given amount of leisure over the lifetime.[1]

Measuring work in terms of hours per week, we begin at a zero level in early childhood. At some point the individual might start a paper route, do some baby-sitting, or engage in some other type of part-time work. In the teenage years, part-time work may increase, and some people begin full-time work. Others go to college and "stop work." Through the middle years most men and over one-third of all women work in the labor force full-time; most women also work in the nonmarket sector, and some work part-time in the labor force.[2] At ages 62 to 65 (or, increasingly, earlier) paid work stops abruptly for many. Individuals shift to nonpaid work and increasing amounts of recreational activities.

This brief summary approximates the work pattern of the typical American worker today. Granted, of course, there are lots of variations to this pattern. Should this pattern be changed?

Back in 1966, Kreps and Spengler developed estimates of the growth-leisure trade-off confronting the United States in the 1960s. Although the projections are out of date, they illustrate well some of the options a nation and its workers face as they look to the future. Figure 3–1 presents their projections of the various possibilities of additional gross national product (GNP) and/or leisure available over a 20-year period (1965–1985). As the various factors influencing economic growth (technological change, **investment,** rising quality of labor, and so forth) increase **productivity,** new opportunities for increased leisure and/or increased consumption arise:

> *With regard to the possible future growth in leisure and its probable distribution . . . at one extreme, assuming no change in working time, per capita gross national product could rise from $3,181 in 1965 to $5,802 in 1985, or by about 80 percent. At the other extreme, if one supposes that all growth is taken in leisure time except the*

---

[1] The work-leisure dichotomy is not as simple as we make it seem. See Robinson et al. (1984) for a good discussion of the difficulty in defining leisure.

[2] Nearly three-quarters of all women age 35–44 are employed full- or part-time. And over three-fifths of those age 45–54 are employed.

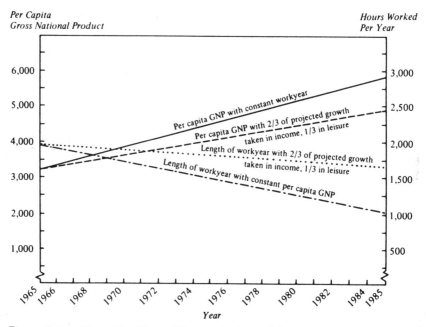

Per Capita
Gross National Product

Hours Worked
Per Year

Figure 3-1   Alternative Uses of Economic Growth Per Capita Gross National Product and Hours Worked, 1965-1985. Source: Juanita Kreps and Joseph Spengler, "The Leisure Component of Economic Growth," in National Commission on Technology, Automation and Economic Progress, *The Employment Impact of Technological Change,* Appendix Vol. II (Washington, D.C.: U.S. Government Printing Office, 1966), pp. 353-389.

> *amount necessary to keep per capita GNP constant at $3,181, the possible changes in work time would be as follows: the workweek could fall to 22 hours, or the workyear could be limited to 27 weeks per year, or retirement age could be lowered to 38 years, or almost half the labor force could be kept in retraining programs, or additional time available for education might well exceed our capacity to absorb such education. [Kreps and Spengler, 1966]*

If we took all the increased growth potential in the form of greater per capita output, Kreps and Spengler estimated (in 1966) that by the year 1985 we could almost double the level of per capita output achieved in 1965. In fact, this projection is close to what we actually did. Average weekly hours have declined moderately from 39 to 35 hours per week in the nonagricultural sector of the economy. And at the same time real per capita GNP (i.e., taking into account **inflation**) has increased by about two-thirds.

Projections like those of Kreps and Spengler assume that there are no "costs to growth," an assumption increasingly questioned by economists. Some of the growth, for example, will have to go into pollution control devices, sewage treatment plants, and defense expenditures (such as tanks and bombs); to say that this growth in output represents an increase in our standard of living is stretching a point.

Also, the projections assume that the government encourages the potential growth by use of appropriate **monetary** and **fiscal policies** and that the assumptions about future changes in technology and the growth of capital based on past occurrences are correct. Accepting these qualifications, we can extrapolate from Figure 3–1 into the future. One major option available to the nation is a sizable increase in the future real standard of living of individuals in the society. Alternatively, we can choose fewer goods and services but more leisure.

The Pattern of Leisure

In addition to the choice between work (more output) and leisure, there is the question of when leisure is taken. The increases in leisure experienced early in this century came primarily in the form of shortened workweeks and longer vacations. In contrast, much of the new leisure in recent decades has been allocated to the end of the lifespan.

Suppose that a country wants to hold constant the total amount of work and leisure over the lifespan but wishes to alter the way in which they are currently distributed. One procedure would be to determine at what point in the life cycle it might be appropriate to taper off weekly hours of work, if the option were available. Providing more leisure by reducing hours of work, however, means that some people *must work more* at some other time—later or earlier in their lives. Providing a significant increase in leisure without a significant drop in lifetime income probably means working longer when older.

Of course, past increases in the productivity of workers have permitted both leisure and income to simultaneously increase historically. But it is important to see that a different mix (both in amount and timing) was possible in the past and will be possible in the future.

Why do many professionals advocate changes in our present mix of work and leisure? Why do some urge, for example, that we stop the trend toward earlier retirement?

Some people are concerned about the rising trend toward "no work"; they claim that some people die earlier, partly as a result of the change from an active to a more sedentary life-style (Bradford; 1979), although there is little but anecdotal evidence to support such claims (Ekerdt, 1987). Some social gerontologists argue that termination of work results in psychological problems connected with the loss of social role and adjustment to retirement realities.[3] Economists worry about the problems of financially supporting a growing retired population with its accompanying rise in public and private pension costs. Some analysts, anticipating a possible future shortage of workers brought about by low fertility and rising retirement, call for incentives to keep people working longer.

While gerontologists and advocates on behalf of the elderly have been almost unanimous in calling for more flexibility in retirement age policies, much of the movement has been in the opposite direction. For example, as we will show in later chapters, public and private **pensions** have been designed to *encourage* retirement to help deal with America's chronic unemployment problems. Economist Juanita Kreps has succinctly summarized the current situation:

> *Retirement, a relatively new lifestage, has quickly become a . . . device for balancing the number of job seekers with the demand for workers at going rates of pay. Insofar as retirement practice is used to drain workers from the labor force, a reversal of the downward pressure on retirement age would seem to be possible only if labor markets tighten. Extensions beyond the usual retirement age are granted when there is a demand for specific talents. Given current levels of unemployment, however, there is no incentive to prolong worklife in general. . . . Except for current concern for the solvency of the public and private pension funds, labor market conditions would probably signal moves to encourage retirement as early as sixty. [Kreps, 1977]*

Legislation passed to prohibit mandatory retirement based on age is a step in the opposite direction. But, as we argue later in this chapter, the impact of such laws has been minimal (see pp. 81–84).

Changing Labor Force Participation

There is general agreement that one of the most important labor force developments of recent decades has been the dramatic rise in labor force withdrawals by older men. Figure 3–2 shows the

---

[3]In a later section of this chapter we discuss mounting evidence that disputes this pessimistic view.

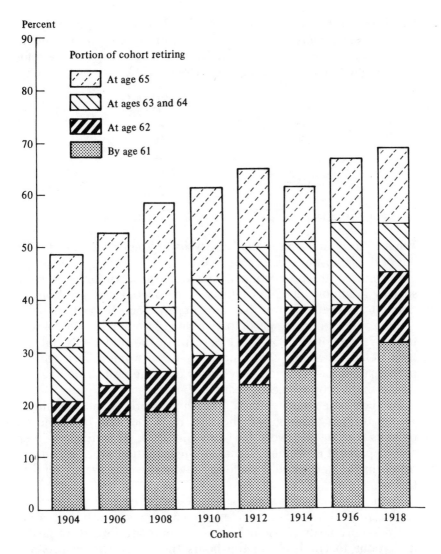

Figure 3-2 Percentage Out of the Labor Force at Specified Ages, Selected Cohorts of Older Men. (Source: Philip L. Rones, "Using the CPS to Track Retirement Trends Among Older Men," *Monthly Labor Review,* 108 (February 1985), Chart 1.

percentage of men born between 1904 and 1918 who were out of the labor force at various ages. Note the steady upward trend of labor force withdrawal at all the age levels.

Withdrawals tend to cluster around the eligibility ages for initial (age 62) and regular (age 65) social security pension benefits. As a consequence, the labor force participation rate for men over 64 has dropped from 57 percent in 1955 to less than 10 percent. But perhaps even more striking is the relatively recent decline in participation at earlier ages. The labor force participation rate for men age 60 to 64 continues to fall (Rones, 1978):

Year	Ages 60 to 64
1957	82.5%
1962	80.2
1967	77.6
1972	72.5
1977	62.9
1982*	57.2
1985*	55.4

*Unpublished estimate by the U.S. Bureau of Labor Statistics.

What is truly amazing is that nearly half of older men are totally out of the labor force *before* age 65.

In contrast, the proportion of females in the labor force has risen sharply in almost all age groups, with an overall increase from 26 percent in 1940 to over 55 percent in 1986. Regarding older women, the labor force participation rate of women age 55–64 rose from 27 percent in 1950 to 41 percent in the mid-1960s but has been relatively stable ever since. For those women over age 65, participation has declined very slowly over the past three decades with a slight drop in recent years to about 5 percent.

For both men and women, part-time work is most common among the very young and the elderly. About half of employed persons over age 64 work part-time (in 1985, 47 percent of men and 61 percent of women). Much of this part-time work is concentrated in the service and trade occupations where wages tend to be low.

Some older persons work part-time out of necessity; others do so by preference. Some need to supplement other income sources—primarily pension income. Others are forced by health limitations to cut back on the hours they work. Some prefer a gradual withdrawal to an abrupt stop. And finally, there are no doubt many who want more leisure but still value highly the various social and monetary benefits arising from some amount of labor force attachment.

Table 3–1 shows variation among nine nations in the proportion of people working after age 65. Compared with other industrialized countries, United States labor force participation by the aged falls in the upper range. Only Japan (where pensions are very low and many workers continue in lower paid work out of financial necessity) has higher participation rates.

Table 3–1 Labor Force Participation Rates of Older Workers in Nine Countries

	Age 55–64		Age 65 +			
	Men	Women	Men		Women	
Country	1984		Early 1960	1980	Early 1960	1980
United States	76%	41%	33%	19%	11%	8%
Australia	79	24	23	11	4	3
Canada	79	31	30	15	6	4
France	NA	NA	24	9ᵃ	9	4ᵃ
West Germany	69	25	25	8	8	3
Great Britain	NA	NA	23	9	6	3
Italy	NA	NA	25	8	7	2
Japan	86	44	57	41	24	15
Sweden	82	50	35	12	9	3

Source: Data for 1960 and 1980 are from Constance Sorrentino, "International Comparisons of Labor Force Participation, 1960–1981," *Monthly Labor Review* (February 1983), Table 4. Data for 1984 are from P. J. McMahon, "An International Comparison of Labor Force Participation, 1977–84," *Monthly Labor Review* (May 1986), Table 4.
ᵃData are for March 1979.

Economic Problems of Older Workers

Over the years there has been increasing recognition that a variety of special economic problems confront middle-aged and older workers: (1) age discrimination in hiring, (2) job obsolescence, (3) changing job-performance capabilities, necessitating job shifts (or job redesign), and (4) adverse institutional structures (such as mandatory retirement). In addition, older workers, while often protected by seniority against job loss, generally find themselves as vulnerable as younger workers to plant shutdowns and many of the dislocations arising from mergers and government spending cutbacks. Not only do these problems create immediate difficulties for workers and their families, but they often have an economic impact on their situation during the retirement years. Long-term unemployment, for example, makes saving difficult if not impossible. Moreover, periods of unemployment often result in lower public and private pension benefits in retirement.

These special employment problems associated with age are part of a larger set of factors influencing individuals in their decisions to work or not to work. In this regard, economists research factors influencing labor force participation and seek to understand the choices made in the relative amounts of time allocated between work and leisure. We emphasize in this section the institutional pressures and constraints placed on individuals in their determination of *when* to retire. We begin with a discussion of the retirement decision.

An important distinction in terminology must be kept in mind here. Throughout most of the book when we talk about the aged or older persons, we are usually referring to people in their 60s (often age 65 or older). In this chapter we talk about older workers but are not focusing exclusively or even primarily on persons over age 65. Rather, the major focus of this chapter is on workers who have reached middle age and those approaching retirement age (generally, the 45–65 age group).

Work Problems

As shown in Table 3–2, unemployment rates vary little with age but tend to be slightly higher in the later years than in the middle ones. Insulated from unemployment by job-dismissal customs and formal seniority rules, older workers are not as likely to lose their jobs. With changing consumer expenditure patterns, however, many established industries have experienced a stagnation or gradual decline in sales and hence employment opportunities. In contracting businesses or those that are closing, even senior job-holders are adversely affected. Declines, for example, in the textile, agriculture, steel, shoe, and automobile industries have encouraged or forced millions of workers to seek alternative jobs. Once unemployed, older workers find themselves faced with a variety of serious problems.

Table 3–2 shows that prior to the late 1960s the official unem-

Table 3–2 Unemployment Rates for Men, by Age Groups, Selected Years, 1968–1981

	25–54		Age 55–64		65+	
Year	U^a	$U + D^b$	U^a	$U + D^b$	U^a	$U + D^b$
1968	1.7	1.8	1.9	2.3	2.8	6.6
1970	2.8	2.9	2.8	3.1	3.3	5.5
1972	3.1	3.2	3.2	3.6	3.6	6.2
1974	3.1	3.2	2.6	2.9	3.3	6.0
1976	4.9	5.2	4.2	4.7	5.1	8.9
1978	3.5	3.7	2.8	3.3	4.2	7.2
1980	5.1	5.4	3.4	3.9	3.1	6.5
1981	5.5	5.8	3.6	4.2	2.9	6.3

Source: Philip L. Rones, "The Labor Market Problems of Older Workers," *Monthly Labor Review* 106 (May 1983), Table 1.
ªThe official unemployment rate, calculated by dividing total unemployment by the civilian labor force.
ᵇAn unemployment rate that includes all "discouraged" workers.

ployment rates for men 55 and over tended to be slightly *higher* than for those age 25–54. This relationship began to change in the 1970s. By the 1980 recession, the rates for men 65 and older were well below those 25–54 by the 1980 recession. But Rones (1983) shows that these statistics may be deceptive. Using data from the Current Population Survey, Rones estimates the number of workers who report that they want a job but are not looking because they believe they cannot find one—that is, "discouraged workers."

Table 3–2 shows that when discouraged workers are added to the official **unemployment rate**, the rates for men over age 64 rise dramatically—doubling and surpassing the other age groups. In part this results from the fact that since most persons in this age group are outside the labor force, there is a huge pool of potentially discouraged workers. It takes only a relatively small number from this pool to be identified as "discouraged" to shift the percentages in the table. While interpretation of the data is not easy, the statistics do suggest that many older persons who want to work do not think that acceptable job opportunities are available.

There has been a clear bias in private and public employment policy against older workers. They are discriminated against in job hiring. Work and job structures have been made relatively inflexible, making midcareer adjustments very difficult. Various policies encourage or force workers to retire from their "regular jobs." They are then discouraged or prevented from returning to the work force in new jobs.

In 1965 the nation was made aware of the extent and nature of discrimination toward older workers through a report issued by the Department of Labor. This report documented that at that time more than 50 percent of all available job openings were closed to applicants over age 55 because of employers' policies *not* to hire any person over that age. Moreover, about 25 percent of the job openings were closed to applicants over age 45.

Since its passage in 1967, the federal **Age Discrimination in Employment Act** has attempted to protect individuals from age discrimination in hiring, discharge, compensation, and other terms of employment. This law originally covered (with some exceptions) persons between the ages of 40 and 65. It was amended in 1978 to include workers up to age 69 and again in 1986 to prohibit mandatory retirement at any age.

As a result of this legislation, the more blatant signs of discrimination—such as newspaper ads restricting jobs to younger persons and forced retirements—have declined significantly. It is difficult to determine, though, the extent to which actual discrimination has in fact lessened, for little comprehensive evidence exists on the matter. Data on the duration of unemployment, however, may be one important indicator that serious problems still exist. While unemployment is relatively low among men age 45–65, men in this age group who become unemployed typically remain unemployed much longer than younger workers.

This longer average duration of unemployment is not all caused by age discrimination, however. Often older workers lack the necessary skills to qualify for available jobs or are not living in areas where job opportunities exist. Competing for jobs in the growing electronics and computer industries, for example, is difficult for many older workers. Many skills developed in the old established industries cannot be readily used in the new high-technology industries. And no large-scale programs exist in the United States to provide these older workers with the required newer skills.

Moreover, the problems arising from this incompatibility of skills have been aggravated by shifts in industries from their locations in the Northeast, Middle Atlantic, and North Central states to the Southeast, Southwest, and West. Many older workers with usable skills (reluctant to leave communities where they have established "roots") have been left behind, with little hope for suitable new employment.

With the growth of social security and **private pensions** has come the recognition that the nonmoney-employee-benefits part of compensation represents another possible factor contributing to the reemployment problems of older workers. Management may be reluctant to hire older workers because it is usually more costly to provide such workers with many of these benefits. Private pension are a good example.

The higher costs of pensions for older workers result primarily from two factors: (1) a shorter work history over which employer pension contributions must be made and thus lower investment income arising from the pension contributions and (2) a declining probability with age of employee withdrawal (job turnover) between hiring and retirement. That is, the later the age of job entry, the shorter the period over which contributions can be made, the shorter the period over which interest is earned on pension funds, and the less likely the worker will die or leave the plan before qualifying for full benefits.

Finally, evidence indicates that older workers have difficulty finding new jobs because of their "job seeking" behavior and the lower priority given to them by various manpower agencies. Sobel and Wilcock (1963) in a study of 4,000 job seekers found that older workers displayed less willingness to (1) change types of work methods or methods of looking for work, (2) engage in job retraining, (3) adjust salary expectations, and (d) move to areas of higher employment opportunity. Sheppard and Belitsky (1966) in a study of 500 workers in one locality found that older workers were also "more restrictive" in their job-search techniques and less persistent in their activities.[4] Rones (1983) reports that in 1981 only about one-half of discouraged workers age 65 years and older indicated plans to look for work during the subsequent 12-month period. In contrast, two-thirds of persons age 55–64 and six out of seven age 25–54 were looking.

What evidence there is indicates that older workers often get lower priority from government agencies set up to aid the unemployed. A 1973–1974 study by the National Institute of Industrial Gerontology reaffirms earlier findings of the Sheppard and Belitsky study: There are no age differences in the proportion of unemployed persons seeking job assistance from the employment service, but there is differential treatment by age (Heidbreder and Batten, 1974). Figure 3–3 shows by age group the proportion of various employment service applicants receiving employment services, referral to a job, and placement in a job. Significantly fewer older workers were (1) tested, counseled, or enrolled in training,[5] (2) referred to employers for job interviews, or (3) actually placed in a job.

Although older workers constitute a large proportion of the long-term unemployed, they have always been an almost insignificant proportion of the persons trained under the various manpower training programs operated or financed by federal and state governments. In general, most government officials and employers do not consider it worthwhile or cost-effective to train older persons (compared to younger persons) because of the expectation of shorter work lives, lower levels of education, and a belief that learning abilities decline with age. For example, the Comprehensive Employment and Training Act (CETA), a major federal program up to 1983, did little to help older workers (Schram and Osten, 1978). Kalman Rupp (1983) reports that in 1980 only 1 percent of the approximately 7 million persons age 45 and older who were eligible for CETA training actually participated. While limited program funds and many other factors explain this result, the fact remains that federal programs continue to serve older workers poorly.

---

[4] See also U.S. OTA (1985).

[5] Similar but more recent findings on counseling and testing are reported by Pursell and Torrence (1979).

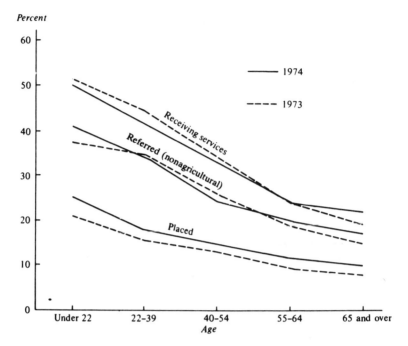

Figure 3-3   Action Taken: Employment Service Applicants by Age. Source: Elizabeth M. Heidbreder and M.D. Batten, "ESAR II—A Comparative View of Services to Age Groups," *Facts and Trends* No. 4 (Washington, D.C.: National Council on Aging, 1974). Used by permission.

CETA was replaced in 1983 by the Job Training Partnership Act (JTPA). Unlike CETA, this program reserves 3 percent of the training funds to serve low-income individuals age 55 or older. Hopefully, this will improve job services to older workers.

There is one major employment program specially designed for older workers: the Senior Community Service Employment Program. Administered by the Department of Labor, this program provided about 54,000 part-time jobs in 1982 for workers age 55 and over. To be eligible, workers have to have been chronically unemployed and have an income below 125 percent of the official poverty level.

There are also a number of private agencies specializing in job services for older persons seeking employment. Studies by Rosenblum and Sheppard (1977) and Doctors et al. (1980) indicate that significant numbers of older workers have been placed in jobs by these agencies. However, older workers using these services are typically not hired in jobs that utilize their skills and abilities to any high degree. Instead, they are most likely to be placed in part-time positions, usually with small employers in various low-paying service occupations.

The Retirement Decision

Interviews of older men soon after they claim social security benefits reveal dramatic changes since the early 1940s in stated reasons for leaving their last job. Table 3-3 contrasts the reasons given in 1941–42, 1968, and 1982. In the early 1940s, only 10 percent of the men said their departure was voluntary; most left because of employer-initiated action (56 percent), such as mandatory retirement, or because of health problems (34 percent). In 1982, however, 63 percent said that they themselves initiated their departure. Perhaps even more interesting is the finding that more than half of nonworking men ages 62 to 64 (i.e., early retirees) reported that *they initiated* the decision to leave their last job.

The term "voluntary" or self-initiated retirement, as used here, is meant to convey the basic idea of more freedom in making the decision. One should remember, however, that these decisions are often influenced by health limitations and by subtle (and sometimes not so subtle) threats and economic incentives from employers and social pressures from co-workers.[6]

What are the implications of retirement? In view of traditional work-oriented values in the United States and the importance of income derived from work, retirement is one of the most important decisions made by persons in our society. Aging in general and the

Table 3–3 Primary Reason for Older Men Leaving Their Last Job[a]

	1941–42	1968		1982	
Reason	65 +	62–64	65 +	62–64	65
Employer-initiated	56%	17%	57%	17%	20%
Health problems	34	54	21	29	17
Worker-initiated	10	29	22	54	63
Total Percent	100%	100%	100%	100%	100%

Source: Virginia P. Reno and Susan Grad, "Economic Security, 1935–85," *Social Security Bulletin* 48 (December 1985): Table 20.
[a]Nonemployed men receiving retired-worker benefits from OASDI. (For 1968 and 1982, the self-employed on the last job are excluded.)
[b]Age at entitlement to benefits in the 1941–42 and 1968 surveys and age at receipt of first benefits in the 1982 survey.

---

[6]On this point see, for example, Scott and Brudney (1987).

retirement decision in particular involve more complex choices than just deciding between more or less income. The amount of income and assets available is certainly one of the major considerations in deciding when to retire, but there are other *personal considerations*. For example, the individual must consider his or her health and evaluate the physical and emotional difficulties of continued employment on a specific job vis-à-vis the benefits and problems of alternative employment or of leaving the work force.

Deterioration of health, which Burtless (1987) has shown varies systematically among different occupations and industries, is one of the most important factors encouraging early retirement. Some persons are unable to continue working because of disabling illness. Even those persons who, despite health problems, could continue to work in their current job, or perhaps in a less demanding one, may decide to retire at age 62—given the alternative income available from a pension.

Many studies have documented the importance of health in the retirement decision. An especially important one is the 1966–1981 National Longitudinal Survey (NLS) of men, initially ages 45–59. The survey found, for example, that, other things being equal, men with health problems in 1966 were twice as likely to have retired between 1966 and 1971 as those who were free of health limitations (Andrisani, 1977).

The NLS findings are of particular interest because they measured the influence of health problems *before* retirement on *subsequent* withdrawal from the work force. Most other studies have asked people *after* they retire why they retired. Are a high proportion of those who cite health reasons, in actuality, giving what they consider to be a more socially acceptable reason for retirement? Joseph Quinn (1975), for example, reports that in the Social Security Retirement History Survey, 11 percent of the men and 18 percent of the women reporting good health and "no health limitations" gave (in another part of the survey) health as a prime motivation for their *early* retirement.

Later years of the NLS also included a series of questions inquiring about the extent of particular physical or mental impairments—such as difficulty in standing, walking, and dealing with people. From these questions an **index** of impairment was constructed. When this index was related to labor force participation or hours worked (controlling statistically for other factors), a strong relationship was found between health and participation. "For instance, an average blue-collar worker with even a moderate degree of impairment is 9 percent less likely to be in the labor force and works 9 percent fewer hours per year than a comparable individual with no impairments" (Parnes, 1981).

The availability of pension income and/or poor health are powerful influences in the retirement decision. Moreover, many researchers have pointed to the growing role of social/demographic and institutional factors *that interact* with these two factors. Sheppard (1977), for example, finds that early retirement decisions are influenced by the presence of children still living at home and by the general economic conditions in the local employment area.

Various *institutional realities* also affect the individual's retirement decision—factors that, in part, are beyond the person's own control. Included among these factors are such things as:

1. The specific provisions of public and private pension plans such as eligibility ages.
2. Changes in the level of pension.
3. Earnings opportunities in paid employment.
4. Job security and the prospects for continuing employment.
5. The institutional setting prescribed by work rules and government legislation.

Prior to 1962, men could not get social security benefits before age 65. In that year, the law was changed to allow men the same option granted to women in a 1956 amendment—early retirement at ages 62 through 64 with actuarially reduced benefits. The result was an immediate and major increase in the number of men accepting early retirement benefits.

Some workers apparently retire before age 65 because they can afford to, often supplementing their reduced social security benefits with a private pension or other income. There is another group of workers who have already stopped working before reaching age 62. The Social Security Administration's Survey of New Entitled Beneficiaries provides information on this group of workers: "Forty-one percent of the nonworking men entitled [i.e., becoming beneficiaries] at age 62 had been out of work for six months or more; 33 percent had not worked for at least a year; and 17 percent had been out of work three or more years" (Reno, 1971).

The labor force participation impact of various social security provisions is currently being hotly debated in the pension literature.[7] What is the impact of the earnings test, payroll taxes, early and delayed retirement benefit adjustment provisions, disability regulations, and the asset value (or wealth effect) of future benefits? While evidence to date is relatively meager, studies indicate that

---

[7] See the survey in Mitchell and Fields (1982).

the earnings test and wealth effects do encourage earlier retirement.

While there is widespread belief that the availability of social security benefits facilitates and encourages retirement, few people realize the powerful impact of employer-sponsored pensions. In recent years it has become common practice for employers to encourage earlier retirement by setting the age of normal retirement specified by the pension plan below age 65. In addition, employers provide "early retirement options," often absorbing all or most of the added costs of paying pensions out over a longer period of time. This practice allows workers to retire early without major penalties in the form of significantly lowering their pension benefit. Workers who continue on the job are often severely penalized. In fact, Kotlikoff and Wise (1985), using data or pension plans in 1979, report that it was not unusual for the reduction in pension benefit accruals at later retirement ages to equal the equivalent of a 30 percent reduction in earnings!

More recently, employers are also encouraging early retirement using another device, the "early retirement incentive program." Workers eligible for pensions are also offered a lump-sum payment (typically equal to one or two years salary) if they terminate employment during a limited "window" period ranging from one month to a year (Leavitt, 1983). In the 1980s, early retirement incentive programs swept the country. There is hardly a major company that has not used this mechanism as a way of adjusting the size and age structure of its labor force.

Concern has been voiced (AARP, 1987 and NOW, 1987) that older workers are increasingly expected to bear the major burden of staffing adjustments in companies. Corporate consolidations, buyouts, mergers, and restructuring (in response to shifting demand, international competition, and "financial entrepreneurship") are causing cuts in the work force of many companies. Particularly hard hit, for the first time, have been managerial and professional workers, many of whom are at older ages. One barometer, say critics of current practices, of the trend to "downsize" the work force of various firms by getting rid of older workers is the rise in age discrimination legal complaints in recent years (see Figure 3-4).

Finally, regarding the factors influencing retirement, Foner and Schwab (1983) point out the increased availability of organizational supports to facilitate and reduce the stress of retirement. Over the years there has been a significant expansion of activity clubs and centers, retirement counseling, senior citizen organizations, spe-

In Thousands

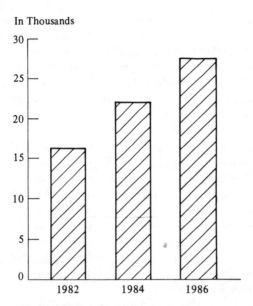

Figure 3-4   **Age Discrimination Legal Complaints.** Source: Equal Employment Opportunity Commission.

cial housing, and volunteer organizations to provide community service opportunities.

Mandatory Versus Flexible Retirement Options

There used to be a stigma to going out. He was over the hill. But now it's a looked-for status. Those retirement parties, they used to be sad affairs. They are darn happy affairs now. The peer pressure is for early retirement.

The above observation (Flint, 1977) is by Victor M. Zink, Director of Employee Benefits at General Motors Corporation. Early retirement is increasing, and workers' attitudes toward retirement seem to be changing dramatically. The statistics show the average age of retirement dropping rapidly in many companies.

At the same time, many recent gerontological studies show retirement to be less traumatic than was initially perceived.[8] Atchley (1976) observes, for example, that "the general trends very definitely contradict the myth that retirement causes illness. . . .

---

[8] Shanas et al. (1968); Cottrell and Atchley (1969); Atchley (1971); Streib and Schneider (1971); Atchley (1976); Atchley and Robinson (1982); Foner and Schwab (1983); and Palmore et al. (1984).

It appears that retirement is a welcome change for couples in good health who enjoy middle or upper socioeconomic status." Barfield and Morgan (1978b) reach a similar conclusion but state it in a different way. Analyzing data from two surveys taken at the beginning and end of the last decade, they derive "a view of the dissatisfied retiree as one whose health problems contribute significantly to leaving the labor force and whose retirement income is low, but not extremely so."

Paradoxically, as retirement ages decline and retirement living becomes increasingly popular, public policy has taken a big step toward allowing workers to continue longer on their jobs. A bill amending the Age Discrimination in Employment Act swept through Congress in 1977.[9] The House passed legislation prohibiting mandatory retirement with only four dissenting votes. The Senate quickly followed with only seven dissenting votes. The resulting law extended protection against age discrimination to nonfederal employees up to age 69 and eliminated the upper age limit entirely for most federal workers.

In October 1986, the Age Discrimination in Employment Act was again amended. The new provisions prohibit job termination on the basis of age, *at any age*. The only employees excluded are those working in businesses with fewer than 12 people. (Also temporarily excluded for a period of seven years were police officers, firefighters, prison guards, and tenured academic faculty.)

Congressman Claude Pepper (the oldest member of the U.S. Congress at age 87 in 1987) hailed the new law. He saw mandatory retirement as "a mean and arbitrary indignity imposed on our senior citizens when they, though of sound mind and sound body, are told they are too old to earn a living" (Lawrence, 1986). In contrast, University of Chicago economist Gary Becker (1986) summarized the opposing view this way:

> *These [mandatory retirement] rules surely hurt some elderly persons who continue to be productive, but they are not motivated by a desire to discriminate against productive older workers. Rather, these rules are a recognition both of the decline in the health and productivity of a significant fraction of elderly workers and of the inability of most large companies to pick and choose among their older workers in order to retain only the productive ones.*

What was the impact of the now illegal mandatory retirement provisions? How many older persons want to work? Will the continued employment of older workers interfere with the employ-

---

[9]The original act was passed in 1967 and applied to workers age 40 to 65.

ment opportunities of younger workers? Data are now available to help answer these questions.

During the 1950s and 1960s, mandatory retirement rules were introduced by a large number of organizations in both the private and public sectors. A comprehensive study (Slavik, 1966) of the prevalence and nature of retirement-age rules was carried out in 1961. Perhaps the study's most important finding was that industrial establishments without pension or **profit-sharing plans** overwhelmingly had flexible retirement policies (over 95 percent of establishments without pension plans, about two-thirds of those with only profit-sharing plans).

But this surprisingly high incidence of flexible retirement rules was strongly related to establishment size. For example, 68 percent of the establishments with 50 to 99 employees had flexible rules as compared to only 30 percent of establishments with 500 or more. In fact, of 6 independent variables investigated, the study found that only "size of company" and the "retirement benefit" showed any significant association with the existence of flexible retirement age policy.

If mandatory retirement during the 1960s was more prevalent in large firms, what proportion of workers in the labor force were subject to such rules? Research findings indicate that the overwhelming number of retired workers were not directly affected by mandatory retirement rules.[10]

To understand more clearly why so few workers' jobs were actually terminated by mandatory retirement rules, it is useful to break down the retirement population into categories. First of all, many workers were not subject to mandatory retirement rules because they worked for establishments without such provisions. And, of course, all self-employed persons were unaffected by such provisions.

Next, it is important to realize that many workers potentially subject to such rules left establishments *before* reaching the age maximum. Early retirement has become a normal occurrence in recent years, while retirement at or after the normal retirement age has become less common. Furthermore, as Streib and Schneider (1971) have documented, "not *all* persons subject to retirement at a certain chronological age are reluctant to retire; some welcome the step." And, of those who do *not* want to retire, a certain proportion are encouraged by health or physical condition to "accept" mandatory retirement and do not try to reenter the work force. Finally, some of those able and willing to work do, in fact,

---

[10] See, for example, Parnes and Nestel (1979) and Clark et al. (1979).

seek and find new jobs on a part-time or full-time basis. Figure 3–5 illustrates these various alternatives.

The percentage estimates shown in Figure 3–5 are based on a 1968–1970 survey of social security beneficiaries and exclude those not covered by social security (e.g., federal and certain state and local government workers). The data show that about two out of five males (age 65 or less) *who reach a compulsory retirement age* are able and willing to work but are not working. As Figure 3–5 shows, however, these workers represent less than 10 percent of the total cohort of retired males.

Now that mandatory retirement is illegal, has anything changed? A recent survey by Charles D. Spencer & Associates, Inc. of 96 employers with nearly a million workers shows that *the old exit patterns continue despite the new law*. The Spencer report concludes that "the trend towards retirement prior to age 65 among employers with pension plans continued unabated from 1978 through 1986, with five out of six retirements (not counting disability retirements) currently occurring before age 65" (La Rock, 1987).

The Economics of Encouraging or Forcing Retirement

Each year, then, before 1986, there was a small but significant number of workers forced to retire who would have preferred to continue working. The overwhelming proportion of workers, however, were unaffected by mandatory retirement provisions.

Far more important than mandatory retirement over the years has been the design of pension and other financial inducements to encourage workers to leave their jobs at increasingly early ages. Throughout this century, and especially over the past two decades, employers have used financial retirement incentives as a major way of dealing with issues of labor redundancy, promotion policy, and concerns about worker productivity. What are the economic implications of these developments?

Whether the firm gains economically from arbitrarily terminating older workers at some specified age depends in large part on the **productivity** and earning levels of those terminated versus (1) those of workers hired as replacements (in the case of constant or expanding output) or (2) those of other employees of the firm who would be otherwise terminated (in the case of contracting output). The question is not easy to answer because of the great difficulty in measuring the productivity of particular workers.

It has often been asserted that mandatory retirement provisions

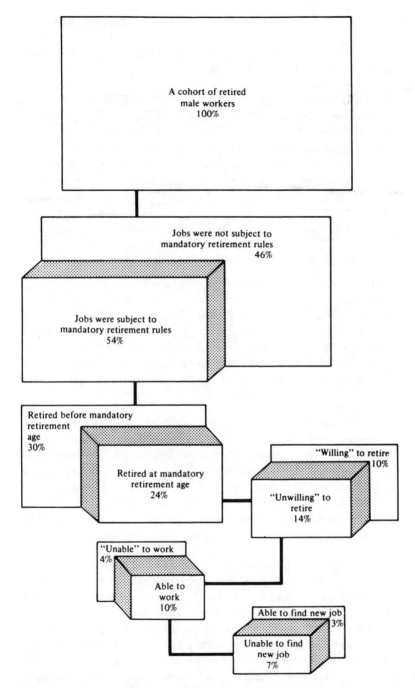

Figure 3-5 The Incidence of Mandatory Retirement. Source: James H. Schulz, "The Economics of Mandatory Retirement," *Industrial Gerontology,* Vol. 1, New Series (Winter 1974): 1-10. Used by permission.

can increase the productivity of a business. A leading pension authority, Professor Dan McGill, states in his pension book that one of the most important reasons why private pensions with mandatory retirement provisions were introduced was the desire of management to increase levels of work force productivity. He argues that private pensions permit "the employer to remove overage employees from the payroll in an orderly fashion, without fear of adverse employee and public reaction, and to replace them with younger, presumably more efficient workers" (McGill, 1975). The evidence, however, on the question of whether retiring older workers raises productivity indicates that one should be cautious about generalizing. The results of a relatively large number of research studies bearing on this issue are available, but the findings are far from conclusive:

> *Collectively, leading studies on various aspects of the effects of aging document the conclusion that chronological age alone is a poor indication of working ability. Health, mental and physical capacities, work attitudes and job performance are* individual traits *at any age. Indeed, measures of traits in different age groups* usually *show* many *of the older workers to be superior to the average for the younger group and many of the younger inferior to the average for the older group. [U.S. Department of Labor, 1965]*

> *Studies under actual working conditions show older workers performing as well as the younger if not better on most, but not all, measures. . . . Age patterns of actual performance do not necessarily reflect the comparative capacities of all older persons versus younger people, but are traceable in part to labor market conditions and to selective processes that may, for example, retain in their jobs the competent older workers, promote the superior . . . or recruit [the] younger . . . of entirely different types. [Riley and Foner, 1968]*

> *(1) While some declines with age in productivity have been observed in certain industries (e.g., clerical, manufacturing, sales), older workers are more productive than younger workers. (2) There are wide differences in productivity within age groups. (3) There are some declines with age in physical capacity, but environmental conditions are important in mitigating the effects of decline . . . (4) Older employees score well or better than younger employees on creativity, flexibility, facility of information processing, absenteeism, accident rates, and turnover. [Robinson et al., 1984]*

> *. . . it is apparent from a number of well-designed studies that age often has no real influence on performance. Wide individual*

differences exist and experience often counteracts any age effects. Where age differences are found, it appears they may be caused often by psychosocial factors, such as reduced work commitment because of limited career advancement opportunities. [Sparrow, 1986]

Factors working against older workers are (1) their on-average *formal* education deficit compared to younger workers (which may or may not be offset by their greater on-the-job experience); (2) their greater risk of chronic illness and the possibility of declining physical and mental capacity; and (3) some degree of work assignment inflexibility due to the interaction of work rules, seniority systems, and pay scales.

It is probably reasonable to assert that many employers recognize that the productivity of some of their older employees is as high or higher than that of younger workers. These employers argue, however, that it is difficult (and costly) to identify such workers. Thus, they argue, retirement rules and pensions provide a practical administrative procedure that is objective, impersonal, and impartial. These rules avoid charges of discrimination, favoritism, or bias in the termination process.

Without operational measures of fitness, employers are faced with choosing among three options: (1) terminating workers arbitrarily at a specific age, (2) allowing workers to decide when to retire, or (3) undertaking potentially expensive activities for "sorting out" the insufficiently productive older workers. More importantly, the employer must justify these termination decisions so that general worker morale will not be adversely affected. Historically, employers have been reluctant to terminate workers solely on the basis of age—especially given past levels of social security old-age pensions. But with the establishment of supplementary private pension plans, management (especially in larger firms) apparently thought such practices were much less inequitable. With the passage of legislation prohibiting employers from using age as a basis of job termination, there has been renewed interest among management in techniques of measuring performance.

A 1974 national opinion survey conducted by Louis Harris and Associates for the National Council on the Aging collected interesting information on the public's mixed reaction to this issue:

The public 18–64 and the public 65 and over were somewhat ambivalent about their attitudes toward mandatory retirement. Eighty-six percent (both groups) felt: "Nobody should be forced to retire because of age, if he wants to continue working and is still able to do a good job." About three-fifths agreed that "most people can continue to perform as well on the job as they did when they were younger." On the other hand, almost half (48 percent) of the 18–64 group and more than half (54 percent) of those 65 and over agreed that "since many people are ready to retire at 65 years of age, and it's hard to make exceptions for those who are not ready, it makes sense to have a fixed retirement age for everyone." [Meier, 1975]

Do the Aged Want to Work?

The 1974 Louis Harris poll sought to examine "the myth and reality of aging in America." One of the most widely publicized findings from that survey relates to the number of older persons wanting employment. For example, *Newsweek*, in a cover story on "The Graying of America," reported the Harris poll finding that "nearly a third of the nation's over-65 retirees said if they could they still would be working" (February 28, 1977).[11] When this finding is cited, it is almost invariably (as in the *Newsweek* story) a part of a discussion examining the importance of work to the aged and the problems caused by mandatory retirement. Yet earlier in this chapter we presented data for the late 1960s that indicated less than 10 percent of those approaching retirement were forced to retire because of mandatory retirement provisions. Are the two findings compatible?

What most discussions of the Harris surveys on this issue fail to report are the answers to a related question asked in the surveys. Those older persons not working who said they would like to work were asked, "What's keeping you from working?" The answers broke down as follows (National Council on the Aging, 1975):

Poor health	57%
Too old	28
No work available; lack of job opportunities	15
Lack of transportation	10
Other interests	8
Would lose pension benefits or pay too much in taxes if worked	4

As we discussed previously, the high number of people giving health as a reason for not working is difficult to interpret. Some people may use this answer as an excuse in place of less socially

---

[11] Another Harris poll in 1979 reporting on the high proportion of people desiring to work in old age also received national publicity. The same qualifications discussed in the text apply to this newer survey.

accepted reasons—although existing research indicates that the number who do is relatively small. It is clear, however, that there are a wide range of reasons why people who "would like to work" do not work. Thus, when those aged who were retired or unemployed were asked if they would come back to work or take on a new job that "suited them well," only 11 percent responded that they would definitely consider it. Moreover, only 12 percent of the retirees reported in the survey that they had some skills they would like to use but that no one would give them a chance to use the skills.

Another relevant and interesting set of findings is reported by Dena K. Motley (1978) from the Social Security Administration's Retirement History Study. Motley investigated men and women age 62–67 in 1973 who had retired since 1969. She measured their availability for work through survey questions on attitudes about work and their need for income. Again, the study found that very few retirees were actually available for work:

> It appears that no more than 12 percent of such retirees would be very likely or even able to return to work. . . . Twenty-four percent of the respondents constitute an ambivalent group whose members might return to work if the drawing power of their need for more income were strong enough to override a disinclination for work or if a preference for employment were strong enough to prevail over the comfort of an adequate retirement income.

A 1979 Louis Harris poll (Johnson and Higgins, 1979) reported that nearly half (48 percent) of workers age 50–64 said they intended to continue working instead of retiring at the usual time. From such findings, Harris concluded that in the future more people will want to defer retirement.

But a study by Goudy (1981) indicates that work expectations change dramatically during the preretirement years.[12] Using data from the Longitudinal Retirement History Survey, Goudy discovered that survey findings like those from the 1979 Harris poll are unreliable predictors of actual practices. His study indicates that retirement "attitudes are relatively volatile; many change within 2 or 4 years, and *large numbers retire shortly after they've stated that they never expect to stop working for a living.*" [Emphasis added.]

Once retired, most older persons adapt quickly to their new life situation and indicate a high degree of satisfaction with their life. As we previously noted, a variety of studies over the past two

---

[12] See also Morgan (1980) and Burkhauser and Quinn (1985).

decades have documented that a high proportion of the elderly are relatively satisfied with their lives after retirement. Those who express dissatisfaction often perceive themselves in poor health and/or without adequate income. But these persons are a small minority, with most elderly expressing general satisfaction with their health and income (Liang and Fairchild, 1979). In 1981, another NCOA/Harris survey asked retired people: "Do you now think you made a right decision to retire when you did; did you retire too early; or do you now think you retired too late? The response (NCOA, 1981):

Made the right decision	90%
Retired too early	6
Retired too late	1
Not sure	3

The evidence is now very clear that most older workers want to retire as soon as financially possible, and that once retired, they adjust well to their new situation in society and enjoy their increased leisure. In their review article on work and retirement, Foner and Schwab (1983) provide a provocative answer to the question, "to work or not to work?":

> Many if not most newly retired persons welcome the opportunity to slow down. . . . It is well to remember that many jobs are not intrinsically satisfying, they do not enhance feelings of self-worth, encourage autonomy, or permit the exercise of independent judgment. Many jobs—in factories, mines, and some types of institutions—are actually harmful. . . . Retirement can be a rewarding experience for what it does not entail. Failure to appreciate this factor may be a result of the relatively privileged positions of those who write about retirement—reporters, professors, and physicians, for example, all of whom have some degree of control over the pace and direction of their work. Indeed generalizations about work and retirement on the basis of such work experiences may have contributed to myths about retirement.

Thus, increasing numbers of workers are looking forward to the retirement period—retiring at increasingly early ages and raising their expectations about retirement living standards. The issue of planning financially for the retirement years, therefore, moves right to the top of the decision-making agenda for most *older* workers.

Planning for Retirement

President John F. Kennedy once remarked that "it is not enough for a great nation merely to have added new years to life—our objective must also be to add new life to years." For those approaching retirement, the challenge is to take advantage of those years in a creative and fulfilling manner. And there is little doubt that preretirement planning by individuals can help many achieve this end.

As we will see in the succeeding chapters of this book, however, the problems involved in preretirement planning are very complex. Hence, most people, having a natural inclination to live for today and avoid thinking about old age and death, give very little systematic thought to the financial issues of old age until they come face to face with them—when it is usually too late. The flood of criticism about the adequacy, financial viability, and equity of social security and private pensions (regardless of their merits) creates confusion and distrust among workers—further discouraging early thinking about retirement preparation.

In recent years, the major efforts to deal with this problem have shifted from the individual to private and public collective efforts. Businessmen, labor leaders, and gerontologists all bring different perspectives to their efforts to deal with and improve preretirement planning. Their goal, however, is similar: to generate a greater awareness among workers and their spouses of the problems and potentials of approaching old age and to assist where appropriate in the preparation for successful retirement.

Studies by Reich (1977) show a significant growth in group preretirement education and the range of institutions offering programs: community colleges, adult education schools, social service agencies, chambers of commerce, religious institutions, universities, unions, private companies, government, senior citizen organizations, and profit-making organizations. For example, 75 percent of Fortune 500 companies now have some kind of program designed to ease the transition to retirement (EBPR, 1987b).

The development of preretirement programs is still in a very early stage. In 1981, for example, fewer than 4 percent of a national sample of older men had participated in such a program (Beck, 1984). Moreover, there is still disagreement over the need for such programs and whose responsibility it is to provide them (NCOA, 1980). A number of studies have argued that many programs are neither suitably designed nor well implemented (see, e.g., Kasschau, 1974). Many employers, for example, offer little more than

fringe benefit information, and many are skeptical about the worth
of preretirement programs.

The challenge is to (1) increase the availability of preretirement
education to persons seeking such information, (2) improve the
quality of available programs, and (3) encourage people to begin
preparing for retirement at a relatively early age.

As we shall see in the chapters that follow, financial planning for
retirement is a difficult and complex matter. Planning shortly
before retirement (even 10 or 15 years before) is usually too late.
In the chapters that follow, we look at the options for dealing with
this dilemma.

Chapter 3 Highlights

Given the increasing numbers of people no longer working in the
later years, much attention has been given to understanding the
various factors influencing older workers' choices between work
and retirement. Some of the important points made in this chapter
are:

1. When an economy is growing and is at a full-employment
   level, a choice must be made on how to divide the higher
   productive potential between more leisure and/or more income (i.e., more goods and services). But when there is high
   unemployment, nations often encourage and facilitate more
   leisure through retirement mechanisms—attempting to deal
   with the unemployment problems by encouraging older
   workers to retire.
2. Few Americans are still working after age 65, and about half
   of those still employed work only part-time.
3. Health, potential retirement income, and, increasingly, early
   retirement incentives are the three most important factors
   influencing the decision by workers to retire.
4. Even though their productivity does not necessarily fall as
   they grow older, most older workers face a variety of barriers
   to reemployment when they become unemployed and receive relatively little help from private and government organizations in dealing with the problem.
5. Historically, few workers were "forced" to retire; currently,
   mandatory retirement policies are illegal at any age.
6. Most workers retire as soon as they think it is financially
   feasible and, once retired, usually adjust well to their new
   situation.

Suggested Readings

FONER, ANNE, AND KAREN SCHWAB. "Work and Retirement in a Changing Society." In Matilda White Riley, B. B. Hess, and K. Bond, eds., *Aging in Society: Selected Reviews of Recent Research*. Hillsdale, N.J.: Lawrence Erlbaum Associates, 1983. An excellent overview article, with many references to the literature.

GINSBERG, HELEN. "Flexible and Partial Retirement for Norwegian and Swedish Workers." *Monthly Labor Review* 108 (October 1985): 33–42. Norway and Sweden have been world leaders in developing alternatives to the "either-or" dilemma confronting older workers eligible to retire. This article explains the innovative approach of these two countries to retirement and their experience to date.

GRAEBNER, WILLIAM. *A History of Retirement*. New Haven, Conn.: Yale University Press, 1980. The best book available that gives in-depth consideration to the historical relationships between pensions and the employment policies of management, unions, and the government in the United States.

KAHN, HILDA. *Reconceiving Part-Time Work*. Totowa, N.J.: Rowman & Allanheld, 1985. A book focusing on the current and potential role of part-time work in the lives of women and older workers.

MIGLIACCIO, JOHN N., AND P. C. CAIRO. "Preparation for Retirement: A Selective Bibliography, 1974–1980." *Aging and Work* (Winter 1981): 31–41. A useful guide to the retirement planning literature.

"Older Persons in Employment." A special edition of *Aging International* 13 (Autumn/Winter, 1986). An excellent collection of articles on older workers—looking at job performance, ways to prolong life, job matching, and experiences in foreign countries.

PALMORE, ERDMORE B., B. M. BURCHETT, G. FILLENBAUM, L. K. GEORGE, AND L. M. WALLMAN. *Retirement: Causes and Consequences*. New York: Springer Publishing, 1985. Using data from three national and four local longitudinal data sets, the authors undertake a comprehensive investigation of the retirement decision.

PARNES, HERBERT S. (AND OTHERS). *Retirement Among American Men*. Lexington, Mass.: Lexington Books, 1985. A collection of articles presenting findings from the National Longitudinal Survey of Older Men. This book is the sixth publication in a series of reports and covers the full 15-year period of the survey cohort, from 1966 through 1981.

ROBINSON, PAULINE, SALLY COBERLY, AND C. E. PAUL. "Work and Retirement." In Robert H. Binstock and Ethel Shanas, eds., *Handbook of Aging and the Social Sciences*, 2d ed. New York: Van Nostrand Reinhold, 1984. A review and synthesis of the work and retirement literature.

SCOTT, HILDA, AND JULIET F. BRUDNEY. *Forced Out*. New York: Simon & Schuster, 1987. An eye-opening study of older workers driven from their careers. Based on interviews of over 100 people between the ages of 50 and 70, the book explores the difficult and often shocking problems encountered by many older workers who lose their jobs and then try to find new ones. Also discussed is the limited help provided by most public and private employment agencies.

TRACY, MARTIN B. "Older Men's Earnings Tests and Work Activity: A Six Nation Study." *Research on Aging* 5 (June 1983): 155–172. The study examines the impact on older worker labor force activity of changes in the social ·security retirement test in six countries. The basic finding is that labor force participation rates have not increased when the test has been eliminated or liberalized.

Chapter 4

RETIREMENT INCOME
PLANNING

We now turn from employment problems and the retirement decision to the issues of financial provision for retirement. There are various ways in which individuals can provide income in the retirement years, when normal income received from work declines or stops. Table 4–1 lists the major mechanisms and institutions available in the United States today for providing economic support in retirement. These are divided into two broad groups:

Table 4–1 Options for Retirement Income Provision

Private		Public	
Individual Provision	**Collective Arrangements**	**Means Tested**	**Not Means Tested**
Physical assets	Family gifts & transfers	Medicaid	Medicare
Insurance claims		SSI	OASDI
Other financial intermediary claims	Private pensions	State property tax reductions[a]	Special federal tax benefits
	Charity assistance		
Direct financial investment claims	Help from friends and neighbors	Veterans' benefits (nonservice-connected disability)	Veterans' benefits (service-connected disability)
		Housing programs	
		Food stamps	
		Government financed elderly services[a]	

[a]Some elderly tax reductions and services are not means-tested.

95

private and public. The private mechanisms are either individual preparation or preparation undertaken by the individual as a part of group action. For the public mechanisms it is important to distinguish between two major categories: those mechanisms for which there is a means test and those without a test.

In this chapter the focus is primarily on private mechanisms, especially the task that faces individuals who want to prepare for retirement. In the absence of *group* mechanisms, both public and private, what must the individual do to have adequate retirement income?

We begin with this focus or emphasis not because this is the principal way that preparation for retirement is currently being carried out, nor because it is the most important way that we would expect it to be carried out in the future. Rather, beginning with individual preparation is a useful way of developing a good understanding of many of the concepts and issues involved in providing adequate income in old age. By starting at this level, it is easier to show some of the personal options, the major problems, and the magnitude of the task the individual faces. This allows us to obtain some needed perspective on the whole problem.

Retirement Provision by Individuals

Some of the problems faced by an individual in preparing systematically for retirement include the following:[1]

1. He doesn't know with certainty when he will die.
2. He doesn't know exactly what his future income flow will be.
3. He doesn't know what his basic retirement needs will be nor what life-style he will ultimately prefer for that period.
4. He doesn't know when he will retire.
5. He cannot easily predict the future rate of inflation, which, if it occurs, will depreciate the value of those retirement assets that do not adjust fully and reduce the buying power of income from those assets.
6. He cannot easily predict the rate of economic growth—which is likely to affect his economic position relative to the working population.

The number and magnitude of problems just listed indicate that individual retirement planning is a very difficult job. There is no doubt that the personal decision-making process involved in prep-

---

[1] The pronoun "he" is used generically in this list.

aration for retirement is a very complex one. First, not knowing when one is going to die is a major complicating factor in ascertaining the amount of money needed for retirement. To plan for adequate income the individual needs to know the number of years for which income is required. Thus arises a major justification for not providing for retirement entirely by *individual* actions alone; one can simplify the decision-making process and reduce uncertainty by entering into an insurance arrangement, either public or private, that provides collective protection by grouping those who live short, medium, and long lives. (This "insurance principle" is discussed later in the chapter.)

The second problem is the uncertainty of the income flow the individual will receive over his or her working life. The problem here arises from such possibilities as child bearing, ill health, or disability (either short-term or long-term). Problems are also created by unemployment in the labor market, job obsolescence, and unequal economic opportunity for various groups. For example, the recurrent periods of recession and **inflation** are outside the control of the individual and are very difficult to predict, yet these factors have a significant, if not dominating, impact on the flow of income and the total amount of income individuals receive over their lifetimes.

A third problem arises from not knowing what retirement needs will be. A major factor here is the great uncertainty that exists with regard to the state of one's health when one gets old. Will chronic or serious illness develop? Will nursing care be required? Will institutionalization be necessary? Not only is health status directly related to medical costs, it also affects retirement mobility—influencing recreation and transportation expenditures.

Yet another difficulty arises if one is married. There is uncertainty as to whether the family unit will break up (divorce) and uncertainty about how long each spouse will live. Pension benefit rights often change if the eligible worker dies. Thus, the amount of money a *spouse* will need or will have in retirement is essentially unpredictable as far as the individual is concerned. This is one of the major factors involved in the current high rate of poverty among unmarried older women.

A fifth problem occurs because of the variability in the age at which people retire. Although individuals have a large measure of control over when they retire, increasingly the decision is based on factors they do not control. Such factors as deteriorating health, pension rules, the growth of early retirement options (sometimes accompanied by management and/or union pressures to retire), and discriminatory practices in hiring older workers often dominate.

Perhaps one of the most difficult retirement preparation problems is that of predicting the rate of inflation that will occur before and during retirement. To the extent that an individual accumulates assets (or pension rights) for the retirement period that do not automatically adjust in value for inflation, he or she is faced with the possibility that these assets may shrink in value—perhaps being of little worth in the retirement period.

Finally, individuals preparing for retirement may be concerned about changes in their *relative* economic status in retirement. After one retires, the real incomes of the working population will continue to rise over the years. Retirees who want to keep up with the general rise in living standards will have to make some estimate of the economic growth that will occur during retirement. They must then provide additional funds before retirement that can be drawn upon to keep their economic status rising along with that of everybody else. Some people will decide that they do not want to bother dealing with this issue; they will be content just to keep their retirement standard of living constant. Some may even prefer to allow it to decline. Nevertheless, this is an important issue that should not be overlooked in retirement planning. There is a choice to be made, and it should not be made passively because individuals are unaware of the nature of that choice.

Required Rate of Saving for Retirement

To see the retirement preparation issues clearly, let us assume certain answers to most of the questions listed earlier in order to answer the following question: Suppose an individual (on his or her own) wants to save a sufficient amount for retirement; how much should the person save? To put the question another way, suppose you were a preretirement counselor and someone came to you and said, "I'm 25. I don't have much confidence in the present pension mechanisms available to prepare for retirement; I just don't trust them. Instead, I want to sit down and work out a financial plan for myself that will provide me with adequate income in retirement. How much should I save?"

The answer to this question depends on a great many factors. Most important are the following:

1. The standard of adequacy one chooses.
2. The number of years one plans to be in retirement.

3. The number of years one plans to work and the earnings (and other income) that will be received over that period.
4. The yield one can anticipate on one's savings.
5. The rate of inflation that is expected over the period.

Let us look first at the standard of adequacy. Two standards were described extensively in Chapter 2: the Social Security Administration's poverty index and the Bureau of Labor Statistics' Retired Couple's Budget. They are possibilities, but a retirement counselor would probably argue that these are not the best measures for most people to use. Instead, it is common to propose that individuals with near- or above-average incomes choose a standard of adequacy based upon the concept of "income replacement." *An income replacement standard seeks to provide the individual with income in retirement that is a certain specified percentage of the individual's average income prior to retirement.* Immediately, a key question arises: What should that replacement goal be; what rate should be chosen—100, 80, or 50 percent?

What Must I Save for Adequate Retirement Income?

The amount of financial resources needed in retirement depends on the standard of adequacy used. If the retired person's living standard is to be related in some way to a standard of living experienced before retirement, sources of retirement funds must enable the individual to replace a certain proportion of the income lost when work stops.

It is generally agreed that expenses in retirement will be somewhat lower than before retirement and, hence, that a 100 percent income replacement is not necessary. Various estimates of the differences in pre- and postretirement expenditures have been made by different researchers. For example, the Bureau of Labor Statistics (BLS) has developed an "equivalency income scale" for families of different size and age (on the basis of the relation between food and expenditures and income). BLS estimates that an elderly couple generally requires 51 percent as much income for goods and services as a younger four-person husband-wife family living on the same standard. While the BLS equivalence scale shows a difference of 51 percent in expenditures needs when comparing a *middle-aged four-person family* with an *aged couple,* the difference between couples age 55–64 and couples aged 65 or more is much less. The scales show only a 13.5 percent difference in goods and services needs.

One reasonable goal is to keep one's living standard not too different from what one has been accustomed to in the not too distant past. We can use the **equivalency scale** to help establish such a retirement living standard: maintaining the same living standard in retirement as existed just prior to retirement. In addition to the 13.5 percent expenditure difference, one should also take into account the reduced income tax burden in retirement due to special federal and state income tax provisions for persons age 65 and over. Also, presumably the individual upon reaching retirement can discontinue saving for retirement—a requirement that reduces the person's disposable income during the working years. Taking these three factors into account, the appropriate replacement is about 60 to 70 percent of *gross* income for a middle-income worker (Schulz et al., 1974).

In 1980, Preston Bassett, a staff member of the President's Commission on Pension Policy, calculated a whole set of target replacement rates for a presidential commission considering pension policy. Using a slightly different methodology from that discussed above, Bassett estimated target replacement rates for single and married persons. Table 4–2 shows his estimates for a wide range of preretirement income levels. Target replacement rates vary from 86 percent for a low-income couple with gross preretirement income of $6,500 to 51 percent for a single individual with an income of $50,000.

Using the appropriate target, one can calculate the saving rate necessary to achieve a specified living standard in retirement. That is, one can determine what amount must be saved every year out of income up to the point of retirement. The year one begins saving can vary. One could decide to start saving at, say, age 25, or one could decide to postpone the task till age 45 and then save more over a shorter period. However, the longer one waits, the more difficult the job becomes.

Let us assume, for example, that one begins to save a certain percentage of annual income starting the first year of work and that one saves the same proportion of income throughout one's whole lifetime. Assume a **life expectancy** equal to the current average life expectancy and retirement at age 65. Assume an investment return on savings of 4 percent.

Suppose one's goal is to provide retirement income equal to 60 to 65 percent replacement of average earnings during the last five years prior to retirement. To do this, one would have to save about 20 percent of one's earnings each and every year.[2]

---

[2]A full description of how this estimate was made can be found in Schulz and Carrin (1972). Alternate estimates are found in Morgan (1977) and Diamond (1977).

Table 4–2   Target Replacement Rates Needed to Maintain Preretirement Living
Standards in 1980

			Single Person			
Gross Pre-retirement Income	*Federal and State Taxes*[a]	*Work Related Expenses*[b]	*Savings*[c]	*Net Pre-retirement Income*	*Post-retirement Income Tax*[d]	*Target Rate*
$ 6,500	$ 1,003	$ 330	$ 0	$ 5,167	$ 0	79%
10,000	2,008	480	240	7,272	0	73
15,000	3,703	678	678	9,941	0	66
20,000	5,783	853	1,280	12,084	198	61
30,000	10,355	1,179	2,357	16,109	1,282	58
50,000	22,249	1,665	4,163	21,923	3,752	51
			Married Couple			
$ 6,500	$ 578	$ 355	$ 0	$ 5,567	$ 0	86%
10,000	1,444	513	260	7,786	0	78
15,000	2,860	728	734	10,684	0	71
20,000	4,488	922	1,405	13,185	0	66
30,000	8,047	1,317	2,646	17,999	63	60
50,000	17,824	1,931	4,841	25,419	1,965	55

Source: Adapted from Tables 19 and 20 in President's Commission on Pension Policy, *Coming of Age: Toward a National Retirement Income Policy,* Report of the Commission (Washington, D.C.: The Commission, 1981), pp. 42–43.
[a]Includes federal income and OASDHI taxes. State and local tax estimate based on state and local income tax receipts, which were 19 percent of federal income tax receipts. Property taxes are not included.
[b]Estimated as 6 percent of income after taxes.
[c]Savings rates vary with income after taxes and are based on survey data.
[d]Postretirement taxes are on income in excess of social security benefits, which were not taxable in 1980.

An individual might desire, however, to save at a lower rate in the earlier years when earnings are relatively low compared to anticipated earnings later in his or her career. In this case, later savings rates would have to be much higher, and disposable income in the years prior to retirement would be lower.

In addition, the question of child-rearing expenses arises. A family with children has a lower standard of living than a family without children but with a similar income. Once a couple's children are self-supporting, the couple's standard of living may rise as a result of the reduced expenditures of this sort. This depends in part on whether the family has incurred previous debts—arising, for example, from educational or unusual medical expenses. Paying off these debts might prevent any significant increase in living standard in the preretirement years.

Not everyone agrees that the most appropriate replacement rate adequacy standard is *the years before retirement*. In a recent book on social security, economist Michael J. Boskin (1986) argues that "with some intertemporal borrowing and saving going on, it does not make sense to compare a flow of income during retirement to a particularly biased small subset of years prior to retirement." Instead, Boskin argues that one should use the average of real (i.e., adjusted for inflation) earnings throughout the entire work career of the individual. But the standard of living measure resulting from averaging these earnings will be much lower and, for most workers, would mean a sharp drop in living standards upon retirement. That is the reason so many retirement planners and pension analysts reject such a measure.

The Role of Pensions

Our estimated required savings rate of about 20 percent assumed that one saved for retirement without the help of either public or private pension plans. In reality, pensions in the United States play a major role—we will argue a dominant role—in providing retirement income. Before looking at the operation of the social security program and other pensions in the United States, we first need to understand the basic rationale behind their development.

The Great Depression of the 1930s went a long way toward exposing the great political lie of American welfare debates: that poverty was generally the result of the laziness or personal unworthiness of particular individuals. In the 1930s it became painfully obvious to everyone that this was not the case. Millions of jobless workers and their families suffered severe financial problems because of an economic catastrophe caused by factors unrelated to their own personal activities. Moreover, the cures for their problems lay almost entirely outside the range of their individual reactions.

Until this depression there had been a great deal of controversy in the United States with regard to the role of (and need for) some sort of public pension system. Many other countries quickly followed the example of Germany, which established the first comprehensive social insurance program in the 1880s. But in the United States the idea of public pensions received no widespread public support until the economic upheavals of the Great Depression. And although there was a scattered handful of employer-sponsored pensions provided by government and private firms in existence during the first half of the 20th century, the significant growth of these pension programs occurred in the relatively recent years of the 1950s and 1960s.

Thus, the social institution of pensions has had a relatively short history in the United States. And there has been continuing discussion and debate over just what are the appropriate roles to be played by both public and private pensions. We now look at this question and discuss some of the important goals for a good pension program; in later chapters we look at social security and private pensions as they currently operate in the United States.

Why Pensions?

Some of the debate over pensions has revolved around the advantages and disadvantages of public versus private pensions, but there are two even more basic questions that should be discussed: Why is there a need for *any kind* of pension program, and should individuals be compelled (either by the government or an employer) to join a particular pension program?

You will recall that earlier in this chapter we listed and discussed a number of problems confronting individuals making economic preparations for retirement on their own. The first problem listed was that the individual does not know exactly when he or she will die—that is, how long a period to provide for. This means that any person (or family) preparing for retirement must assume the "worst"—a long life—and put aside enough money to take care of that eventuality. Or one must be prepared to rely on private or public charity if one lives "too long" and exhausts one's own economic support.

A pension program provides an attractive option by utilizing a basic insurance principle. If the number of individuals in a pension program is sufficiently large, mortality tables of life expectancy can be constructed that estimate average life expectancy at particular ages. Retirement preparation costs can then be geared to *average* life expectancy, with the "excess" payments of individuals who die before the average age going to those who live beyond it. The result is that no one has to pay more than one would need to put aside personally if it was known with certainty that one would live for a period of years equal to the average life expectancy.

The second problem discussed earlier in this chapter in connection with individual retirement preparation is the lack of predictability of future income. For example, chronically low earnings, ill health, or periods of unemployment (as a result of a variety of factors) may make sufficient saving for retirement very difficult or even impossible. Also, health or employment problems may force an individual to leave the labor force unexpectedly and much earlier than was originally planned.

Collective arrangements to deal with this problem are not new. Since earliest times people have attempted to mitigate or eliminate economic insecurity by banding together in groups—families, tribes, associations, or guilds. Especially important has been the family. Throughout history individuals have relied heavily on family ties to provide protection from economic insecurity in old age. Even today in the United States, the family still remains an important source of economic and social support for many older persons when they get seriously ill. And in some other countries— particularly those less industrialized—the family still remains the major source of economic protection and security in old age.

The major problem with the family (and many other group associations) for sharing risk is that the number of people involved is relatively small. As Kenneth Boulding (1958) has observed, "It is when the 'sharing group' becomes too small to ensure that there will always be enough producers in it to support the unproductive that devices for insurance become necessary. When the 'sharing group' is small there is always a danger that sheer accident [illness, crop failure, unemployment, etc.] will bring the proportion of earners to nonearners to a level at which the group cannot function."

The commonly held view that in earlier America most of the aged lived in rural communities together with, or in close proximity to, adult children who provided financial support in the later years is not supported by the facts (Tibbitts, 1977). Nuclear parent-child families have always been the more common family type in the United States, and the three-generation family has been relatively rare.

Thus, the need for better collective arrangements to deal with the economic problems of old age has probably always been with us. The earliest available statistics on the economic status of the elderly prior to the establishment of pensions indicate that most of the aged were poor and that, in fact, many were completely destitute. The reasons why pension programs were not developed sooner are not entirely clear, but various writers have pointed to the *relative* economic prosperity throughout America's history, the country's decentralized governmental structure, and (most importantly) the individualistic ethic of much of the population.

Why Compulsory Pensions?

Individual self-reliance and voluntary preparation for retirement— together with family interdependence—dominated the early discussions of old age security provision. It is now generally accepted, however, that this is not the appropriate cornerstone of an income maintenance policy for the aged. Instead, there is widespread support for relying on *compulsory* pensions. A number of prominent American economists have written about the rationale for compulsory pensions. In a chapter in his book on the *Principles of Economic Policy*, Kenneth Boulding (1958) concisely states the principal argument:

> *[If an individual] were rationally motivated, [he] would be aware of the evils that might beset him, and would insure against them. It is argued, however, that many people are not so motivated, and that hardly anyone is completely motivated by these rational considerations, and that therefore under a purely voluntary system some will insure and some will not. This means, however, that those who do not insure will have to be supported anyway—perhaps at lower levels and in humiliating and respect-destroying ways—when they are in the nonproductive phase of life, but that they will escape the burden of paying premiums when they are in the productive phase. In fairness to those who insure voluntarily, and in order to maintain the self-respect of those who would not otherwise insure, insurance should be compulsory.*

Richard Musgrave (1968), writing on the role of social insurance, makes a similar point:

> *Insurance could be purchased privately, but becomes a matter of public concern only because [some] will not do so, while [others] will. Given their humanitarian premise, Calvin and Homer must bail out Jack should the contingency arise. They will require therefore that Jack should insure. Social insurance is not insurance in the technical sense, but its basic function (and especially the rationale for making it mandatory) is again to avoid burdening the prudent.*

Pechman et al. (1968) in their book on social security, after an extensive discussion of the rationale for pensions, conclude:

> *There is widespread myopia with respect to retirement needs. Empirical evidence shows that most people fail to save enough to prevent catastrophic drops in post-retirement income. . . . Not only do people fail to plan ahead carefully for retirement, even in the later years of their working life, many remain unaware of impending retirement needs. . . . In an urban, industrial society, government intervention in the saving-consumption decision is needed to implement personal preferences over the life cycle. There is nothing inconsistent in the decision to undertake through the political proc-*

ess a course of action which would not be undertaken individually through the marketplace.

The first empirical studies of this issue have been carried out by Peter Diamond (1977) and Kotlikoff et al. (1982). Both studies conclude that without social security (or its equivalent), a substantial fraction of the population would be inadequately prepared for retirement. The data analyzed in both studies indicate that a large number of the population, if left on their own, are likely to undersave for old age.

Social Security Decision Making

J. Douglas Brown, who helped draft the original social security program, writes in his book on the history of social security that the drafting group never seriously considered anything other than a compulsory program. The drafting group did worry, however, about whether a national compulsory program would be constitutional.

Hoping that it might be possible to avoid a court test of the constitutionality of social security, the drafting group did consider briefly a plan that would have permitted elective social security coverage by states and various industrial groups but rejected it. According to Brown, the plan was "so cumbersome, ineffective, and actuarially unsound that no further attempt was made to avoid a head-on constitutional test of a truly workable system" (Brown, 1972).

As it turned out, during the debates that followed, the principal argument for compulsion was a financial one. It was argued that an optional coverage program would make it **actuarially** impossible to project both benefits (costs) and revenue. It was feared that this problem would create financial instability and make it difficult to guarantee adequate, equitable, and improved benefits as social security developed.

The original Social Security Act required participation by all workers in commerce and industry except those working for railroads.[3] A number of groups, however, were specifically excluded from coverage—the major groups being farm workers, the self-employed, and government employees (including military personnel). Over the years, as coverage was extended to these groups,

---

[3] Railroad workers were exempted because similar legislation on their behalf had already been enacted in 1934. Although this original legislation was later declared unconstitutional, new (and still separate) railroad pension legislation was enacted in 1935 and 1937.

optional coverage was introduced for certain specific groups: employees of nonprofit institutions, state and local governments, and most clergymen. But in each case, coverage was not optional for the individual, depending instead on the collective decision of the organizational unit. Today, all these groups are covered mandatorily by social security, except certain state and local employees (who are covered by their own mandatory systems).

The decision of the United States to have a compulsory pension program is in no way unique. There is no country in the world with a social security old age pension program that has designed a large amount of voluntary coverage into the program. Like the United States, many countries have special public pension programs for certain groups of workers (especially government employees), and many exclude from coverage certain groups (such as farm workers, the self-employed, or employees of very small firms). Some countries—for example, Ghana, the Federal Republic of Germany, Kuwait, Liberia, Peru, Uganda, and Zambia—have voluntary coverage, but these noncompulsory provisions *are all limited* to certain (usually small) groups in the country.

If we shift our attention from public pensions to *private* pensions in the United States, we find that the situation is not very different. Most of the workers who are covered (or not covered) by private pension plans have *not* achieved that status by personal election. Not all firms have established private pension plans for their employees, but almost all private pension schemes that have been set up are compulsory. Typically, once a worker joins a firm, he or she automatically becomes a member of the pension plan—sometimes after a short waiting period. There are a few private plans, however, that provide for an employee contribution out of salary; such plans sometimes make coverage optional.

In summary, we see that the usefulness of pensions in helping to provide for economic security in old age is generally accepted and that compulsory coverage remains a feature of both public and private programs.

What Makes a "Good" Pension Program?

If one wants to evaluate a pension program or a pension proposal, what characteristics or features of the plan should be examined? With an institutional arrangement as complex as pensions, one can generate a long list of plan features that might be studied. Opinions differ widely as to which of these are most important. Moreover, there is little agreement on the relative weights that should be assigned to each feature when making an overall judgment about a particular pension plan. Some important characteristics of pension plans, however, that would probably appear on everyone's list, are discussed in the pages that follow.

The Adequacy of Pension Benefits

Any discussion of a particular pension plan's adequacy must explicitly recognize the variety of means available to the individual (or society) in achieving a particular level of income in old age. A particular pension plan is rarely designed to be the sole source of such income. Thus, in evaluating the adequacy of any particular pension benefit, it is necessary to relate such analysis to a general framework for evaluating individuals' general economic status and the variety of means available to achieve or change that status: Are individuals expected to accumulate personal savings for their old age? Are all individuals *able* to save for old age? What noncash programs (such as health insurance) are available to provide economic support? How large are both public and private pension benefits? Who is currently covered by each? Who should be covered?

There will never be complete agreement about the appropriate roles for the various means of providing income in old age—collective pension schemes are only one major way (see Table 4–1). Rather, it is almost certain that there will be continuing political debate and private discussion among bargaining groups over these matters. Out of such discussions come decisions on legislation, employment contracts, and employer policies in the area of pensions. As these decisions are made, it is possible to evaluate their economic implications for retirement income adequacy, estimating the contribution the resulting pensions will make to a particular individual's or group's goal.

The Certainty of Benefits

In addition to estimating or projecting the size of pension benefits, one can examine particular pension plans and estimate the degree of uncertainty associated with the *promised* benefits. Three major contingencies should be evaluated:

1. Plan termination: What provisions are made to ensure that the plan will survive economic or political adversity, such as a change in government (public pensions) or bankruptcy of the firm (private pensions)?

2. Inflation: How well are the workers' future benefits and the pension recipients' actual benefits protected from general increases in the level of prices?
3. Job termination: What happens to pension rights if a worker involuntarily or by choice stops working or changes jobs?

Flexibility and Discretion for Varying Conditions or Preferences

The larger the pension program in terms of people covered, the greater the differences in the circumstances and preferences of these participants. It is generally desirable for pension plan provisions and rules not to be too rigid. The introduction of greater flexibility, however, usually results in greater administrative costs (see Administrative Costs, below). And by complicating the program, flexibility often makes it more difficult for participants to become knowledgeable and to understand their pension program.

Adequate and Nondiscriminatory Coverage

The determination of eligibility for pension coverage is a very complex but important factor in assessing pension plans. Most people would agree that individuals in similar circumstances (e.g., working for the same employer) should not be arbitrarily excluded from coverage under a pension plan or excluded because of age, sex, race, and so forth. But the actual determination of who should and who should not be included is often difficult because of a variety of administrative, technical, political, and economic considerations. For example, should workers be excluded from protection because they do not (or cannot) work full-time?

Equity

Whether a pension program is perceived as fair depends in large measure on how the program treats different individuals and how these individuals think they *should* be treated. The major issue around which equity questions usually cluster is financing: How much do the benefits received cost the individual in contrast to other benefit recipients and, possibly, nonrecipients?

Administrative Costs

Apart from the benefits paid out by a pension program, there are a variety of expenditures connected with keeping records, regulatory supervision, determining benefit eligibility, collecting and managing the funds used to pay benefits, and informing individuals of their rights under the plan.

Boulding (1958) has argued that one valid criterion for choosing between private and public programs is whether there can be significant economies of scale in their operation:

> *If there are these economies—that is, if the cost of administering the insurance declines with every increase in the amount of insurance written—then a state monopoly will almost inevitably be cheaper than a number of competing private companies. . . . We may venture a hypothesis that where the operations of insurance are fairly routine, the case for state or national monopoly is stronger than where the operations involve great difficulties of definition of rights.*

Simplicity and Ease of Understanding

It is important that individuals know whether they are covered by a pension plan, what the conditions of entitlement are, what benefits they (or their family) can or will receive, what the risks of losing benefits are, and various other facts about the plan. Over the years a large amount of evidence has accumulated that indicates a great lack of knowledge and much misinformation exists among workers in the United States with regard to their own expected pensions, both public and private (see, for example, U.S. GAO, 1987). As the number and variety of pension programs grow and many of these programs become more complicated, this problem will also grow. Therefore, in reviewing existing programs or proposals for pension changes, the complexity of the program should be considered. An assessment should be made of the resultant impact on the employees' ability to understand the pension program and to incorporate it realistically into their pre-retirement planning.

Integration

A particular pension plan is almost always only one of a number of collective programs operating to provide economic assistance. It is not sufficient to view a particular pension program in isolation from these other programs. For example, eligibility or benefit determination under one program is sometimes related to benefits received from another program (see Schulz and Leavitt, 1983).

This is an especially important issue with regard to public

programs. The value of social security pension benefits to the elderly depends, for example, on (1) the tax treatment of these benefits and (2) whether the benefits are counted as income in determining eligibility for Supplemental Security Income, food stamps, Medicare and Medicaid, housing subsidies, and so forth (see, for example, Federal Council on Aging, 1975).

What Mix of Public and Private Pensions?

Despite the fact that the first pension plans were established about a century ago, there is still little agreement about the relative virtues of public versus private pensions and what the ideal combination of the two types should be. There is great diversity in the mix of pensions existing in various countries, but there are fewer countries where private programs assume a major role than there are countries that rely primarily on public pensions.

Relatively little has been written that attempts objectively to approach the question of the most desirable pension mix and present data for evaluation purposes. In the United States, well-known economist Milton Freidman has been a consistent critic of social security and one of the few academics actually to advocate complete abolition of public pensions. He argues that "social security combines a highly regressive tax with largely indiscriminate benefits and, in overall effect, probably redistributes income from lower to higher income persons. I believe that it serves no essential social function. Existing commitments make it impossible to eliminate it overnight, but it should be unwound and terminated as soon as possible" (Cohen and Friedman, 1972).

There has been very little support for Friedman's extreme position. Instead, the more common negative view toward social security advocates a small role for it and, consequently, seeks to limit any future growth of the program—either by expansion of real benefits or by adding additional functions.

Robert J. Myers, chief actuary for the social security program between 1947 and 1971, labels advocates of a greater role for social security in aged income maintenance as "expansionists" and designates as "moderates" those persons who believe the program should not be expanded. Myers (1970) summarizes the moderate viewpoint as one that seeks a governmental program that would provide benefits "sufficient so that, with assets and real estate normally accumulated, the vast majority of beneficiaries will be able to have at least a *reasonable subsistence*." [Emphasis added.]

Arguments Against and for Social Security

Over the years concern about further expansion of the role for social security and raising social security benefits has not been the major issue raised by critics. Rather, most of the concern and criticism has centered on the way benefits have been financed. In Chapter 6 we discuss many of the issues connected with social security financing. In general, critics assert:

1. Social security places a heavy tax burden on the poor and nearpoor.
2. There are very great differences in contributions paid in versus benefits received among different socioeconomic groups and between current and future generations.
3. Individuals lose control over money put aside for old age.

Criticism of social security, however, has been relatively limited in comparison to support voiced for it. On the positive side, four major arguments have been advanced in its favor:

1. Social security's payroll tax is offset for low earners by special federal income tax provisions, and the program will remain a "good buy" for most people in the future.
2. The (per capita) nonbenefit costs of social insurance are much lower than the costs for private pension administration, fund investment, mobility, disclosure to recipients, supervision and regulation, and reinsurance.
3. It is easier to make social security pensions both inflation proof—adjusting for inflation at and during retirement—and adjustable for economic growth.
4. It is relatively easy to cover all workers and provide complete portability of credits under social security, whereas private pensions present formidable problems in this regard (unless coverage is mandated by the government).

Administrative Costs

Although the structure of social security in the United States is far from being uncomplicated, there are many aspects of its operation that are relatively simple. Consequently, the collection and benefit payout process permits the extensive use of computers. This in turn permits the handling of large numbers of claims in a way that allows significant economies of large-scale operation to be realized. In fiscal year 1985, for example, administrative expenses were about 1 percent of payroll contributions for the old age and survivors program (OASI). These low expenses are in sharp contrast to public perceptions. A Roper opinion poll found that only 2 percent of those interviewed thought that social security administrative costs were less than 10 percent of contributions collected (Social Security Administration, 1981). The median estimate was 52 percent!

Comparing costs between social security and private pensions is complicated by the fact that social security financing in the United States is essentially on a pay-as-you-go basis, whereas private pensions are funded (see Chapter 8). Private pension funding costs generated as a result of financial investment on behalf of employers (and, in part, indirectly benefiting the economy) have no analogous counterpart in the United States social security program. Also, another difference between the two types of pensions is the fact that employers and the Internal Revenue Service give lots of "free" administrative services to the social security system.

Insurance companies, unions, corporations, and banks administer private pension plans. Although there has been no study of the costs of private pension plans compared to social security, it is hard to imagine that the current conglomeration of thousands of private plans, many covering fewer than a hundred workers, can have lower administrative costs. A study by Mitchell and Andrews (1981) analyzes expenses in multiemployer plans. Annual plan expenses in the early 1980s were estimated to range from about $13 per participant for large plans (20,000 participants) to $138 per participant for small plans (100 participants).

Pension Adjustments for Inflation

Another important argument made in favor of public pensions is their ability, in contrast to private plans, to deal with the need to respond to inflation and economic growth. The problem of inflation has plagued pension programs since their inception. All countries have had to struggle with this problem, continually adjusting pension programs and benefits to offset increases in price levels. Inflation has varied, for example, from the catastrophic rate in post–World War I Germany (which completely wiped out the monetary value of that country's social security reserves and benefits) to the relatively mild price increases averaging less than 2 percent in the United States during the 1958–1968 period to the much higher rates in later years (including double-digit inflation in 1974 and 1979/80).

Gradually, most industrialized countries (including the United States in 1972) have introduced some sort of automatic benefit adjustment mechanisms into the social security program to deal more effectively with the inflation problem. In contrast, private pension plans, with few exceptions, virtually ignore the need for *regularized* adjustment mechanisms.[4] This results, in large part, because of employers' unwillingness to make financial commitments based on guesses about future price levels and fear that the cost of these adjustments may be too high. In addition, most private pension analysts believe that it is virtually impossible to devise an acceptable inflation-proofing mechanism without indexed bonds issued by the government (see Munnell, 1979).

It is much easier for governments to deal with the inflation problem, given their inherent taxing powers and their ability to minimize the size of the monetary fund necessary to guarantee the financial soundness of the pension program. A pay-as-you-go system, for example, makes it easier to increase revenues to pay for inflation-adjusted pensions because the earnings base is also rising with inflation. In contrast, many securities in a reserve fund will not adjust upward in value with the inflation.

The actual history of social security programs in various countries dealing with inflation supports that conclusion; even after runaway inflations, countries have been able to adjust pensions to the price level. In addition, public pension programs have shown an ability to devise equitable ways of permitting retired persons to share systematically in the real growth of the country. Social security programs in some countries—such as Belgium, Canada, Norway, and West Germany—provide for automatic or semiautomatic adjustments in *real* benefit levels. Still others adjust systematically by various ad hoc processes.

Coverage

It has proven to be a relatively easy matter in all industrial countries to extend social security coverage to large segments of the labor force. Coverage of agricultural workers and the self-employed has presented problems—especially in developing countries—but, in general, extension of coverage all over the world has been quite comprehensive. In the United States, for example, coverage of the gainfully employed is now complete (see page 123).

In contrast, as we discuss in Chapter 8, extension of private pension coverage beyond current levels presents serious problems. It has been especially difficult to extend coverage to workers in small firms (page 220). As a result, a sizable proportion of the work

---

[4]This issue is discussed more extensively in Chapter 9.

force in countries with private pensions may not be covered by such pensions.

One possible solution to the coverage problem is for the government to require that all employers provide private pension benefits. Some countries have done this (Switzerland and Great Britain). In Britain, employers must provide pension protection equal to government minimums or contribute to a quasi-public funded pension scheme.

In 1981 the President's Commission on Pension Policy recommended mandatory private coverage for the United States, but thus far the recommendation has received little support in Congress.

Arguments in Support of Private Pensions

There are two major arguments supporting the existence and expansion of private pensions:

1. That social security—because of its broad coverage—must remain very uniform in its benefit provisions, while private pensions are more flexible and can be tailored to meet differing situations and conditions (e.g., hazardous conditions) of various industries, particular firms, or different occupational groups.
2. That private pensions are vital to assure the saving necessary to provide sufficient **investment** in a growing economy.

Flexibility

On the one hand, a private pension can be a flexible management tool. As Charles A. Siegfried (1970) of the Metropolitan Life Insurance Company has observed, "A pension plan can be devised to attract and hold employees or it can be devised to facilitate the separation of employees from employment." On the other hand, pension objectives may vary to accommodate different employee wishes and aspirations, these being determined by decisions of the employers (unilaterally or in consultation with workers) or by collective bargaining.

The late Edwin S. Hewitt, a well-known pension consultant, arguing the case for private pensions before the U.S. Senate Special Committee on Aging, emphasized the flexibility factor:

> *It is extraordinary how flexible an instrument for providing adequate security the private plan has proved to be. There are two*

*kinds of flexibility and perhaps this fact is underrated when we
oppose what private plans are doing.*

*First is their flexibility in terms of adapting to different needs.
Very real differences in security problems exist among different
companies, different industries, different age groups. . . .*

*The second dimension is the flexibility between periods of time.
Private plans have exhibited amazing flexibility to make their provisions meet the different needs that a group may have at different
times.*

*The initial job of most pension plans when first established is to
concentrate on retirement income for the older worker, hence the
importance of past service benefits.*[5] *As plans become better funded,
they tend to branch into other areas. Variety increases as plans are
able to spend more money and give attention to tailormade benefits
to meet specific needs. [Hewitt, 1970]*

Pension Saving and Capital Formation

A much more controversial argument made in favor of private
pensions is their role in the mobilization of national saving for
economic investment. Charles Moeller, an economist for the Metropolitan Life Insurance Company, argued the positive aspects
this way:

*The key to any nation's economic growth is its ability to direct
substantial portions of its output into real investment, i.e., to defer
current consumption of output through saving and to permit investment in productive facilities for use in future production processes.
. . . In effect, what pension funding operations and other forms of
contractual saving do is to improve the efficiency and stability of the
capital markets. . . .*

*The importance of the saving function for private pension plans
cannot be too strongly emphasized. The need for encouraging the
accumulation of individual saving flows and for recirculating these
funds back into the economy through the investment process has
been spotlighted by the dramatic events of recent years including
the "crunch" of 1966 and the "liquidity crisis" of 1970. [Moeller,
1972]*

It is a common misconception that there is a direct relationship
between the personal saving of individuals (for retirement and

---

[5] Past service benefits are credits for years of work in the firm prior to the establishment
of the pension plan (page 238). Most benefit formulas pay benefits that rise with years of
service with the company.

other reasons) and economic growth. While there is a need for saving to facilitate investment in the economy, there are a variety of ways such saving can be accumulated. Hence, there is no agreement on the need or importance of any one accumulation process—such as through personal saving or private pensions.

In the key growth sector of *corporate* production, the overwhelming majority of funds needed to finance new investment comes from the *internal* funds saved by the corporations themselves. "If you substract housing investment from total capital investment funds, more than 99 percent of real capital investment funds took the form of corporate **retained earnings** or **depreciation allowance** in 1973" (Thurow, 1976). That result would not be very different today.

Other possible sources of savings are unincorporated business, individuals, and government budget surpluses. Moreover, there is a disagreement over the extent to which there is any insufficiency of saving in the United States relative to investment opportunities and the willingness of business to undertake investment. Economist Arthur Okun (1975) observed that "the specter of depressed saving is not only empirically implausible but logically fake. . . . The nation can have the level of saving and investment it wants with more or less income redistribution, so long as it is willing to twist some other dials."

A *New York Times* article reviewing this issue reiterates the caution of many economists that even if the savings rate were to rise, this would not necessarily increase investment, **productivity,** and growth. Quoting Nobel laureate Robert M. Solow, the article stated:

> *Increasing savings only matters when what is limiting investment is capacity, and that is not the case now. The problem affecting investment now is one of profitability. How will more saving make the automobile or steel industry more profitable? [Arenson, 1981]*

Or as Franco Modigliani (1987), another recipient of a Nobel prize in economics, states, "One of the interesting implications of the life-cycle theory [of savings] suggests that when a country needs capital to drive rapid growth, capital will be forthcoming."

Economists also disagree about the impact of social security on personal savings. In 1974 economist Martin Feldstein was the first to present statistical evidence indicating that growing social security benefits may have reduced total personal savings in the United States. A great deal of additional research and debate followed Feldstein's original article. For example, Barro (1978) argued that evolving social security has changed the pattern of voluntary intergenerational transfers (from parents to children and vice versa). Barro presented statistical evidence (disputed by Feldstein) indicating that this changing pattern of family transfers offsets the savings impact of social security. Lesnoy and Leimer (1981) then demonstrated a serious error in Feldstein's original study and reached the opposite conclusion using the same data. Reviewing these and other studies to date, both Munnell (1982a) and Aaron (1982) conclude that *there is little evidence that the pay-as-you-go social security system has depressed personal saving in the United States*.

Finally, it should be noted that the generation of savings through pensions is not limited to private pensions. Public social security reserve funds can also be generated. For example, there is a growing debate in the United States over whether to allow the OASDI trust funds to grow dramatically over the next two decades (pp. 166–168). In Sweden, the financing rates for the social security program have been deliberately set high enough to help generate savings in the Swedish economy. In fact, public pension reserves may be a particularly attractive means of mobilizing savings in developing countries where private pensions are virtually nonexistent.

The Pension Mix in Various Countries

If we look at the pension programs currently in existence in various industrialized countries, we find a tendency to rely heavily either on public pensions or on some sort of private/public combination *with extensive regulation of the private sector*. In countries that rely heavily on private pensions, the tendency is for the private and public pension programs to be closely coordinated by a large number of complex legislative and administrative mechanisms and regulations. In France, for example, it is difficult to make a distinction between social security and the widespread private pension programs—given the elaborate coordinating mechanisms that have been established.

In the United States, both public and private pension plans have assumed a growing share of responsibility for providing retirement income needs. The indications are that this collective share will continue to grow. But it is not yet clear how that responsibility ultimately will be divided.

Chapter 4 Highlights

What are the mechanisms available for providing economic support in retirement? How should choices be made among the alternatives? In this chapter we emphasized the following points:

1. While there are many ways of providing for retirement, a major choice is between personal saving and collective pension programs (both public and private).
2. Planning for retirement by individuals is complicated by (a) a variety of uncertainties, such as future health and employment possibilities, and (b) the need to take action far in advance of the actual event.
3. A reasonable planning goal for a middle-income worker is retirement income equal to 60 to 70 percent of preretirement gross income.
4. Assessments of pension alternatives should be based on differences in adequacy, the certainty of receipt, flexibility, coverage, equity, costs, simplicity, and integration mechanisms.
5. A more controversial criterion for assessing pension alternatives is the impact of particular types of pensions on national saving.

Suggested Readings

BOULDING, KENNETH. "Income Maintenance Policy." In *Principles of Economic Policy*. Englewood Cliffs, N.J.: Prentice-Hall, 1958, pp. 233–257. One of the best discussions of the rationale for pension insurance and one of the few discussions available on the relative merits of public versus private pensions.

CATES, J. R. *Insuring Inequality*. Ann Arbor: University of Michigan Press, 1983; and C. L. Weaver. *The Crisis in Social Security*. Durham, N.C.: Duke Press Policy Studies, 1982. Two very different views regarding the origins of social security in the United States.

ESPOSITO, LOUIS. "Effect of Social Security on Saving." *Social Security Bulletin* 41 (May 1978): 9–17. An explanation for noneconomists of the relationship of social security to saving and capital formation. A variety of relevant data and research findings are summarized.

HEIDENHEIMER, ARNOLD H., HUGH HECLO, AND CAROLYN TEICH ADAMS. *Comparative Public Policy—The Politics of Social Choice in Europe and America*. New York: St. Martin's Press, 1975. Chapter 7 of this book is an excellent comparative discussion of various social welfare programs. Included in the discussion is consideration of issues influencing how and when social insurance was introduced in each country.

MEIER, ELIZABETH, C. C. DITTMAR, AND B. B. TORREY. "Retirement Income

Goals." Chapter 5 in the Appendix of the President's Commission on Pension Policy, *Coming of Age: Toward a National Retirement Income Policy*. Washington, D.C.: The Commission, 1981. A discussion of adequacy goals and estimates of amounts required to achieve them.

SCHULZ, JAMES H., AND THOMAS D. LEAVITT. *Pension Integration: Concepts, Issues and Proposals*. Washington, D.C.: Employee Benefit Research Institute, 1983. A comprehensive discussion of the historical development of social security integration provisions in private pension plans and the controversial issues arising from them.

SCHULZ, JAMES H., ET AL. *Providing Adequate Retirement Income—Pension Reform in the United States and Abroad*. Hanover, H.H.: New England Press for Brandeis University Press, 1974. This book presents a more extensive treatment of the topics in this chapter. It emphasizes the replacement of average preretirement earnings by pensions as a measure of adequacy. Innovative pension systems in five countries are analyzed.

Chapter 5

SOCIAL SECURITY: OLD AGE AND SURVIVORS' BENEFITS

The first American social security benefit ever paid was $22 a month and was received by Miss Ida Fuller, a retired law firm secretary, in early 1940. Ida Fuller's experience with social security dramatically illustrates one of the major benefits of public pensions discussed in the prior chapter. Miss Fuller (who died in 1975) lived to be over 100, paid into the program less than $100, and over the years received about $21,000 in social security benefits.

One of the reasons Miss Fuller received much more than she paid in was because she lived far beyond the average **life expectancy;** pensions are designed to pay more to those who live an "unexpectedly" long life. But as we discuss further in Chapter 6, there is another reason why many Americans like Ida Fuller receive significantly more benefits than the contributions they paid into social security. Congress decided in the early years of the program to reduce the eligibility requirements (i.e., the length of the work/payment period) for older workers approaching retirement when the program was first established (and later when new groups were brought into the program).

In response to the pressing needs of Ida Fuller and millions of other persons unemployed or approaching old age with little money, the United States social security system was created in 1935. It has grown over the years to be one of the major programs of the federal government.

121

The Changing Social Security System

The Social Security Act of 1935 established the basic federal old age benefits program and a federal-state system of unemployment insurance. Various key events occurred in succeeding years. In 1939, survivors' and dependents' benefits were added (OASI). In 1956, social security was expanded to include disability insurance to protect severely disabled workers (OASDI). In 1965, Medicare was added, establishing a comprehensive health program for the elderly (OASDHI).[1] **Indexing** of earnings used to compute benefits was legislated in 1972.

Total annual OASDHI expenditures have grown from less than $1 billion in 1950 to nearly $300 billion in 1988. This chapter focuses primarily on the social security old age pension program (OASI). The discussion focuses mainly on benefits, however, since Chapter 6 is devoted to a discussion of financing issues. Chapter 7 discusses the medical, disability, and supplemental security income programs.

Encouragement of Retirement

Paradoxically, the major motivating force behind the passage of the Social Security Act in 1935 was not the provision of adequate retirement income but the creation of jobs. Passed in a period that at one point witnessed more than a quarter of the labor force without jobs, the social security legislation was one of many New Deal laws aimed at job creation and relief for those out of work. The 1935 legislation encouraged the creation of state-administered unemployment programs to help unemployed workers find work and to provide them with financial support while they looked. Old age pensions were provided to help the elderly financially but were also provided to *encourage older workers to leave or remain out of the work force*. Old age benefits to otherwise eligible persons age 65 or over were made conditional on meeting a "retirement test." In the original 1935 act, benefits were *not* to be paid to persons receiving any "covered wages from regular employment."

Regular employment, however, was not specifically defined in the 1935 act. In the 1939 social security amendments, the retirement test was made less ambiguous; it specified that no benefits

---

[1]The railroad retirement program was integrated with the social security system in 1974. We do not discuss the railroad retirement system in this book. Those interested in developments should read Skolnik (1975).

would be paid to anyone earning more than $14.99 a month in covered employment. Over the years the earnings exemption rules have varied by age, and the level has been increased periodically by specific increments. In 1988, the exemption amount for persons age 65 to 69 was $8,400. (See page 135 for more detail.)

Changes

Over the past three and a half decades there have been a great many adjustments in the social security system. However, except for the introduction of disability insurance in 1956, medical insurance (Medicare) in 1965, and automatic cost-of-living benefit adjustment procedures in 1972, there have been few, if any, major programmatic changes. Four historical developments are of particular importance, however.

First, as a result of a series of legislated liberalizations (listed above), there was an expansion of persons covered by the system. Over the years successive groups of workers have been brought into the system: certain self-employed, farm, and domestic workers and employees of charitable, educational, and religious organizations (1950), most other self-employed and ministers (1954), (optionally) employees of state and local governments (1950 and 1954), members of the uniformed services (1956), Americans employed by foreign governments or international organizations (1960), physicians (1965), and new federal employees (1983). Currently, the only major groups of gainfully employed workers not covered are (1) federal employees hired before 1984,[2] (2) certain state and local government employees, (3) farm and domestic workers who do not earn or work "enough," and (4) self-employed persons with very low net earnings.

Second, as discussed in the next section, coverage and benefit liberalizations over the years have prevented the accumulation of large monetary reserves—consistent with the pay-as-you-go basic financing principle adopted by Congress in 1939.

Third, adjustment of the pension formula's preretirement earnings using a wage index was introduced to stabilize the earnings replacement rates provided by benefits. The objective of this indexing was to provide successive cohorts of workers with equivalent average monthly earnings over their working lifetimes (relative to the average earnings of the economy) the same replacement rates at the time of retirement. In addition, cost-of-living adjust-

---

[2] Unless a federal employee has voluntarily transferred to the new retirement system for civil servants (page 244).

ments were introduced to protect benefits from inflation occurring during retirement. (Benefits are adjusted every January to reflect increases in the consumer price index (page 56).)

Finally, beginning in 1984, beneficiaries have been required to pay income tax on up to 50 percent of their social security benefits if adjusted gross income plus 50 percent of their benefits exceeds $25,000 (individual) or $32,000 (married couple filing jointly). (See Chapter 6, page 184, for more details.)

Financing

Although we discuss financing in Chapter 6, some initial remarks are appropriate here. Currently, the social security system is almost completely "unfunded" (i.e., historically only a limited amount of reserves have been allowed to accumulate, and obligations have been met essentially on a pay-as-you-go basis). From the very beginning social security was never completely funded.[3] It was recognized from the start that this was not necessary since (1) mandatory participation resulted in the involvement of a large part of the employed population, (2) the pension system could be assumed to operate indefinitely, and (3) the taxing power of the government ultimately stood behind the system.

As initially enacted in 1935, legislated social security contribution rates were expected to provide the money for a fairly large trust fund as payments came in over the years. But as this reserve fund began to accumulate and **actuarial** projections predicted that it would grow much bigger, congressional leaders began to argue that there was no reason for the fund to grow so big. Instead, the decision was made in 1939 (and years thereafter) to liberalize the system and to use the scheduled increases in contributions to pay for these liberalizations.

Historically, the gradual adoption of an almost completely pay-as-you-go funding policy facilitated the liberalization and improvement of the system. New groups were added to the system with retroactive benefits provided. Cost-of-living increases in benefits were legislated periodically. And, in 1972, a major increase in real benefits was provided to current and future participants in the system.

The historical evolution of social security financing is important to keep in mind. Some argue that the financial problems of the recent past and those projected for the 21st century are, in part, a

---

[3] President Roosevelt initially insisted on an almost fully funded program, but this approach was not accepted by Congress (Leonard, 1986).

result of overly liberal expansion decisions made in earlier years. In response, others argue that Congress deliberately legislated benefits considerably in excess of contributions, to keep millions of elderly out of almost certain poverty; the aim was to deal with the problem through a program that avoided the stigma of needs-tested public assistance programs (see page 209 for a discussion of this history). In the opinion of the latter group, the future costs of this approach are to be expected and should not be viewed with alarm. In fact, the original designers of social security in the 1930s called for later government contribution out of general revenues to meet the costs of providing benefits to the several initial generations who had not contributed very much into the system. As we discuss later (page 181), this proposal has never been implemented.

The Principles of Social Security

The social security legislation that was accepted by President Roosevelt and the Congress was based on a number of principles. First, participation was to be compulsory for the designated groups. Workers could not opt out of the system. Nor were covered individuals with either high earnings or high total income entirely excluded.

Second, social insurance was set up as an earnings-related program. When this decision was made in the 1930s, it was not at all obvious that social security should be based on an earnings-related principle. At the time, many countries in Europe had flat-rate pensions. And Dr. Francis E. Townsend, a California physician, had proposed in 1933 a flat pension of $200 per month for all persons aged 60 and over—resulting in the Townsend movement of 7,000 clubs with 2 million people.

The decision against the flat rate is explained by J. Douglas Brown (1972), one of the architects of the system: "It was early recognized that a single flat rate of benefits for a country as diversified as the United States would fail to meet the needs of those living in the high-cost urban areas of the Northeast while being unduly favorable to those in the rural South." Moreover, a *high* flat pension for all the aged would have been very costly and more than most government decisionmakers thought was financially feasible.

Third, social adequacy was to be taken into account in the determination of benefits for various recipients, A weighted benefit formula that favored workers with lower earnings was established.

Also, a contribution cutoff point (the maximum contribution ceiling) was established; the earnings above the ceiling of very highly paid earners were excluded. The intent was to focus the program on those people with the greatest problems and with the greatest need for a public benefit (while allowing all eligible earners to participate).

Fourth, it was decided that social security should be only one of many sources of economic protection and that further supplementation, either through group or individual means, would be needed to maintain an adequate standard of living in retirement. In the early years, social security was often referred to as providing "a floor of protection."

Fifth, funds for operating the program were to come from earmarked taxes, called contributions. Social insurance was to be "a cooperating institution taken over by the state, but still a reflection of the responses of workers who are willing to contribute from their earnings today to protect themselves and their families from the hazards of tomorrow" (Brown, 1972).

Sixth, social security benefits were to be a matter of right through participation as workers; there was to be no **means test**. Individuals were to earn their benefits through participation in and contributions to the program. The system was to be self-supporting through these worker contributions, together with so-called employer contributions.[4]

Seventh, as indicated above, a retirement test was established. Pension benefits were to be withheld, initially, if an age-eligible person worked for pay and later if a person earned above a specified amount.

Retirement Benefit Provisions[5]

To be eligible for retirement benefits under the old age and survivors insurance program, a worker must have worked in covered employment for the required number of calendar quarters. Prior to 1978 a quarter of coverage was defined as a calendar quarter in which the worker in covered employment was paid at least $50. In 1978 the reporting of social security wages was changed from a quarterly basis to an annual basis (to reduce

----

[4] We discuss in Chapter 6 the question of who actually pays the employer contribution—the employee through reduced wages, consumers through higher prices, or the firm itself.

[5] The disability program is not discussed until Chapter 7. Some students of social security, however, see it as an important part of a retirement program, providing transitional protection for many of those unable to continue working up to the OASI eligibility ages.

administrative costs). Currently, therefore, the number of quarters credited depends on annual earnings, one quarter (up to four) credited for each $470 (in 1988) of wages paid.[6]

The number of quarters required for eligibility varies by age— to make it easier for older workers to achieve eligibility during the early history of the program (see page 161). A worker attaining age 62 in 1988 needed 37 quarters. The total number of quarters required increases by one quarter in each succeeding year. The maximum number of quarters required will ultimately be 40, or about 10 years of covered employment.

The various types of benefits paid under the old age and survivors insurance program to eligible workers and their spouses are first briefly listed and then discussed below in more detail.

1. The *basic benefit*, based on a "normal retirement age" of 65, is based on the worker's average indexed monthly earnings (AIME) in covered employment. It is derived from a legislated benefit formula that is weighted to provide workers with lower average earnings a relatively greater percentage of earnings replacement than workers with higher earnings. Credited earnings (and hence benefits) are limited by an "earnings ceiling" limiting the earnings on which a worker previously paid contributions. Only taxed earnings below this ceiling enter into the calculation of the average monthly earnings used in the benefit formula. Also, total family benefits are limited by prescribed maxima.

2. A *minimum benefit* ($2,556 in 1988) is provided workers (and their survivors) who attained age 62 before 1982 and who would otherwise be eligible for very low basic benefits. A *special minimum benefit* is paid if larger than the minimum benefit or regular benefit and is increased annually by the consumer price index. However, it is available only to workers attaining age 62 who have *10 or more years of covered employment*—the size of the benefit being dependent on the number of years of covered employment between 10 and a 30-year maximum.

3. *Spouse and dependent benefits*, equal to 50 percent of the worker's basic benefit, may be paid to a spouse and to each child under age 18 (and elementary or secondary school students under age 19), subject to the "family maximum." Benefits for some spouses, however, are reduced by federal, state, or local pensions payable to the spouse based on earnings in noncovered employment. Aged parents, disabled adult children, and divorced persons may also receive a benefit if certain specified conditions are met.

---

[6]The amount is adjusted annually using an index of average earnings.

4. *Early retirement benefits* may be paid to beneficiaries at ages 62–64, but these benefits are actuarially reduced (by 20 percent at age 62) to take into account the longer period over which they will be paid.

5. *Delayed retirement credits* are given to workers age 65 or older who continue working and, as a result, do not receive their entitled benefits after age 65. An additional 3 percent is added to benefits (for those reaching age 62 in 1979 or later) for each year between ages 65 and 70 that they delay benefit receipt. (Higher credits begin in 1990.)

6. *An earnings test* reduces benefits paid persons under age 70 (and their dependents) who earn more than a certain amount. Benefits are reduced one dollar for every two dollars earned above the exempt amount. The exemption for beneficiaries age 65 to 69 ($8,440 in 1988) increases automatically with increases in average wages. A lower exemption applies to beneficiaries under age 65 ($6,120 in 1988).

7. *Survivors' benefits* are payable to a surviving spouse beginning at age 60 or, if disabled, at age 50 or, if there is a disabled adult child or a nondisabled dependent child under age 16, at any age. This benefit equals 100 percent of the basic benefit (see 1 above) for widows age 65 or over or a widow with a child in her care. Reduced benefits are paid to widows age 60–64 and to disabled widows age 50–59. Unmarried minor children and disabled adult children, dependent parents, divorced wives, and remarried widows are also eligible for survivors' benefits of various levels when meeting certain specified conditions. Benefits for surviving spouses are partially reduced for receipt of a government pension based on noncovered employment income (see 3 above).

Table 5–1 lists the major steps in the benefit calculation process. Each of the components listed above, or mentioned in the table, are discussed in more detail below.

Benefit Levels

Benefits generally are based on *all* years (except as noted below) of earnings after the year 1950. Only earnings covered under the social security program are counted. Earnings up to age 60 are adjusted upward based on changes in average wages throughout the whole economy. The adjustment process is called **wage indexing**. The highest indexed earnings are used to calculate the benefit. The calculation is based on five less than the number of years elapsing after the year one attains age 21 and before the year one

Table 5–1 Major Steps in the Old-Age Benefit Calculation Process

1. Check eligibility (required "quarters" of coverage).
2. Calculate average monthly indexed earnings (modified "lifetime earnings").
3. Determine primary insurance amount (from benefit formula or table).
4. Check if eligible for a minimum benefit:
    (a) Regular minimum or
    (b) Special minimum.
5. Reduce benefit if "early retirement."
6. Raise benefit if "delayed retirement."
7. Apply retirement test if covered earnings.
8. Calculate spouse benefit if married (and compare with spouse's own benefit).
9. Determine if other family benefits apply.
10. Check to make sure total benefits do not exceed family maximum.

attains age 62. The resulting total earnings are averaged to produce a measure called "average indexed monthly earnings" (AIME).

The law specifies a formula to determine the amount of benefit based on the worker's calculated AIME. The benefit formula for those reaching age 62 in 1988 is 90 percent of the first $319 of AIME, plus 32 percent of AIME over $319 and through $1,922, plus 15 percent of AIME over $1,922. The AIME dollar amounts in this formula change each year as part of a mechanism to stabilize replacement rates over time (see Chapter 6).

One of the best ways of evaluating the resulting level of social security benefits is to look at **pension replacement rates**. You will remember from Chapter 4 that a pension replacement rate specifies the proportion of a worker's prior earnings that is replaced by the pension he or she receives.

Table 5–2 shows the amount of earnings replacement provided a single person by social security at various earnings levels. Given the target rates (also shown in Table 5–2), we see that social security provides a significant proportion of the income required. The last column of the table shows the gap between the replacement rate necessary to maintain living standards upon retirement and the replacement rate provided by social security retirement benefits.

The Social Security Administration's Retirement History Study provides us with information on the actual amount of earnings replaced by public and private pensions. Using these data, Fox (1982) reports on the pension replacement rates achieved by social security recipients who were married and began receiving benefits during the 1968–1976 period (see Table 5–3).

Table 5–2   Target Replacement Rate Goals and Social Security, Single Person in 1980

Gross Preretirement Earnings	(1) Replacement Goal[a]	(2) Social Security Replacement[b]	(1)–(2) Gap
$ 6,500	79%	57%	22%
10,000	73	49	24
15,000	66	42	24
20,000	61	34	27
30,000	58	23	35
50,000	51	14	37

Source: Preston C. Bassett, "The Cost of Providing an Adequate Retirement Income." Background paper for the President's Commission on Pension Policy (Washington, D.C.: mimeo, 1980).
[a]The goal is to provide sufficient retirement income in order to maintain prior living standards upon retirement.
[b]Assume retirement at age 65.

Minimum Benefits

Since its inception, the old age pension program has had a minimum benefit. In the original legislation, the guarantee was $10 per month. Over the years the original minimum benefit has been periodically increased and in 1988 was $2,556 per year for most workers who qualified.

Pechman et al. (1968) succinctly summarize the major problem that arises when a minimum is provided:

If minimum and low benefits were paid exclusively to aged house-holders with little or no other money income, the case for sharply

Table 5–3   Total After-tax[a] Earnings Replacement Rates for Social Security Recipients First Receiving Benefits in 1968–76

Replacement Rate	Couples	Nonmarried Men	Nonmarried Women
0.1–19.9	1	1	0
20–39.9	18	·32	18
40–59.9	44	44	50
60–79.9	27	14	21
80–99.9	7	4	6
100 or more	4	4	5
Total Percent[b]	100	100	100
Median	55	46	52

Source: Alan Fox, "Earnings Replacement Rates and Total Income: Findings from the Retirement History Study," Social Security Bulletin 45 (October 1982), Table 9.
[a]Includes federal, state, and local income taxes and FICA taxes, on both preretirement earnings and pension benefits.
[b]May not add to 100 percent due to rounding.

*increasing the minimum would be overwhelming. In the absence of
an income test, however, many beneficiaries receive minimum or low
benefits because they had had limited attachment to occupations
covered by social security, not because they have had low lifetime
earnings. Former employees of federal, state, and local governments
can enter covered employment late in life and acquire insured status
sufficient to entitle them to low or minimum benefits.*[7]

Congress recognized the problems associated with the minimum. In 1972, it created a special minimum for long-term workers; in 1977, it froze the level of the regular minimum for future beneficiaries; and in 1981, it eliminated the regular minimum for those turning age 62 after 1981.

In the spring of 1981 the Reagan administration proposed a number of social security amendments. These proposals included elimination of the minimum benefit. The administration argued that "the main beneficiaries of the minimum . . . [were] those with a modest work history in employment covered by social security." In response to this proposal, Congress passed legislation terminating the minimum. It restored the provision almost immediately, however, for "the current aged"—reacting to intense lobbying and a growing awareness that a significant number of low-income beneficiaries would be seriously harmed by the elimination. The regular minimum is currently available only to very low earners who attained age 62 before 1982 or were first eligible for disabled-worker benefits before that year. It is also available to survivors of workers who died before 1982.

Under the provisions of the special minimum, persons with 10 or more "years of coverage" under social security have a guaranteed level equal (in 1988) to $20.10 per month times the years of coverage in excess of 10 years (but not exceeding $402 per month). The special minimum is adjusted automatically over time for increases in the cost of living. Currently, relatively few workers qualify for this benefit.

Dependent Benefits

In 1939 the social security program was amended to provide dependent benefits for wives over age 64 and for children under age 16. Successive legislation liberalized these provisions and extended benefits to students age 18–21, disabled children age 18 and over, divorced wives, and "dependent" husbands meeting

---

[7]*New* federal employees are currently covered by social security (see Chapter 8).

various eligibility conditions. In 1977 the Supreme Court further liberalized benefits by ruling unconstitutional the social security provision that men must prove they were financially dependent on their wives in order to get dependent benefits. As a consequence, widowers can now qualify for benefits based on their deceased wives' records without demonstrating "dependency."

As indicated above, an eligible dependent can receive a benefit based on the related worker's earnings and work history. Spouses who work and become qualified for benefits based on their own work experience can receive a benefit based just on their own work history. However, if their spouse benefit is larger, they receive their own pension *plus the difference* between the spouse benefit and their own worker's benefit. That is, in effect they receive either the dependent benefit based on the spouse's earnings or a benefit based on their own work history, whichever is greater. Thus, a wife may pay social security taxes without adding to the family's retirement income.[8] The problem is further aggravated by the fact that the husband and wife are treated as separate taxable units and consequently may collectively pay more social security taxes than a family with only a single worker earning the same amount. This occurs as a result of the taxable earnings ceiling that limits the taxed earnings of the single-earner family to the ceiling but taxes each earner of the dual-earner family up to the maximum.

Table 5–4 provides examples of the differences that can arise. The table shows the benefits four retiring couples would have received in 1987 if they had four different combinations of earn-

Table 5–4   1987 Benefits for Four Retiring Couples[a]

	Couple A	Couple B	Couple C	Couple D
Earnings				
Husband	$24,000	$12,000	$16,000	$24,000
Wife	0	12,000	8,000	8,300
Monthly benefits				
Husband	797	499	606	797
Wife	398	499	393	400
Total benefits	1,195	998	999	1,197
Survivor benefits	797	499	606	797

Source: Edith Fierst, Chair, Technical Committee on Earnings Sharing.
[a]Benefits are calculated assuming individuals begin benefits at age 65.

---

[8]If a husband and wife both work, the working wife has several advantages not available to the nonworking wife. She can retire and draw benefits at 62 or over, even if her husband works on. Survivors' benefits—lump-sum, children's benefits, and parents' benefits—may be paid on her earnings record. Also, before age 65 she may draw disability benefits on her own record.

ings. The first three examples show couples with equal *total* earnings that are divided differently between spouses. The fourth case shows a couple with more earnings (earned by the wife) but with no greater benefits.

As with the weighted benefit formula and the minimum, the justification for the spouse benefit is made on social adequacy grounds: On a given earnings history, two people are less able (than one person) to provide for retirement and need more income in retirement. Pechman et al. (1968) argue, however, that the greater amount a couple receives (currently 50 percent more than the single worker) is too large. They think that "the benefits of single workers should be raised substantially, relative to those of married couples. A smaller increment than 50 percent is justified because, at any given earnings level, single persons now receive smaller benefits relative to their previous standard of living than do married couples." Robert Ball, former Commissioner of Social Security, has in fact proposed that we reduce the spouse benefit and, at the same time, raise the basic benefit; he sees this as a way of making the progam more adequate for survivors.

Other arguments against the spouse benefit are (1) that a majority of women (but not all) in the future will be covered by social security on the basis of their own earnings, (2) that since few husband-wife families are poor, the spouse benefit is an extremely inefficient way to channel money to low-income families, and (3) that with rising female earnings, most families are now characterized by the mutual economic dependence of husbands and wives (Munnell, 1977).

The treatment of women under social security provisions has been studied intensively both inside and outside government (see page 147). In the area of spouse benefits three approaches are most frequently proposed as changes:

1. To eliminate the spouse benefit and split the combined earnings of the husband and wife for purposes of calculating benefits (see page 149).
2. To increase the worker benefit level, and at the same time reduce the spouse benefit (see Ball, 1978b).
3. To extend coverage and benefits directly to nonsalaried household workers, as is currently done in West Germany (see Task Force on Women and Social Security, 1975).

Early Retirement

Up until 1956 workers could not receive their old age benefits until they reached the age of 65. The selection of age 65 for the receipt of benefits was a somewhat arbitrary decision of those who drafted the legislation. In large part the decision was simply to copy the age provisions of existing public and private pension programs, almost all of which used age 65.

In 1956 the social security law was changed to permit women workers to receive reduced benefits between the ages of 62 and 64; and in 1961 this option was extended to men. In both cases the reduction was to be the full actuarial amount. That is, persons receiving benefits before age 65 were to receive over their remaining lifetime amounts that—based on average life expectancy— would not exceed (on average) the total amounts received by those retiring at age 65.

From the very beginning, the early retirement option was exceedingly popular and has been exercised by the great majority of workers. The Social Security Administration reports that over half the men awarded initial retirement benefits each year since 1962 have received reduced benefits. Table 5–5 shows the rise in the proportion of social security beneficiaries receiving reduced benefits. Over 70 percent of women and 60 percent of men do not receive full benefits.

Delayed Retirement

In 1939 the calculation of the social security pension was changed to include a 1 percent increase in benefits for each year that

Table 5–5   Social Security Worker Beneficiaries[a] Receiving Reduced Early Retirement Benefits

	Men		Women	
Year	Number[b] (000s)	Early Retirement[c] %	Number (000s)	Early Retirement %
Prior to 1970	274[d]	05[d]	115[e]	08[e]
1970	2,758	36	3,308	59
1975	4,465	49	4,904	66
1980	5,889	56	6,307	69
1985	7,166	61	7,553	71
1986	7,465	62	7,817	72

Source: U.S. Social Security Administration, *Social Security Bulletin* (September 1987), Table Q2.
[a]OASDI benefits in current payment status.
[b]Number of individuals receiving reduced benefits.
[c]Percent of all beneficiaries receiving reduced benefits.
[d]1961.
[e]1956.

credited earnings were at least $200. "This provision thus gave an individual who postponed his retirement after 65 a larger benefit when he retired than if he began to draw his benefits at 65. This provision was the subject of much controversy and was repealed in the 1950 law . . ." (Cohen, 1957).

In 1972 a provision was again added to the social security law that raised benefits for those who delayed retirement beyond age 65. Between 1950 and 1972, persons who continued to work beyond age 64 lost the value of all pension benefits potentially available while they worked. The 1972 provision reduced the loss somewhat but did not totally eliminate it. For there to be no loss in the actuarial value of a worker's benefit would require an increase in the worker's benefit level by about 8 percent a year, instead of the 3 percent adjustment in effect. In 1983 Congress moved to achieve that result, legislating future liberalizations in the delayed retirement credit. The credit will gradually rise from 3 to 8 percent over the 1990–2008 period.

The Retirement Test

The retirement test reduces or eliminates social security benefit payments if an otherwise eligible recipient has earnings above an exemption ceiling. Over the years officials of the Social Security Administration have acknowledged that this test generates the most questions and the most criticisms among people covered by the social security program. Further evidence of the controversy is that in every session of Congress since 1940 numerous bills have been introduced to eliminate or liberalize the test. In 1987, the Commissioner of Social Security called for elimination or major liberalization of the test. This was the first time that any commissioner of the program called for such a reform.

A past Advisory Council on Social Security[9] (1975) gave the following rationale for the test:

> *The Council has reviewed the provisions of the retirement test and believes that the test is consistent with the basic purpose and principles of social security: to replace, in part, earnings lost because of retirement in old age, disability, or death. Complete elimination of the retirement test is inadvisable. The retirement test has been criticized because it does not take into account a beneficiary's income from such nonwork sources as dividends, rent, or pension payments. If the test took account of income other than*

---

[9] Under current law, a new council is appointed every four years. Its function is to review all aspects of the social security program and to recommend improvements.

earnings from work, it would no longer be a retirement test but an income test. If it became an income test, the fundamental idea that social security benefits are intended as partial replacement of earnings from work would be diluted or lost.

While the reasoning advanced by the Advisory Council has also been the official position (until recently) of the Social Security Administration, it is important to recognize two other arguments that are frequently made in support of the test.[10] First, since there are still many workers age 62 or older who do not receive social security benefits and since many of them work full time, repeal of the retirement test would be relatively expensive and benefit most those who need help the least. For example, about 93 percent of the increased benefits resulting from the liberalizations in the earnings test legislated in 1977 went to individuals at the top or in the middle of the earnings distribution (Esposito et al., 1980). Second, given the fact that relatively high rates of unemployment have been a frequent phenomenon in the American economy, the retirement test encourages older workers to retire. Many people think that this opens up job opportunities for younger workers. Moreover, it is argued that older workers with pensions are discouraged from competing for jobs with younger workers by offering their services at wages below prevailing levels.

The work disincentive result of the retirement test arises principally from the fact that, in effect, earnings above the maximum are "taxed" at the relatively high rate of 50 percent. Studies have shown that some older workers have a strong aversion to loss of benefits at this tax rate (Campbell and Campbell, 1976). The effect of the test, therefore, is to discourage some workers from staying in the labor force and also to set a limit on part-time work activity so that earnings do not go beyond the maximum.

Whereas complete elimination of the retirement test would be costly and benefit many high earners, it can be argued alternatively that the test should be liberalized significantly to encourage and allow those people with low or moderate pension incomes to work in retirement. Various proposals have been advanced that would effectively exclude people with high earnings from the receipt of benefits but would not penalize low earners who wanted or needed to supplement their pension income. Complete *elimination* of the test was estimated in 1987 to cost 11 billion in the first year (BNA, 1987), but substantial liberalization, while maintaining some earn-

---

[10] For a more detailed listing and discussion or arguments for and against the test, see Schulz (1977) or Colberg (1978).

ings ceiling, could reduce the cost by as much as 80 percent (Schulz, 1978).

The second argument—that older workers should retire to make room for younger workers—raises a number of very complex issues. Ideally, an appropriate mix of monetary and fiscal policy by the government could promote an expansionary economy with jobs for almost everyone—thereby avoiding the dilemma of the older versus younger worker trade-off. The problem that arises, however, is that as the economy approaches full employment, inflationary factors tend to push up the general level of prices. Economic policymakers are thus faced with the unpleasant trade-off of less employment to prevent more **inflation.** In addition to having to choose between inflation and unemployment (sometimes referred to as the problem of "fine tuning" the economy), there is the problem of the **recessions** and **depressions** that have occurred throughout the century. The result of these has been millions of unemployed workers.

The causes of downturns in the economy are varied. While it is generally agreed that increased economic sophistication now provides nations with the necessary tools to prevent or moderate economic instability, the application of this knowledge has been far from perfect. Given, then, the recurring instability and joblessness that have characterized the American economy, it is not surprising to find workers and unions supporting policies that promise to moderate the situation. The retirement test appears to be one policy that falls into this category.

In contrast, the recent aging of the population is a factor that may undermine future support for the retirement test. As the cost to the working population of providing pensions to a growing segment of the total population significantly increases, there is apt to be better recognition that a relatively high price tag is associated with our present policies, which encourage or force people to retire. As indicated above, *significantly liberalizing* the test would probably encourage work without incurring the high costs of completely eliminating the test.

Responding to intense political pressure to abolish the test completely, Congress has instead retained it but has enacted in recent years three liberalizations:

1. It reduced the maximum effective age for the test from age 72 to 70, effective in 1983.
2. It increased the annual exempt amount and wage indexed the amount.
3. It scheduled for beneficiaries older than the "normal retire-

ment age" a reduction in the "take-back" rate after the "normal retirement age" from 50 to 33.3 percent, effective in 1990.

Only one *restrictive* provision has been enacted in recent years. The 1977 social security amendments eliminated the monthly exemption test (except for the first year of entitlement). Under this monthly measure a beneficiary who did not earn over the specified monthly exemption or render substantial services in self-employment in a month received a benefit for that month regardless of the level of his or her *annual* earnings. Now only an annual test applies.

Survivors' Benefits

We are apt to forget that social security provides more than worker retirement benefits. Currently, about 18 percent of the OASDI benefits being paid are to survivors—totaling about 7 million pensions in 1987.

When a worker protected by social security dies, a modest $255 lump sum payment is made to the surviving spouse who was living with the worker or who is eligible for a survivor benefit (or if there is no such spouse, to an eligible child). Qualifying widows, surviving divorced wives, children, and dependent parents may also be eligible for monthly benefits. Conditions for receipt of a survivor's benefit vary considerably.

Probably the two most important categories are widows and children. A widow who was married to a fully insured worker for at least nine months and who has reached age 60 may be entitled to a benefit. This benefit equals 100 percent of the worker's age 65 pension if payments begin at age 65 and is reduced if benefits begin at an earlier age (71.5 percent at age 60). Benefits are also subject to reduction if earnings exceed the retirement test exempt amount. Younger widows with eligible children, unmarried dependent children under age 18, and disabled adult children may also be entitled to a benefit equal to 75 percent of the deceased's basic benefit amount. [11]

Supreme Court decisions in 1975 and 1977 struck down provisions of the Social Security Act that prohibited men from receiving survivor benefits based on their wives' earnings. The number of widower benefits received by men remains relatively small. For example, in November 1987, there was 1 widower receiving bene-

---

[11] Special benefits are available for disabled widows age 50 to 59.

fits for every 207 widow beneficiaries. The main reason for the relatively small number of widower beneficiaries is (1) that most men are entitled to higher benefits based on their own earnings records than the benefits based on the earnings of their wives and (2) that most men die before their wives.

The monetary value of survivors' benefits is often very large. Ball (1978b) reports, for example, that a male worker with median earnings in 1977 who died at age 35—leaving a wife age 32 and two children ages 3 and 5—"would have left his family the social security equivalent of an estate worth $129,265." (This amount would be almost doubled in today's dollars.) And a study by Lucy Mallan (1975) found that if social security were omitted from the total 1971 income of widows under age 60 with children, the proportion with poverty incomes would have doubled, rising from one-third to almost 60 percent.

Until recently one of the major factors resulting in low (and often inadequate) benefits for widowers has been the way earnings were indexed to calculate benefits. A survivor benefit was based on the amount of benefits that would have been payable to the deceased worker, as determined by applying a benefit formula to the worker's covered earnings. These earnings were indexed by a wage index reflecting the national wage trend. However, this wage indexing was applied to reflect nationwide wage increases only through the second year before the death of the worker. The benefit was calculated based on these wages and then indexed to take account of only price changes in subsequent years.

When the worker died long before retirement age, the benefit for which the widowed spouse ultimately became eligible in old age (or at disability after age 50) was based on outdated wages. Thus, the spouse who became widowed at a relatively young age but who did not become eligible for benefits for many years was deprived of the worker's unrealized earnings, as well as the economywide wage increases that occurred after the worker's death.

The social security amendments of 1983 changed this calculation procedure. For newly eligible widows and widowers after 1984, deferred survivors' benefits are wage indexed until the year the deceased worker would have been age 60 (or indexed up to 2 years before the widow(er)'s own eligibility, if earlier). This significantly increases benefits for many survivors.

Social Security Pension Reform

In recent years mounting criticism of the old age and survivors program has centered on five major issues:

1. The adequacy of benefits
2. Separating welfare from social security
3. The treatment of women
4. The retirement age
5. Financing current and future benefits

The last of these issues will be discussed in Chapter 6. In this section we discuss the other four.

Benefit Adequacy

Are benefits too low or too high? Until recently, nearly everyone thought social security benefits were too low. A national survey by Peter D. Hart Associates Inc. (1979) for the National Commission on Social Security found "most Americans neither extremely satisfied nor totally dissatisfied with Social Security." The most frequent complaints, however, were about benefit levels. Although most respondents recognized that social security is intended to supplement other sources of retirement income, most felt that social security alone should provide enough income to meet the basic needs and obligations of retirees.

Increasingly, however, arguments are made that social security benefits are now adequate—maybe even too large. The current controversy over benefit levels centers on the changes legislated by Congress in 1972.

Early in his first term (1969), President Nixon sent a message to Congress proposing changes in social security. The key recommendations were, first, a 10 percent increase in benefits; second, and more important, a proposal that the consumer price index be used to adjust future benefits automatically and that a wage index be used to adjust the contribution and benefit base.

At the same time that the President proposed changes in social security, he proposed a welfare reform bill—the Family Assistance Act. The House Ways and Means Committee and the Senate Finance Committee held hearings that *simultaneously* considered both the social security and welfare reforms. The major focus of these hearings, however, was on welfare reform and not on social security. Therefore, most of the testimony did not even mention the social security proposals.

At about the same time, the Social Security Advisory Council issued a report. This council had been appointed in the early part of the first Nixon administration. Nixon took the position that aside from the changes recommended in his social security message, he would make no other legislative suggestions until the Advisory

Council made its report. He argued that it would be premature for the administration to propose legislation while this blue-ribbon group, which was given the job of surveying the whole situation, was still deliberating.

This position, of course, set up expectations that something significant would come out of the council's report. Nothing did. The council looked at a number of incremental changes, mostly equity changes, and rejected most of the major benefit proposals people had made. Instead, the Senate passed an unusually large benefit increase (20 percent) that had been proposed by Senator Frank Church on the floor during debate. The increase was subsequently supported by the then powerful (and usually fiscally conservative) chairman of the House Ways and Means Committee, Wilbur Mills (who was, at the time, a presidential hopeful).

The Advisory Council's only important recommendations were in the area of financing. Their report argued strongly in favor of moving further toward a pay-as-you-go system with a "one-year reserve." They also strongly recommended changes in the static actuarial assumptions in use for projecting benefit outlays and contributions. They called for introducing *dynamic* assumptions, arguing that one should expect earnings levels to rise over time, that the contribution and benefit base would increase as earnings rose, and that benefits would be increased as prices rose. Both recommendations facilitated the large benefit increases that were legislated, but the council itself never recommended the increases.

The increased benefit levels and indexing enacted in 1972 have caused some pension experts to argue that there is little need for most future retirees to supplement social security. For example, Robert Ball, a former Commissioner of Social Security, writes: "At average wages, the [social security] replacement rate for the couple is approaching adequacy" (Ball, 1978a). Similar opinions have been voiced by other pension experts (see, for example, Bassett, 1978).

Perhaps the very strongest views on this point come from prominent conservative economist Martin Feldstein. Feldstein (1977) has asserted that the high earnings replacement rates resulting at retirement from public and private pensions are "quite inappropriate for middle and higher income couples." Feldstein argues that retirement on social security now brings little decline in an average family's standard of living and that, furthermore, workers often receive additional income from private pensions. It is important to see how Feldstein reaches this debatable conclusion, since it is a view shared by others.

Feldstein and almost all recent discussants of social security reform focus on the replacement rate for an average (male) earner—that is, a hypothetical worker who earns the average annual wage each year of the working period. The social security benefit formula provides a retiring worker who has earned (each year) an amount equal to the average wage with a retirement benefit equal to about 42 percent of earnings just prior to retirement.[12] But if the worker has a nonworking spouse, the replacement rate jumps to about 63 percent as a result of the additional spouse benefit. Given estimates that 65 to 75 percent of gross earnings for nonpoor families allows these families to maintain their living standards in retirement, we see that social security has the potential of providing most of the normal retirement needs for these so-called average workers.

For those who are eligible, we must then add the contribution of private pensions to retirement living. A study of 1979 **defined benefit plan** formulas (Schulz et al., 1982) indicates, for example, that these formulas often provide 25 percent earnings replacement for hypothetical long-service workers.

Combining the replacement rates from social security with those from private pensions raises the average pension replacement rate for the "average" one-worker couple to almost 100 percent. Can there be any doubt that we are overpensioning some workers today?

The truth is that the overpensioning characterization suffers from a number of major limitations. There is no doubt that severe economic deprivation faces far fewer retiring persons—at least as long as they stay well and avoid institutionalization. But the picture is not quite as rosy as the replacement rate percentages usually cited would suggest.

The statistic for average earnings before retirement selected by Feldstein and others for the hypothetical earnings calculations is an average for both part-time and full-time workers at all stages of their earnings career (i.e., for all age groups). In estimating pension replacement adequacy, do we really want to use the earnings of workers about 30 years of age as a measure of preretirement earnings for workers currently retiring? That is what the statistic chosen is equivalent to. In contrast, workers close to retirement have earnings that are much higher than the chosen statistic and, consequently, much lower replacement rates from social security. In 1984, for example, the "average annual wage"

---

[12]This figure appears in almost all recent reports and publications discussing social security benefit levels and is based on a methodology and estimates developed by the Office of the Actuary, Social Security Administration.

was $16,135. In contrast, average earnings for men and women working full-time and *ages 60 to 64* were $21,252.[13]

In addition, the couple replacement rates of 70 percent (social security alone) and nearly 100 percent (with a private pension) are for a couple with one worker earning median wages and retiring at age 65. But most people retiring do not fall into that particular category. To begin with, more than half of married women approaching retirement age are working in the labor force. The relevant replacement rates for many two-worker couples are very different from those for one worker; the combined higher earnings of the couple *are not replaced proportionately* by higher social security benefits. In fact, if the spouse doesn't earn enough to become entitled to a benefit greater than 50 percent of the other worker's benefit, there will be no increase in social security benefits at all! Thus, the pension replacement rate from social security for an "average" two-worker family will often be much lower.

An equally important consideration in the determination of actual (rather than potential) replacement rates is the age at retirement. The dramatic rise in the numbers of workers retiring before the retirement age of 65 has made early retirement the norm. Once again, because of the actuarial reduction provisions in social security (and reductions in some private pensions), the actual replacement rates of a great many retirees will be lower than the percentages originally cited.

While no individual is required to retire before age 65 and many retire early because they want to, numerous studies have shown that there is also a sizable group of early retirees without a meaningful option. These workers have little or no potential to engage in substantive employment activity because of poor health or structural unemployment problems.

Finally, as we discuss in Chapter 8, the private pension supplement that boosts the replacement rate for many is not available to all; many workers are never covered or lose pension credits before retiring. Failure to meet vesting requirements or being covered by a plan that terminates, for example, results in lost service credits for many workers, especially women. Not all of those who are covered long enough to receive a pension achieve the long periods of service required for *large* private pension benefit amounts.

If we look at *actual* replacement rates for retiring workers, we

---

[13]The $16,135 number is published in the Social Security Bulletin's *Annual Statistical Supplement, 1986*. The age 60 to 64 earnings are based on the author's tabulations of the Survey of Income and Program Participation.

see how all these considerations affect pension adequacy levels. An important study by Alan Fox (1982) provides estimates for couples, nonmarried men, and nonmarried women retiring over the 1968–1976 period. Fox calculates the proportion of after-tax earnings[14] replaced by pensions (also after taxes). The median replacement rate for social security benefits is only 43 percent for married couples—in contrast to the 70 percent estimate by Feldstein. Even when private and government pension income is taken into account, replacement rates fall far below that level necessary to maintain living standards in retirement. Table 5–3 (page 130) shows the replacement rates estimated by Fox using data from the U.S. Social Security Administration's Retirement History Survey. The data indicate that, despite improvements over the years, a gap still exists between the retirement income goals of most retirees and the benefits they get from social security.[15] We will return to this issue in Chapter 8, when we discuss the roll of private pensions.

Separating Welfare from Social Security

Pechman et al. argue in their book *Social Security—Perspectives for Reform* that the aged should be eligible for either an earnings-related pension or welfare payment—whichever is the greater. They argue further that the earnings-related pension should have a replacement rate that is roughly the same at all earnings levels between subsistence and the level of median earnings. They also recommend that there be no spouse benefits but that pensions be based on total family earnings instead.

Their major point is that the social security system *should not operate both as a welfare system and a pension system*. People who receive income in old age (including a social security pension) that places them in a taxable bracket should pay taxes (regardless of age), in the view of Pechman et al. On the other hand, if an elderly person's income is too low, they argue, that the person should be eligible for a **negative income tax:**

> *The advantage of the dual system is its efficiency and flexibility.*
> *Either part of the system could be altered independently of the*

---

[14] In the study, various definitions of earnings are used. The numbers reported here are based on "price-indexed estimated total earnings in the highest three years of the last ten."

[15] See Boskin (1986) for alternative and much higher replacement rates based on "real career average earnings" (as opposed to the high three of the last ten). We do not think, however, that average lifetime earnings are a good basis for retirement planning or pension adequacy assessment. Most pension planners currently use some type of *final* earnings measure.

other. At present any effort to improve social security with respect to the income support function typically requires substantial improvements with respect to the earnings replacement function. For example, a program to raise minimum benefits to help the aged poor must in practice be joined with a general benefit increase, thereby making the cost of aiding the poor seem greater than it is. This is aggravated, of course, by the fact that the present system supplements income regardless of the income status of the beneficiaries. In many instances higher minimum benefits would be paid to individuals with adequate income. Under the proposed system the earnings related benefit could be set at any desired percentage of past earnings. Negative income tax allowances to those with low earnings histories would be sufficient to keep income above the poverty level. Thus, policy makers and the public could identify immediately the cost of performing the two distinct functions of the system. [Pechman et al., 1968]

The advantage Pechman et al. (and various other economists) see in separating the two issues is considered a drawback by others.[16] Some writers argue that separating the two groups (clearly identifying who is being helped) makes it very difficult to get sufficient political support for improving the situation of the poor. They argue that the only way one can get help for the poor is to piggyback it onto help for middle (and even upper) income groups. For example, one leading authority on social security, Wilbur Cohen, argued:

. . . in the United States, a program that deals with the poor will end up being a poor program. There is every evidence that this is true. Ever since the Elizabethan Poor Law of 1601, programs only for the poor have been lousy, no good, poor programs. And a program that is only for the poor—one that has nothing in it for the middle income and the upper income—is, in the long run, a program the American public won't support. This is why I think we must try to find a way to link the interests of all classes in these programs. [Cohen and Friedman, 1972]

A two-day social security conference in 1976, sponsored by the Brookings Institution, gave major attention to whether the social adequacy function of social security should be reduced or transferred to the supplemental security income (SSI) program (described in Chapter 7). In addition to repeating the opposing arguments summarized above, there was general agreement that

---

[16] See, for example, Brown (1972).

several serious problems had to be dealt with before SSI could assume a larger role (Munnell, 1977).

Most conference participants felt that the SSI asset test was unreasonably stringent and needed a complete overhaul. Some participants pointed out that it would be difficult to reduce the current dollar-for-dollar SSI reduction for social security benefits (after a $20 **disregard**) to, say, 50 cents for each dollar so that low-wage workers would be insulated from a decline in retirement income as a result of a (more) proportional OASI formula. The existence of supplementary state programs that supplement the SSI benefit in many, but not all, states would make it difficult to ensure uniformity of welfare programs in the face of large-scale changes in the relationship between OASI and SSI. And simply changing the federal SSI "tax rate" (i.e., the income offset rules) would not in itself be sufficient; state tax rates would also have to be changed. But that raises issues of state autonomy and whether states would be willing to bear the increased costs of the new program. Finally, a shift to an expanded SSI program would mean that more people would be subject to a more welfare-oriented program.

Still another approach to the matter is the "double-decker." The 1979 Social Security Advisory Council seriously considered but rejected a double-decker social security plan. Under this plan each aged, disabled person and surviving child would receive a flat grant of money (paid out of general revenue) that would be the same for all. In addition, as in the present system, a "second deck" benefit would be paid that was directly proportional to the past covered earnings of social security contributors. However, this second benefit would not be paid to dependents or survivors. (Variants of this type of plan are currently operating in Canada, New Zealand, and Scandinavia.)

In rejecting the plan on a split vote, the majority of the Advisory Council stated in their report that they believed the current system performed its functions well. They saw "no need for the kind of radical changes embodied in the double-decker plan." Their specific objections to the plan included:

1. The resulting reduction of benefits for many dependents and survivors.
2. Fear that the lower deck (financed out of general revenue) would not be adjusted over time for rising earnings and that an eventual result would be lower benefits than under current law.
3. The high costs of the lower deck and hence the large burden on general revenues.

4. Fear that the lower deck would eventually be means tested.
5. Coordination issues related to federal, state, and local pension plans.

Four prominent members of the 1979 council (all economists) strongly supported the double-decker approach. They believed that the major objections raised by the majority of council members were attributable to the specific form of the double-decker that was used as a model—rather than to the principles of such a scheme. In their supplementary statement to the report, they argued that the double-decker: (1) can effectively separate the adequacy and equity elements of the present system and permit separate adjustments of the two components, (2) would prevent high earners with limited coverage from qualifying for benefits on more favorable terms, (3) would reduce reliance on the means-tested SSI program, and (4) would help solve some of the adequacy and equity issues arising in connection with female and disabled workers.

Women and Social Security

There is widespread agreement that social security provisions related to women need to be reformed but no consensus on how to do it. As observed by Flowers (1977), "The social security benefit structure reflects a pattern of marital life and family obligations which is no longer typical in the United States." Benefits (and payments) are designed to provide family protection under an assumption that there are just two major family types: single workers and married couples consisting of lifelong paid workers and lifelong unpaid homemakers.

A number of important social trends have made that assumption increasingly unrealistic. First, female participation in the paid labor force has changed dramatically. Over 70 percent of women age 25 to 54 were in the labor force during 1986, and labor force participation for these women is projected to rise even further—to about 80 percent in the year 2000 (Fullerton, 1987). Moreover, increasing numbers of married women spend part of their lives solely as homemakers and another part in the paid labor force.

Second, there is a changing perception of roles within families. A government report (HEW Task Force on the Treatment of Women Under Social Security, 1978) describes these changes as follows:

As more married women work and have broader employment opportunities, the homemaker role is more frequently viewed as a career choice in itself; the decision to have a spouse at home full-time is viewed as a conscious decision rather than a foregone conclusion. The idea that the homemaker role has economic value—though difficult to measure—is gaining acceptance. . . . Both the rising labor-force participation of married women and the changing perceptions of the homemaker role tend to lead toward a view of marriage as an interdependent relationship between spouses.

Third, there are a rapidly rising number of women who are divorced, separated, or widowed. The United States has one of the highest divorce rates in the world. And there are currently about five widowed women for every widowed man in the United States. Reporting on the economic consequences of families breaking up, the University of Michigan Survey Research Center's five-year study of American families found that "the economic status of former husbands improves while that of the former wives deteriorates" (Morgan et al., 1974). Under social security divorced persons do not achieve eligibility for a spouse or widow's benefit for marriages briefer than 10 years. This results in significant periods of marriage (often with perhaps little or no earnings) and consequent low benefits at retirement. And in past years many of the women becoming widows have found their income falling below the poverty line.

In reaction to the many new issues that have emerged, attention has been given to changing the way social security programs treat women. A number of other countries have already instituted major reforms, and many countries have legislative proposals actively under consideration. Canada, for example, has passed legislation at the federal level for a "child-rearing dropout" provision and "credit splitting" (both provisions are discussed below). Optional credit splitting at the time of a divorce is also available. Paltiel (1982) and Tracy (1987) report, however, that thus far very few people have utilized the option, despite widespread publicity concerning the provision.

In the United States, discussion has centered on three issues: (1) the equity and adequacy of spouse and survivor benefits, (2) fairness of coverage of one-earner versus two-earner couples, and (3) coverage of homemakers and divorced persons. The first two issues are discussed in other parts of the book. With regard to homemakers, persons who stay out of the paid labor force to raise children or maintain a household currently accumulate no earnings credits for that period of their lives. If they later take a job outside the household, they find their average lifetime earnings depressed and hence receive lower social security benefits. Furthermore,

American homemakers who never worked outside the home must depend entirely on the earnings records of their spouses for any social security benefits. Consequently, a divorce, disablement, or death of a spouse (especially in the early years) could result in the homemaker receiving very meager benefits or no benefits at all. Alternatively, the death or disability of the homemaker deprives the household of valuable services, but lack of homemaker coverage precludes any social security compensation.

Homemaker credits are used in several countries. In the United Kingdom, West Germany, and Japan, voluntary contributions by homemakers to the social security system are permitted. In Japan, where the system provides benefits in excess of the value of contributions paid, 80 percent of eligible homemakers participate (Lapkoff, 1981).

In the United States, several proposals have been introduced in Congress that would provide social security credits for people performing homemaker services in the family. A number of issues and problems have been raised in connection with these proposals, however. Disagreement arises over how these benefits will be financed: Financing by general revenue, by a special earmarked tax, or by the covered person are all possibilities. Another issue is the difficulty in determining how much credit the homemaker should receive. Some have suggested that the Secretary of the Department of Health and Human Services should determine the value; others advocate using the median wage for all paid workers (or all women workers). Another issue to be resolved is deciding who would be eligible and determining how to assure proper reporting of homemaker services. Finally, there is a "targeting" issue. The findings of recent research studies indicate that a homemaker credit provision is likely to primarily benefit higher-income families (see, for example, Holden, 1982). Is this a good use of our social security dollars, ask the critics?

The homemaker credit approach has received little political support over the years (see U.S. House Committee on Ways and Means, 1985). An alternative reform approach has received much more attention. It would divide social security earnings credits of married couples equally between spouses. Retirement credits could be split and credit given on three alternative occasions: (1) as the credits are earned, (2) only in case of a marriage dissolution, or (3) at the time of retirement or disability. This type of approach is referred to as "credit splitting" or "earnings sharing." Although earnings sharing is a new idea for social security, the concept has been in use for a long time in community property states.

Over the past 20 years various earnings sharing proposals have been developed and evaluated. The National Commission on Social Security, which reported in 1981, studied this option. They concluded that the most serious problem was the fact that most plans that have been proposed would lower benefits for a significant number of future beneficiaries, even for some whom the plan was designed to help:

> It was the sense of the Commission that changes which erode the adequacy of the system do not help women. The Commission concludes that such changes could not be supported unless the unintentional disadvantages could be remedied at a cost which was deemed reasonable. To be fair to some women at the cost of reducing the protection of others does not achieve fairness. [National Commission on Social Security, 1981]

Instead, the Commission chose "to concentrate on the incremental improvements" that it considered most urgent. It proposed that the special minimum benefit now available for long-term, low-wage workers be computed on a maximum of 35 years of coverage and allow credit for up to ten child care years.[17] A bill which allowed up to two additional years to be dropped from the earnings history of persons leaving the work force to care for a child under age three was passed by the Senate in 1983. The provision was dropped, however, in the conference agreement between the House and Senate.

The issue of earnings sharing continues to receive study and discussion. A study by the Congressional Budget Office (1986) concluded that "the key issues for the Congress . . . are whether it wants to make changes in the social security benefit structure that would raise some people's benefits, and, if so, how it wished to pay for them." Cost estimates for various approaches have ranged from *saving* $600 million a year to *spending* an additional $16 billion (Forman, 1987).

With congressional concerns focused on other spending and deficit issues, few people expect much attention in the short run to this or any other major reform to improve the situation for women covered by social security. The Technical Committee of Earnings Sharing, a private group seeking to improve women's treatment under social security, worked for over five years to design an earnings-sharing scheme that would deal with all the major technical problems and still be acceptable to a broad spectrum of political interests. At the time of writing this revision of

---

[17]They also recommended that the earnings of deceased workers be wage indexed for purposes of calculating survivor benefits. This recommendation was legislated in 1983 (see page 139).

the book, their report and recommendations were about to be released.[18]

The Social Security Retirement Age

Currently, age 65 is the "normal retirement age"—the age when workers can retire and receive an *unreduced* retirement benefit. Over the years, however, there has been increasing support for raising the age. Increasing the retirement age beginning around the turn of the next century was recommended by three major commissions: in 1981 by the National Commission on Social Security and the President's Commission on Pension Policy, and in 1983 by the Republican-appointed majority of the National Commission on Social Security Reform. The major reasons given to support this change are:

1. Americans are living longer and many are healthier.
2. Older workers will be in greater demand in future years.
3. Rising pension costs (especially in the next century) can be partially offset by reversing the trend toward earlier retirement.

Those arguing against an increase in the social security retirement age do so for the following reasons:

1. While life expectancy in later life is increasing, there is no evidence that general health and ability to work at later ages is improving.
2. A large proportion of people retire involuntarily (due to poor health, obsolete skills, and lack of job opportunities) and will not be able to respond to changes in social security by working longer.
3. The presumption that the economy in the future will be unable to support retirement at the current age is questionable.

It seems clear that the predominant factor that has motivated those favoring an increase in the age is a desire to reduce the long-run costs of social security retirement pensions. Faced with a serious shortfall in social security funds in the short run and large projected deficits beginning around the year 2010, Congress began an urgent search in the early 1980s for ways to bring the system into financial balance. One part of the solution voted by Congress in 1983 was an increase in the retirement age. Under the

---

[18]"Earnings Sharing in Social Security: A Model for Reform."

new law, future workers will have to be age 67 before receiving a full benefit. Individuals will still be able to retire as early as age 62 but will suffer a 30 percent reduction in their benefits. The change is scheduled to be phased in gradually, *not beginning until 2003* and achieving its full impact in 2027.

Because this provision of the law is not scheduled to go into effect for many years, proponents and opponents alike see the intervening period as providing an opportunity for careful study of the consequences of the change. In fact, the 1983 legislation called for a study and analysis of the law's implications "for those individuals affected by the change who, because they are engaging in physically demanding employment or because they are unable to extend their working careers for health reasons, may not benefit from improvements in longevity." The report, based mainly on work carried out by the Social Security Administration, focused on the health of older workers and the changing physical demands of jobs. The following are some of the report's major findings (U.S. HHS, 1986):

1. About 19 percent of newly retired workers (1980–1981) were (a) unable to work or had partial work limits and (b) had had jobs with heavy strength requirements.
2. The evidence is unclear with regard to recent trends in the illness and work limitation patterns of persons ages 62 to 67.
3. The growth in other sources of income is not likely to alter substantially the degree to which retirees will rely on social security in future years.
4. It is not clear whether future retirees in physically demanding jobs or ill health will have been able to save in order to offset a potential benefit reduction; however, it seems unlikely that they will substantially extend their work lives.

Several members of Congress have filed bills to repeal the higher retirement age provision and have called for hearings on the issue. The Social Security Administration is starting new research to help clarify many of the unresolved questions and issues. As Associate SSA Commissioner Jane Ross (1987) has observed, "The luxury of knowing that a new law will be implemented 15 years hence is extraordinarily rare."

Chapter 5 Highlights

The Social Security Act passed in 1935 is considered a landmark in social legislation. This chapter—focusing on the old age and survivors' program—explained the major provisions and changing nature of the program as it has evolved over time:

1. OASDI is a universal, compulsory, earnings-related, contributory program that seeks to provide protection against common problems confronted by the whole population.
2. In responding to the economic problems of old age, Congress decided to emphasize a scheme that avoided the need to put most individuals through a means-testing screening device.
3. To reduce the number of people who would have to rely on needs-tested public assistance, Congress incorporated into OASI a large number of provisions that made it easy to qualify for benefits in the early years, raised the adequacy of benefits for low earners, and created dependent benefits. Critics today argue that these early decisions now create serious issues of equity and cost.[19]
4. Important changes in OASI have occurred over the years with regard to coverage, benefit levels, eligibility ages, the retirement test, indexing, and the taxing of benefits.
5. Despite increased benefit levels, there is still a large gap for most workers between OASI benefits and the income needed to maintain living standards in retirement.
6. The evolving roles of women in American society, widening differences in life expectancy between men and women, and changing marital situations have all resulted in much debate (but little action) on how best to reform social security with regard to its treatment of women.
7. One of the major policy issues of the next two decades is whether to increase the social security retirement age (now scheduled under law to begin rising in the year 2003).

Suggested Readings

AARON, HENRY J. *Economic Effects of Social Security*. Washington, D.C. The Brookings Institution, 1982. This short and very readable discussion of social security provides an excellent introduction to the major analytical issues related to the system's economic impact.

BERNSTEIN, MERTON C. AND JOAN B. *Social Security—the System That Works*. New York: Basic Books, 1988. An excellent discussion of the policy issues related to both social security and private pensions.

BURKHAUSER, RICHARD V., AND KAREN C. HOLDEN. *A Challenge to Social Security: The Changing Roles of Women and Men in American Society*. New

---

[19] This point is discussed more extensively in the next chapter.

York: Academic Press, 1982. The best book to date on public and private pensions and their treatment of men versus women.

COHEN, WILBUR, J., AND MILTON FRIEDMAN. *Social Security: Universal or Selective?* Rational Debate Seminars. Washington, D.C.: American Enterprise Institute, 1972. A debate between former HEW Secretary Cohen, who defends social security, and economist Friedman, who argues for its abolition.

LUBOVE, ROY. *The Struggle for Social Security, 1900–1935.* Cambridge, Mass.: Harvard University Press, 1968. An interpretive, historical analysis of the passage of the 1935 Social Security Act.

RIMLINGER, GASTON. *Welfare Policy and Industrialization in Europe, America, and Russia.* New York: Wiley, 1971. Where did American social insurance come from? Rimlinger provides a history and comparative analysis of earlier social security systems in Germany, Russia, and Great Britain—comparing them with programs in the United States.

ROSS, JANE. "Changing the Retirement Age in the United States: A Case Study on Research and Social Security Policy-making." *International Social Security Review* 3 (1987): 231–247. An excellent overview of "the eligibility age for retirement" issue.

STEINMEYER, HEINZ-DIETRICH. "Social Security Reform: Its Consequences for Women in Industrialized and Developing Countries." *Compensation and Benefits Management* 3 (Autumn 1986): 413–416. Women's pension issues from an international perspective.

TRACY, MARTIN. "Removing the Earnings Test for Old-age Benefits in Canada: Impact on Labor Supply of Men Ages 65–69." *Aging and Work* 5 (1982): 181–190. This article examines the Canadian experience following the removal of the earnings test in 1975.

Chapter 6

SOCIAL SECURITY FINANCING: WHO PAYS? WHO SHOULD PAY?

In an article entitled "The Young Pay for the Old," journalist Edwin L. Dale, Jr. (1973) wrote:

> *A funny thing happened to your taxes on the way to 1973. Congress passed the biggest federal increase since the Korean war (and that one was temporary), and hardly anybody peeped except a few intellectuals. This was happening at the time of the "taxpayers' revolt" at federal, state, and local levels. . . .*
>
> *Before anyone wonders whether he missed some important news development, or has been somehow bamboozled, it is best to explain the mystery. The paradox is resolved in two words: social security . . . a $7 billion tax increase enacted in 1972 with scarcely a voice of protest.*[1]

In 1977 Congress again found it necessary to schedule further increases in social security payroll taxes: "President Carter and Congress have a bear by the tail," wrote Hobart Rowan (1978). "Having decided . . . [in 1977] that the only way to rescue the social security system from bankruptcy was to raise an additional $227 billion in payroll taxes over the next ten years, they now have discovered—big surprise!—that this isn't very popular with the voters."

The 1978 report of the Social Security Trustees stated that the 1977 tax increase would "restore the financial soundness of the cash benefit program throughout the remainder of this century and into the early years of the next one." But by 1982 the balance

---

[1] © 1973 by the New York Times Company. Reprinted by permission.

of the OASI fund (after taking into account the taxes to be received in the year) was less than the amount needed to pay benefits for the year, and interfund borrowing from the disability and hospital insurance funds began. And in 1983 Congress had to pass another major social security financing package, including—for the first time—taxation of certain social security benefits.

Then suddenly in the late 1980s the discussion reversed. Social security deficits disappeared and huge surpluses loomed (see page 166). Reacting to another scheduled increase in the payroll tax, Robert Myers, former chief actuary of the social security system asked in *The Washington Post* (1987): "Are these increases desirable or necessary? The answer is clearly 'no'. . . ." In reply, former Commissioner of Social Security Robert Ball argued: "I disagree completely. . . . Let's make sure we have a safety margin for the immediate future" (Ball, 1987b).

For the public, one of the most important aspects of pension policy is the way these programs are financed; yet until recently there has been little controversy over these matters. Why in recent years has pension financing become front-page news?

Rising Pension Expenditures and Growing Controversy

Few people realize the magnitude of the expenditures involved in pension programs and hence the huge amount of funds that must be raised annually through taxes, worker "contributions," returns on pension reserves, and employer allocations for pension purposes. In 1984, $241 billion in public pension benefits were paid to Americans (see Table 6–1). This amount, by way of comparison, was $54 billion *more* than national defense expenditures in the same year; almost four times the amount spent on "public assis-

Table 6–1 Public Retirement Pension Expenditures, 1984[a]

Type of Pension	Billions
OASI benefits	$162
Public employee retirement benefits[b]	59
Veterans' pensions and compensation	14
Railroad retirement benefits	6
Total Benefits	**$241**

Source: Based on data in *Social Security Bulletin, Annual Statistical Supplement* (1986).
[a]Data are for fiscal year.
[b]Federal, state, and local employee pensions.

tance"; and a little less than the total population's expenditures that year on all forms of transportation.

In recent years there has been a sharp increase in criticisms of the techniques used to finance pensions—especially those used for social security. Pension financing involves many complex issues, and, no doubt, part of the recent controversy arises because of the confusion and misunderstanding that generally prevails. Is the social security system bankrupt, as is frequently charged? Will younger workers get back less than they contribute to social security? Does the burden of financing fall disproportionately on the poor and treat racial minorities and women unfairly?

We will divide the discussion of social security financing into three broad aspects: (1) current social security financing practices and short-term versus long-term issues, (2) the equity of present practices, and (3) a review of various proposed changes in social security financing.

Financing Social Security

The OASDHI program is financed by a payroll tax that requires workers in covered employment (regardless of age) to pay a percentage of their earnings into the program and employers to pay an equal percentage based on their employees' earnings. In both cases the percentage paid is limited to the earnings of each employee up to a specified annual maximum. In the original legislation (and up through 1950), this maximum, called the *earnings base*, was $3,000. Between 1951 and 1972 the earnings base was increased periodically on an ad hoc basis. Then, in 1972 legislation was passed that set the earnings base at $12,000 in 1974 and specified that the base was henceforth to rise *automatically* as average earnings rose. By 1988 the earnings base—through a combination of ad hoc and automatic increases—had reached $45,000. $55,500 in 1990

Table 6–2 shows past and future increases in the payroll tax. As legislated by the Social Security Amendments of 1983, the OASDI combined tax is scheduled to reach 12.4 percent in 1990. An additional tax of slightly under 3 percent is currently levied for the hospital insurance programs under social security (Medicare).

The Reserve Funding Issue

It is important to understand that in the past most of the revenues generated each year by these payroll taxes were used to pay

Table 6–2   Maximum Taxable Earnings and Payroll Tax Rates, OASDI for
Selected Years

Year	Maximum Taxable Earnings	Combined Payroll Tax Rate[a]
1937	$ 3,000	2%
1940	3,000	2
1950	3,000	3
1960	4,800	6
1965	4,800	7.25
1970	7,800	8.40
1975	14,100	9.90
1980	25,900	10.16
1983	35,700	10.16
1985	39,600	10.40[c]
1986	42,000	11.40[c]
1988	45,000	12.12[c]
1990 +	[b]	12.40[c]

Source: National Commission on Social Security Reform, *Actuarial Cost Estimates for OASDI and HI and for Various Possible Changes in OASDI and Historical Data for OASDI and HI* (Washington, D.C.: The Commission, 1982), and Social Security Amendments of 1983.
[a]The tax is split equally between employee and employer payments. The amount shown here combines the two. The health insurance tax is not included. Rates for the self-employed are different and not shown.
[b]The amount will be automatically determined by law on the basis of the annual increase in covered employment average earnings in prior years.
[c]As scheduled by the Social Security Amendments of 1983.

benefits to nonworkers *in the same year.* Any surplus of revenue over expenditures is maintained as part of the reserves for future needs and is deposited in one of the three social security trust funds: OASI, Disability, or Hospital Insurance. However, the size of these trusts funds has never been very large relative to future obligations.[2]

Concerning reserves, J. Douglas Brown (1972) writes that "as originally enacted the old age insurance system would have accumulated in time a reserve of $47 billion, more than the outstanding debt of the government in 1935." But before any monthly benefits were actually paid by the new pension program, Congress quickly revised the contribution rates, postponing scheduled increases in the payroll tax rates. This action set the pattern for future financing action, with tax rates being set below the rates that would be appropriate for a private pension or insurance plan.

Over the years there has been considerable controversy over

---

[2]However, see page 166 for a discussion of current and future surpluses.

whether adequate financing of social insurance programs requires the accumulation of large financial reserves. Much of the discussion has centered on the extent to which public insurance programs require financing practices conforming to the traditional tenets of actuarial soundness associated with private insurance.

The term *actuarial soundness* refers to the ability of insurance programs to provide sufficient (i.e., legally obligated) payments to eligible recipients at the time they come due. A private insurance company, for example, must necessarily operate on the basis that it will not sell any new policies in the future. Therefore, it should always have sufficient assets on hand to meet its obligations for existing policyholders, even if they all surrender their policies at once. Similarly, private pension plans generally try to maintain reserve funds sufficient to meet contracted obligations.

This involves putting aside money for **accrued benefits** based on employment *after* the plan is initiated. However, it also involves payments (often spread out over a period of years) for the costs of unexpected new obligations or benefits provided for employee services rendered *before the pension plan began operation*.

The Pay-as-You-Go Approach

There is now widely accepted agreement among pension specialists that social security programs do *not* require the accumulation of large amounts of reserves to be actuarially sound (see, for example, Myers, 1985). It is recognized that the taxing power of the government guarantees the long-run financial integrity of such programs and that, unlike private insurance, it is appropriate to assume that the programs will operate indefinitely—with a consequent continuous flow of revenue. Moreover, the fact that public insurance is usually compulsory and covers most of the population avoids the financing problems arising from a fluctuating number of participants.

This way of financing social security is known as the pay-as-you-go method. Benefits are paid to the current aged out of the payroll tax contributions of the current working population. In return, members of the working population know that they are promised benefits when they become eligible, financed out of the taxes of future workers.

Thus, while OASDI reserves have increased in 36 out of 49 years (1937–1986), total reserves in recent years have been equal to only about one-third of one year's disbursements. Given this small reserve, some people have argued (erroneously) that social security is a bankrupt program that does not have the money to pay its obligations. Without necessarily characterizing the situation as bankruptcy, others have seriously questioned the financial soundness of the program.

In answer to critics of pay-as-you-go financing, five former secretaries of the Department of Health, Education, and Welfare and three former social security commissioners issued on February 10, 1975, a statement emphasizing why they thought that the government did not need to amass vast reserves to keep social security financially sound. In part, they argued:

> By earmarking the proceeds of social security taxes for the payment of benefits and depositing them in a trust fund for this purpose, by entitling the system insurance, by continuing actions to assure its financial soundness, and by innumerable pronouncements of congressional committees and individual spokesmen, Congress has made clear beyond question its pledge to the American people that the social security commitment will be honored. [Ad Hoc Advisory Committee, 1975]

Thus, we see that *the main argument for nonfunding rests on the quality of the pension promise made by the government*. To fulfill this promise requires that Congress ensure that over the long run the flow of funds remains in a "satisfactory actuarial status." But what constitutes satisfactory actuarial status? An expert panel on social security financing—composed of economists and actuaries—argued that this means being able to predict with reasonable confidence (1) that future scheduled flows of income and expenditures will be in harmony and (2) that future scheduled taxes required to support the program be within the limits of practical acceptability to the population paying the social security tax (U.S. Senate Committee on Finance, 1975).

Reviewing the financing experience of social security in the past and research on "reserve adequacy," Munnell and Blais (1984) conclude that:

> . . . [social security] balances should be equal to at least 75 percent of annual outlays plus the additional 10 percent that is required to pay benefits on a timely basis. Somewhat higher balances, however, may be desirable to give Congress more time to act in the wake of back-to-back recessions. In short, trust fund balances somewhere between 85 percent and 145 percent of annual outlays should provide an adequate contingency reserve.

A Benefit Bonanza?

As we indicated earlier, the unfunded liability results from a decision by Congress not to operate a funded system.[3] Historically, *both private and public* pensions have opted to grant significant pension benefits to persons reaching retirement age during the initial years (or start-up) of the programs.

To become eligible for social security benefits, an individual must have a certain number of calendar quarters of coverage based on employment. Congress initially set the required quarters low for the older worker group, which resulted in their receiving benefits that far exceeded what could be "actuarially purchased" from their few years of contributions.

Thus, ever since the social security system began, the vast majority of retirees have received far more retirement benefits than they ever paid contributions into the program. New groups that were covered in the 1950s and 1960s also were granted these "windfall gains." And with liberalizations in the benefit structure, most new retirees will also experience these gains—and for many years to come.

Why did Congress grant these generous benefits (relative to payroll contributions) for early participants in the system? First, because the early participants needed the benefits. Without them, a majority of the aged would have had incomes far below the poverty level. Many had seen their lifetime savings disappear or decline dramatically during the Great Depression. Congress, aware of their economic plight, sought to ameliorate it *without forcing people to confront the stigma of needs-tested public assistance.*

Second, as we discussed in Chapter 5, Congress was confronted by historically high unemployment rates. It initially set benefit eligibility very low to encourage older workers to leave the labor force. And continuing unemployment during downturns in the postwar period again encouraged Congress to expand coverage and liberalize eligibility requirements.

Finally, the growing social security coverage itself and the general economic growth of the post–World War II years resulted in revenues exceeding outlays for the system. These actual and projected short-run surpluses made it politically and economically easier for Congress to improve benefits.

The resulting policy—*not* to exclude persons with relatively few

---

[3] A good discussion of this point can be found in Robertson (1977).

years of participation in the program and not to make them "pay their way"—was financed on a pay-as-you-go basis out of the rising earnings of the working population, with only modest increases in taxes. But it has also added to the future "unfunded" liabilities of the social security program.

Long-Term Financing

Actuarial projections of future benefits and taxes are made annually by the Social Security Administration's Office of the Actuary. The projections and a general assessment of financial status are submitted in a report by the Social Security Board of Trustees to Congress each year. In the early years these reports expressed little concern about any long-term financing problem. In the 1974 report, however, the actuarial projection forecast a significant actuarial deficit over the 75-year period 1974–2048. This projected deficit, higher than any previously forecasted, was *almost doubled one year later* when the trustees issued their 1975 report! This was the beginning of concern about the serious financial problems that plagued the system over the next decade.

The long-term financing concerns of that decade were the result of three major factors: (1) expanding benefit expenditures, including costs arising from the automatic cost-of-living adjustment mechanisms legislated in 1972, (2) rising future cost of the post–World War II "baby boom," and (3) declining revenues due to a projected lower rate of economic growth and a dramatic decline in the American birthrate. Projected deficits were in large part related to the particular way the Social Security Amendments of 1972 specified that pension benefits were to be automatically adjusted for inflation. Soon after this legislation was passed, various experts demonstrated that the particular inflation adjustment mechanism used would have a major unintended effect; depending on economic conditions (with regard to the relationship between price and wage changes), it could have a steadily increasing effect on the **replacement rates** of benefits for workers retiring in future years. The greater the rate of inflation and/or the smaller the rate of growth in real wages, the greater the increase in real benefits, and hence the greater the future financial burden on social security.[4]

The result of what was generally acknowledged to be a mistake in indexing procedures was a dramatic change in *projected* bene-

---

[4] We do not present the relatively technical explanation for this result. Interested readers should see the monograph by Lawrence Thompson (1974).

fits. The social security benefit structure promised (given fore-casted inflation rates) to provide future generations of retiring workers with social security benefits that replaced much larger proportions of preretirement income than were originally in-tended. These replacement rates were projected to get bigger for successive cohorts of retiring workers. Thus, the replacement rates for some retirees in the 21st century were projected to be well above 100 percent of preretirement earnings.

Naturally, the cost of these high benefit levels was also projected to rise. And, as a result, actuarial assessments of the financial status of the social security system (referred to at the end of the previous section) projected sharply rising system deficits in the next century and the need for greatly increased payroll tax levels.

Congress took action in 1977 to correct the **indexing** procedures and to roll back for future retirees most of the real benefit increases (resulting from the "over-indexing" procedures) that had occurred over the five-year interim period.[5] Thus, the projected deficits were significantly reduced by eliminating the unintended indexing increases. But projected deficits in the long-run were not elimi-nated, given two other key factors: the "baby boom" and declining fertility.

The steady rise in births after World War II (reaching a peak in 1957 of 4.3 million) will cause a future rise in the retirement age population relative to the working age population. This will begin around the year 2010, when this baby boom population begins reaching old age. The drop in births in recent years causes the rise in the ratio to be even sharper, since the falling number of births reduces the number of persons who will be in the working popu-lation. The result is a large rise in social security retirement benefits that come due in the 21st century, without as rapid an increase in payroll tax revenues from workers, whose numbers will not be increasing.

Congress took major steps in 1983 toward eliminating the pro-jected deficits of the next century. It passed legislation amending the Social Security Act that contained a number of provisions designed to have a positive impact on long-term financing. A major provision of the legislation was an extension of the normal retire-ment age. This will have a favorable long-term financial impact

---

[5]This corrective action is the origin of the so-called "notch" issue. The cut-back in benefit levels for those born after 1916, below the benefit levels for those just preceding them, produced cries of inequity. The inequity, however, was that those born before 1917 received benefits larger than Congress has intended (i.e., windfalls)—not that those born after 1916 received too little.

(see page 151). However, the age increase is not scheduled to go into effect until early in the next century.

Tax revenues will also increase significantly in the long run as a result of mandatory coverage of workers in the nonprofit sector and new federal employees and an increase in the payroll tax for self-employed persons. In addition, a six-month delay in granting cost-of-living increases from July of each year to the following January not only resulted in expenditure reductions in the short run but will also have a significant impact on outlays over the long run.

The most important change, however, was to impose for the first time federal income taxes on up to half of social security benefits for beneficiaries with income over a specified level. This provision will initially affect relatively few elderly persons, since most have "adjusted gross income" levels which, together with 50 percent of social security, fall below the specified level of $25,000 (for an individual) or $32,000 (for a married couple). Eventually, however, real and inflation-induced income increases will push a significant number of future elderly persons into the taxable range, given that the exemption level is not indexed over time. One result of this tax provision will be more revenue for the social security system in future years. The 1983 amendments specified that the tax revenue from social security income is to be transferred to the social security trust funds.[6]

Despite these actions taken in 1983, issues about long-term financing will continue to demand attention. The lesson from our past experience is clear: unforeseen circumstances and constantly changing economic, political, and demographic considerations make it impossible to plan social security's financing future with complete certainty. As observed by Morrison (1982), for example, "as long as Social Security payments are financed by intergenerational transfers instead of by the contributions of the recipients themselves, the system will be vulnerable to demographic shifts— for example, unforeseen swings in future fertility—that legislation cannot fully anticipate."

This fact need not worry us unnecessarily, however. What is also clear from past history is that attention is constantly being given to the evolving finances of social security. The activities of various government groups (some mandated by law), numerous interest groups, academics, research institutions, and Congress itself result in continuous monitoring of the situation. When problems arise,

---

[6] The taxing of benefits is discussed again later in this chapter (see p. 184).

we are likely to know about them quickly and to have an opportunity to take corrective action.

Short-Term Financing Problems

In 1979 a survey by Louis Harris Associates (Johnson and Higgins, 1979) reported that more than four out of five workers did not have confidence that social security would be able to pay the benefits due them when they retired. Perhaps more startling was the finding that about 40 percent *had hardly any confidence at all* that they would receive their entitlement.

These were startling statistics, but later surveys have produced similar results. What produced such anxiety with regard to social security? Why does that anxiety continue today? To what extent is it the result of concern over the projected long-term deficits discussed in the previous section?

Clearly, media stories about the indexing problem in the 1970s and the specter of the baby boom generation eventually retiring have contributed to the anxiety many people have about the security of their promised social security benefits. It is probably the more recent financing problems, however, that have created the aura of crisis that has prevailed. Off and on over a period of ten years, the American public was told that the social security system was about to run out of money. If we want to understand the anxiety existing among Americans today, we must understand why social security finances over the recent past seemed to bumble along like those of a small corner grocery store on the verge of bankruptcy.

Starting in the mid-1970s, both high inflation and high unemployment rates rocked the country. As far as social security was concerned, there was both a decline in expected payroll taxes and an increase in benefit obligations. The result was unexpected funding deficits, with payment obligations exceeding revenue by billions of dollars. In 1975 a Social Security Administration study (Thompson and Van de Water) of these unexpected short-term deficits concluded that the deficits were "due almost entirely to unforeseen adverse economic circumstances."

In later years the situation became even worse. The nation during the late 1970s and early 1980s was battered by poor economic conditions that were unprecedented in our postwar economic history. Along with double-digit inflation, record levels of agricultural and industrial bankruptcy, the near destruction of whole industries, the agony of millions suffering long-term unemployment, and turmoil in financial markets, financial problems plagued our public and private pension programs. In fact, the pension problems were basically a result of the other problems (unemployment and inflation) and the fact that prices rose faster than wages.[7] Social security reserves over this period continued to dip, despite various congressional actions.

As was discussed previously, social security, run on a pay-as-you-go basis, has never historically accumulated more than a minimal amount of reserves. The reserves that accumulate are, in fact, there to be "nearly exhausted." That is, their function is to provide a cushion against adverse economic conditions that can never be fully and accurately anticipated by Congress and the actuaries who advise Congress. The adverse economic situation over this period was not anticipated, and hence the reserves were needed to meet the drains on the system.

While the short-term problems were real and serious, they were not unsolvable and were not a result of some basic flaw in social security's design. Yet many critics of social security seized on this situation to proclaim disaster and call for major changes in the system. Reacting to these critics, Henry Aaron (1981) argued that "it is intellectually dishonest, though it may be politically convenient, to use the short-run problems as the basis for making changes in the system that are more relevant to the long-run problem." In assessing the viability of social security in delivering promised benefits, it is important to keep the distinctions between short- and long-term development clearly in mind.

The Growing Surplus

The Social Security Amendments of 1983 and the demographic shifts (discussed in Chapter 1) have combined to create a very different financing issue for future years. The social security deficits of the 1975–1982 period have given way to surpluses. But unlike the modest surpluses of the past, legislated payroll tax levels and demographics are projected to send future surpluses in the OASDI trust funds skyrocketing. Current estimates indicate reserves will grow by the year 2022 to about $2.5 trillion (yes, trillion!) in 1987 dollars (Rauch, 1987a). The reserves then are projected to decline very rapidly as the baby boom generation retires, and further increases in payroll taxes will be needed after 2050 to meet these future obligations (unless, of course, benefit levels are cut between now and then).

---

[7] Rising prices meant that more revenue was needed to pay benefits indexed for inflation, while slower rising wages meant less revenue than anticipated was coming into the system from the payroll tax on wages.

The situation has triggered a growing debate. Some argue the surpluses will *cause* problems and should not be allowed to accumulate. Others think the surpluses will *solve* problems and don't want to change current policy. Still others think we need to change the way we record these surpluses in the national accounts. And still others advocate a change in the way the surpluses would be invested.

The main argument for lowering future surpluses is a political one. Many people (especially conservatives) fear that as the funds pile up in the form of government Treasury bonds, Congress will be tempted to either liberalize social security (thus compounding long-term future financing problems) or increase other types of federal spending. Another fear is that government investment of the surpluses in the private sector (rather than buying government bonds) might introduce undesirable interference in the control and operation of private businesses—resulting, in some cases, in government ownership of companies.

The alternative view is that these surpluses, if not offset by dissaving elsewhere, could increase the nation's saving rate. The United States, never a big saver by international standards, has seen national saving plummet to record lows in recent years. Thus, larger surpluses are viewed by some economists and policymakers as an opportunity to counteract the nation's habit (both public and private) of deficit spending. The result, they argue, could be a higher level of output and consumption during the next century than would otherwise occur.

Another view of the surpluses relates to the future demographic situation. The surpluses are consistent with the need for the very large baby boom group to pay into social security while working to help pay for the huge expenditures that will be necessary when they reach retirement ages. The alternative is to finance social security, as in the past, on a mostly pay-as-you-go basis. But this approach, it is argued, will mean a shift of the baby boom financing burden from the "baby boomers themselves to their children, who, because they are a smaller generation, would find the burden heavier" (Rauch, 1987b). As we discuss in the next section, the distributional equity of social security financing is a very complicated and controversial question. The "future surpluses" issue will complicate this issue even further. For example, the accumulation of surpluses through social security, argues economist Alicia H. Munnell, results in "shifting consumption away from a relatively poorer to a relatively more affluent generation" (Clark, 1985). Others see payroll taxes that weigh heavily on lower- and middle-income workers as a poor way to raise national savings rates—given the many alternatives.

Perhaps the one clear action to be taken is to at least accumulate an adequate contingency reserve in order to restore public confidence in social security's ability to pay promised benefits. As we discussed in the previous section, the economic chaos of the post-OPEC period (and the social security deficits associated with those bad economic times) left the nation with widespread fears regarding the future. Many people lost confidence in social security's ability to deliver on its future obligations.

Presumably, we have learned an important lesson from that experience. Social security reserves accumulated to meet unexpected economic bad times should never again be allowed to fall as low as those resulting from our social security policies in the 1960s and early 1970s. Former Social Security Commissioner Robert Ball argues that we need to allow reserves to accumulate, at least in the short run:

> *In its 50-year history, Social Security has had two financial crises, one in the mid-70s and one in the early '80s. In both cases, the short-term crises were caused principally by inadequate reserves and reliance on economic assumptions that turned out to be too optimistic. We cannot afford to take a chance on a third mistake of this kind. [Ball, 1987b]*

The debate on this issue is just beginning. As Milton Gwirtzman (1985) observes:

> *If Congress faces Social Security's coming "prosperity" with the knowledge that it is only temporary, not a newly discovered pot of gold, it can make the kind of decisions that will guide the system through the new few decades in shape to confront the far more difficult (financial) times that will come thereafter.*

But how Congress will behave is probably the heart of the issue. To many, "the question is whether the presence of social security surpluses changes policymakers' behavior by lulling them into doing less to balance the budget than they would have done otherwise" (Rauch, 1987a). And that is a question to which no one has a definitive answer.

Financing Equity

Rising costs of social security now and in the future increase the importance of developing financing methods considered fair by the population. Our first question in assessing the equity of social security is, Who pays? In the United States payroll tax revenue now exceeds all other federal, state, and local types of taxes except the federal income tax. Thus, it is important to look at who pays the tax and the relationship between those taxes paid and the benefits ultimately received.

Who Pays?

Determining "tax incidence" or who ultimately bears the burden . of any tax is one of the most complex issues in economics. Although the general population thinks it knows who pays taxes, economists disagree—especially about who actually bears the corporate income tax, sales taxes, and the property tax. Until recently, the payroll tax had received little attention from economists. Most people have assumed the worker bears the burden of *his or her* payroll contribution, but there has been great disagreement over the employer payments.

A variety of recent economic studies indicate that most of the employer tax is ultimately paid by the worker in the form of wages that are lower than what they otherwise would have been (or, to a smaller extent, by consumers in the form of higher prices). In an early study of the question, economist John A. Brittain found that the worker generally bears all the tax. He reports that given a particular level of productivity, the higher the employer payroll tax rate the lower the basic real wage—the wage rate being lower by the same amount as the payroll tax increase (Brittain, 1972). Not all economists, however, agree with the Brittain findings (see Feldstein, 1972, and Leuthold, 1975).

Is the Payroll Tax Fair?

The payroll tax has been criticized as unfair by numerous people. There have been three major criticisms: (1) that the tax is regressive and a heavy burden on the poor, (2) that the tax is unfair to certain groups of beneficiaries, given the benefits they are likely to receive, and (3) that younger workers who are now paying taxes (and those who will pay in the future) are likely to get an unfair deal. We will examine each of these criticisms in turn.

First is the issue of a regressive tax structure and its impact on the poor. In general, a regressive tax is one in which the amount of tax paid is a *declining* proportion of income as incomes *increase*. Since the payroll tax is levied only on earnings up to the "earnings base" and not on earnings above the maximum earnings ceiling, the tax is partly regressive. The proportion that contributions represent of total earnings falls for *earnings levels above the ceiling*. However, if one looks at the payroll tax in relation to *total* income (not just earnings), it becomes even more regressive.

During the 1950s and 1960s the maximum ceiling was low relative to average earnings. The proportion of total earnings in covered employment subject to the payroll tax fell from slightly more than 90 percent during the early years of the program to a low of 71 percent in 1965. Thus, for example, in 1972, when the earnings base was $9,000, about one-quarter of the workers paying social security taxes had earnings that *exceeded* the maximum. With the significant increase and indexing of the earnings ceiling that began in 1973, the proportion of total earnings in covered employment had risen to slightly over 90 percent. Thus, today the tax is proportional (not regressive) over a wide range of earnings levels but regressive with regard to total income.

Thus, what concerns many critics is not the burden on worker earnings near or above the maximum but, rather, the tax burdens of low wage earners. The payroll tax contrasts sharply with the personal income tax, falling more heavily on persons with relatively low incomes. There are several reasons for this:

1. As discussed above, the maximum taxable earnings ceiling places a limit on earnings subject to the payroll tax.
2. Unlike the federal income tax, the payroll tax rate is a constant percentage at all earnings levels below the maximum.
3. Unlike the income tax, the payroll tax has no exemption or deduction provisions.
4. Income from interest, rents, and profits—the bulk of which is received by people in the higher income brackets—is not subject to the payroll tax.

Why should people with poverty-level incomes have to pay any taxes—including social security? The principal answer given over the years by supporters of the payroll tax is that the *benefit* structure of the program is heavily weighted in favor of low earners and that tampering with the tax structure threatens to turn the program into a welfare program—thereby undermining its general political acceptability. J. Douglas Brown (1973) in a memorandum sent to the U.S. Senate Special Committee on Aging argues:

> *Overall, the advantages of uniform proportionate contributions toward one's social insurance protection are of great psychological, social and political importance. They clearly differentiate benefits*

as a matter of right from those available only on individual proof of need. They reflect a natural desire for self-reliance. They refute a criticism of dependency. They also are a factor in avoiding a class-conscious society in which some classes give and some classes get. Proportionate contributions are a force for political restraint in the evolution of a total system, both in respect to excessive demands for liberality in the benefit structure and the condoning of abuse in unwarranted payments.

Despite growing criticism, little change has occurred over the years in the basic payroll financing mechanism. Concerned about the tax burden on low earners, Congress has approached the problem in a different way. Instead of modifying the payroll tax structure, it has instituted a policy of income tax offsets.

The 1975 Tax Act contained a one-year provision known as the "earned income credit" or "work bonus" for low-income workers *with children*. Under this provision, an eligible individual was allowed a tax credit equal to 10 percent of earned income up to $4,000 a year (a rough approximation of his or her combined payroll tax at the time). The tax credit was reduced (until it reached zero at income levels of $8,000) by 10 percent of "adjusted gross income" (or, if greater, the earned income) that exceeded $4,000 per year.

The major justification given for the amendment was to remove the work-disincentive effect of social security taxes on low-income workers. In 1975 this credit offset most of the payroll taxes paid on earnings of $4,000 or less.

Most of the early opposition to this "work bonus amendment" was based on its welfare character. Senator Sam J. Ervin, for example, charged in one floor debate over the credit that "it is robbery to take social security money and use it for welfare purposes." In addition, the Nixon administration came out against an early version of the work bonus, arguing that the provision would create serious administrative problems and that it would complicate the development of sound income maintenance policy by "adding yet another program to the many present assistance programs." The Ford administration, using similar arguments, also argued against the provision.

Despite this initial opposition, the earned income credit has been continuously renewed in all subsequent tax legislation. The 1978 tax law extended its application to the first $10,000 of earnings. And in the Tax Reform Act of 1986, the earned income credit was increased to 14 percent of earnings; the maximum credit was raised to $800, and the phase-out range was lifted to $9,000–

$17,000. The effect of these changes is to eliminate almost the entire social security tax (including the employer's share) for those eligible.[8] However, the provision has still not been extended to workers without children, a liberalization recommended by many. Other suggested improvements are: increasing the credit amount as family size increases and/or better coordination of benefit provisions with other welfare programs to reduce work disincentives (Steuerle and Wilson, 1987).

Intergenerational Equity

From time to time people argue, and sometimes present calculations to show, that payments to social security by new entrants into the labor force will be much greater than the retirement benefits they can expect to receive subsequently. Such calculations almost always assume that currently legislated contribution rates and benefit levels will remain unchanged in the future, which is an unrealistic assumption.

A better way to investigate this question is to calculate a **lifetime rate of return.** This method mathematically determines the rate of interest or rate of return implicitly earned on payroll tax contributions paid over a worker's lifetime. It is done by comparing the taxes paid (plus an imputed interest rate on them) to the benefits received during the entire retirement period. John Brittain (1972), using 1966 tax and benefit levels, estimated projected yields for hypothetical *average* earners that ranged from about 3 to 6 percent, depending on assumptions with regard to economic growth, birth/mortality rates, the interest rate, and the age when entering the work force. Brittain concluded that "if the model and the official demographic projections are fairly realistic, new contributors will in the aggregate get "neither a very good buy nor a very bad one, but they will fare moderately well." Another study by Chen and Chu of 1974 retirees and entrants also calculates similar lifetime rates of return. Their rates for 1974 hypothetical retirees ranged from 6 to almost 17 percent. Entrants into the labor force in 1974 were estimated to have much lower rates of return, between 1 and 8 percent (Chen and Chu, 1974).

Both the Brittain and Chen/Chu studies calculated measures of individual equity for *hypothetical* case histories that are thought to be representative of the lifetime experience of various individuals. In contrast, Freiden et al. (1976) calculated measures of individual

---

[8] Under the terms of the 1986 law, the maximum credit and the phase-out starting point are to be adjusted in future years for inflation.

equity for a sample of *actual* case histories. Using data from Social Security Administration records, they calculated rates of return for a sample of workers retiring between the years 1967 and 1970. Again, relatively large positive rates of return were found, with higher rates for those with histories of lower earnings.

More recently, Pellechio and Goodfellow (1983) compare the worth of benefits relative to taxes paid by hypothetical workers who were age 25, 40, and 55 in 1983. Unlike earlier studies, Pellechio and Goodfellow take into account the impact of the 1983 social security amendments. Their study finds a substantial drop in gains from the system for younger generations, with some workers projected to receive benefits worth less than the payroll taxes they will pay. Aaron (1982), in a critique of an earlier but similar study by Pellechio, argues that "although their estimates are carefully prepared, they do not support the contention that social security is actually unfair, because they attach no value to important features of social security not available privately—such as complete indexing—and take no account of selling costs associated with virtually all private sector plans that provide similar benefits."

In a similar but expanded study to the one by Pellechio and Goodfellow, Boskin et al. (1986) again find low rates of return in the future. They add, moreover, that "the magnitude of the differences in treatment of households of different income or marital status are enormous and receive little attention relative to the much smaller distributional issues which are prominently debated when considering income tax reform."

An actuarial analysis carried out by Myers and Schobel (1983) focuses on two groups of workers: those with lifetime earnings equal to the average earnings of all workers (see page 142) and those workers earning the social security earnings maximum (page 127). Myers and Schobel conclude that:

> The OASI program remains a "good buy," even for a maximum-earner single man retiring at age 65 in 2025, if only the employee taxes are considered. If both the employee and employer taxes are considered, the benefit/tax ratios gradually drop below 100 percent for single maximum earners, and even for single male average earners.

Just as in the case of asking who pays the payroll tax, determining the relative cost-benefit equity of social security is extremely difficult. The wide range of rates of return estimated by various researchers demonstrates the difficulty of giving an unequivocal answer to the question of whether social security is a "good buy."

Results are highly sensitive to the assumptions made in the analysis. Also, studies usually fail to include in the analysis the federal and state income tax treatment of social security contributions and benefits.

Brittain (1972), moreover, raises another question:

> *Why should one ask whether a person ultimately recoups in benefits the equivalent of his taxes when the same question is rarely asked about other taxes? . . . Since the taxes and later benefits assigned to a person are not at all closely related, as they are under private insurance, a strong case can be made for a completely separate analysis and evaluation of the tax and benefit structures on their own merits.*

While many would agree with this point of view, others see social security taxes differently—as special earmarked taxes associated with a *compulsory* pension program, which necessitates analysis of who pays and who should pay.

Aaron (1982) has correctly pointed out that most, if not all, of the controversy in this area arises from the fact that analysts have approached the various issues with different frameworks. Some view social security as an annual tax-transfer program that redistributes income from wage earners to retirees. Others see it basically as a lifetime compulsory retirement saving program within a "life-cycle model" of individual decisionmaking about saving and labor force participation.

Moreover, Aaron points out that much of the controversy over whether social security is "a good deal" for different types of workers arises from our *not* knowing what is the "correct," "right," or minimum **discount rate** to use. Aaron (1982) argues:

> *Calculations of the internal rate of return or of the present discounted value, though not without interest for certain purposes, miss most of the interesting and important questions about whether different cohorts of workers get their money's worth from social security and whether reserves should be accumulated. They place no value on the full protection against inflation that only social security now provides. In addition, the calculations do not address the fundamental question of the political, economic, and social value at the margin of social security benefits.*

There is general agreement, however, that calculations of returns from social security are useful to help focus attention on possible differences in treatment of various groups within the population. Both Boskin and Brittain emphasize, for example, that the wide spread in social security rates of return indicates substantial income redistribution among categories of participants. Brittain points out, for example, that the college graduate who starts work at age 22 may fare much better than the high school graduate who starts work at 18, if both earn the same average earnings over their respective work lives. Their social security benefits will be very similar, but the college graduate, entering the work force later, will pay less total payroll taxes over his career. Leimer (1979), however, cautions against giving too much weight to such hypothetical findings when evidence indicates that there are more offsetting factors in real life experiences.

Women and Social Security Financing

Certain specific groups have been singled out for attention by some critics of social security. The treatment of women has recently come under careful scrutiny.[9] In the financing area the most controversial issue has been the differential treatment of working and nonworking women. Currently, a spouse first claiming benefits at the normal retirement age is entitled to a benefit equal to 50 percent of the working partner's basic benefit—regardless of whether or not the spouse participates in the social security program. A spouse who works, however, may become eligible for a regular benefit on the basis of that work. In effect, the law stipulates that such a person can get only one benefit—that from the spouse's earnings record or his or her own pension, whichever is larger (see page 132).

An issue arising from this treatment of working spouses is the low rate of return on the contributions of the spouse. A working wife may pay social security taxes toward retirement protection, but the resulting benefits of the family may be *no higher* if the spouse doesn't work a sufficient number of quarters to achieve eligibility or has low earnings. Moreover, because of anomalies in the benefit structure, a couple composed of two retired workers can receive lower total benefits than a couple with the same average lifetime earnings credits all earned by one spouse (see Table 5–4).

Although a working woman's retirement benefits may be little more or no more than a nonworking spouse's, she does receive the following protection under social security not available to a nonworking wife:

---

[9]See, for example, Gibson (1987) or the report of the Task Force on Women and Social Security listed in the Suggested Readings at the end of this chapter.

1. Disability protection.
2. Benefits payable at or after age 62, even if her husband continues to work.
3. Monthly benefits to her children if she becomes disabled or dies.

As we discussed in Chapter 5, the economic role of women has been shifting over time (see also Kahne, 1975). As a result, a number of social security reform bills have been introduced in Congress over the years to deal with the working woman issue. Thus far, no legislative action has been taken. When the 1975 Advisory Council on Social Security recommended no major action in this area, Rita Campbell (1975) gave a dissenting opinion:

It is my belief that because of the continuing trends in the increasing labor force participation rate of women, the declining labor force participation rate of men, the increase in divorce and decrease in marriages, and the decline in the birth rate, it is advisable to begin now to restructure the social security system to adapt to these socioeconomic changes rather than wait for dissatisfaction with the system to so increase as to force hurried changes which may be undesirable.

Differential Life Expectancies

Another issue that has been raised in relation to women, and also by various ethnic minority groups, is the extent to which differences in average **life expectancy** should be taken into account. Women, *on average*, tend to live longer than men; nonwhites, *on average*, have shorter life expectancies than whites. For benefit purposes, social security policy has largely ignored these or any other differences in life expectancies. Some private pensions, however, have paid in the past differential pension benefits based on sex, causing certain women's organizations to successfully challenge in the courts such differentials in benefits.

Some nonwhites argue that they *should* receive preferential social security benefits because of adverse life expectancy rates. For example, the 1971 White House Conference on Aging "special concerns session" on aged blacks recommended: "The minimum age-eligibility requirement for primary beneficiaries of Old Age, Survivors, Disability, and Health Insurance (OASDHI) under social security should be reduced by eight years for black males so as to erase existing racial inequities."

The average life expectancy *at birth* is different for whites versus nonwhites, in large part because of higher infant mortality rates for nonwhites. Differences in life expectancies at other ages are not nearly as great. At age 65, for example, there are almost no differences between white and nonwhite men.

Ubadigbo Okonkwo has investigated intragenerational equity under social security for subgroups of the United States population differentiated by race, marital status, education, and region of residence. Calculating "internal rates of return" by race, Okonkwo finds that returns are higher for all groups of nonwhite workers except nonwhite couples with 16 or more years of schooling. The highly favorable mortality experience of white female college graduates results in a more favorable internal rate of return for these couples. Okonkwo (1975) concludes:

> *In general, the progressivity of the social security benefit structure tended to redistribute lifetime earnings in favor of subgroups with low earnings, exemplified by nonwhites and workers with relatively few years of schooling. However this redistributive effect was weakened, but not reversed, by the relatively smaller probabilities of survival experienced by these subgroups.*

Similar conclusions are reached by Leimer (1979). Specifically, Leimer examines the validity of the arguments made by some critics of social security that the disadvantaged (nonwhites, low earners, and women) get a poorer deal from social security (see, for example, Friedman, 1972; Aaron, 1977). Leimer uses the hypothetical worker approach; projected earnings streams for representative workers are based on cross-sectional age-earnings profiles derived from the 1973 Current Population Survey. Leimer's investigation suggests that future nonwhite, low earner, and/or women retirees will generally fare better than their counterparts.

Viscusi (1979) in his book *Welfare of the Elderly* argues against public pension differentials based on life expectancy. He cites the widespread resentment that would probably be generated by an explicit set of different eligibility criteria or benefit levels. And he points out the administrative and practical difficulties in taking account of all differentials—smokers versus nonsmokers, drivers of safer cars, persons in occupations or industries with environmental settings that may affect health. Finally, he argues that these differentials are not as important as equalizing benefits per unit of need: "Once we accept the notion that the principal focus of Social Security should be on equalizing income for the periods one is alive, the need to adjust for differing lengths of lifetimes is not only unnecessary, but is also detrimental to this more fundamental objective."

Prior hypothetical worker studies in this area have all found that entrants to the labor force at early ages have lower rates of return from social security because they contribute payroll taxes over a longer work life. Since going to college may delay entry into the labor force and result in higher lifetime earnings, most researchers have concluded that the actual impact of delayed entry into the labor force is very important. Leimer, however, analyzes data showing that workers with high ultimate education attainment have substantial earnings *during* the education period. This offsetting factor tends to reduce the importance of the delayed entry factor in actual case histories.

Reform Proposals

Numerous proposals for changing the financing of social security have been put forth. This section will look at four such approaches: (1) the Buchanan proposal to change social security radically, (2) introducing general revenue financing, (3) changing the payroll tax structure, and (4) taxing social security benefits.

The Buchanan Proposal[10]

In an article published in the *Wall Street Journal*, economists James Buchanan and Colin Campbell proposed that a new system of social security financing be devised. Their approach would, in effect, finance the "windfall gains benefits" of current and future social security recipients out of general revenue. Once this is done, they recommend that the payroll tax be set at a rate that would make it actuarially certain that the amount people paid into the program would equal, on average, the amount that is paid out to them.

In a later article, Buchanan amplified the original proposal, calling for a radical change in the social security structure. The purpose of the proposed new program is "to embody the advantages of an intergenerational tax transfer program while at the same time incorporating most of the desirable features of a genuine insurance program" (Buchanan, 1968).

Buchanan refers to the advantages of an intergenerational tax transfer program. As originally described by economist Paul Sam-

---

[10]Three somewhat similar plans have been proposed: Browning (1973), Robertson (1981), and a plan proposed to the National Commission on Social Security Reform by economists Michael Boskin, L. Kotlikoff, and J. Shoven.

uelson (1958), there can be a "subsidy" in public social security programs that moves from one generation to the next as a result of population growth and economic growth. Buchanan seeks to establish a social security program that would embody that subsidy advantage but, at the same time, be more consistent with private insurance principles in terms of a *guaranteed* pension payoff based on the law.

Buchanan proposes that the present payroll tax be repealed. In its place, individuals would be required to purchase "social insurance bonds." The pension benefits paid out at any particular time would be financed from revenues (purchases) of bonds sold during the same period.

Thus, when someone bought a bond for retirement, the purchase money would be immediately transferred to people who were currently retired. This would resemble the current practice of taking social security contributions and immediately paying them out to current social security pension recipients. If these bond revenues were insufficient to meet current benefit obligations, Buchanan proposes that general revenue financing be used to pay for the balance of benefits due. In this way, he argues, current bond purchasers would not be paying for the results of blanketing in certain groups (see page 161) or for higher individual benefits that are not based on prior contributions.

If they wanted to, individuals would be allowed to buy more bonds than the compulsory amount. *In either case, however, individuals would be able to buy bonds from either private companies or government.* When the individual turns 65, the bonds mature, and he or she can then convert them into an annuity.

As far as the government bonds are concerned, Buchanan proposes that the return on them be the higher of either of the following: the interest rate on long-term U.S. Treasury bonds or the rate of growth of the nation's total economic output (gross national product). Thus, the private bonds—in order to compete—would have to promise (with a fair degree of certainty) a rate of return either better than the interest rate on long-term government bonds (if one didn't expect any growth in the economy) or equal to the rate of general economic growth.

Thus, Buchanan accepts the need for compulsory pension programs. He also agrees that there need not be reserve funding—accepting the approach of a nonfunded, pay-as-you-go government program. But he seeks to prevent possible inequities that may occur as a result of combining benefits based on limited contributions (resulting from "blanketing-in" coverage and retroactive benefits), with benefits based strickly on contributions paid over a lifetime.

Buchanan tries to incorporate into the system an adjustment procedure that guarantees that the individual in the social security system will benefit from the general growth of the economy. Adjusting the bonds at the same rate as the changing gross national product also takes care of the problem of inflation, for this procedure will automatically adjust for general price increases in the economy. Thus, one would have both a price adjustment and a real growth adjustment factor built into the social security system.

Buchanan argues that such a program would have much wider acceptability than the current system because of its "individualization." The current system, he argues, is politically acceptable because people think of themselves as paying contributions into it and getting back benefits when they retire based upon *their* contributions. It is not a welfare system; it is a system of forced savings in the minds of most people. But Buchanan is worried that increasingly people will find this rationale unacceptable—given the current divergence between individuals' contributions and the amount paid back. He argues that future generations will be less and less certain that they are going to get their money's worth, losing confidence in the system. The advantage of Buchanan's plan is that the individual gets his or her own financial asset with a guaranteed rate of return. He argues that this is a much stronger guarantee than the *implicit* promise of benefits to be paid inherent in the current system.

Buchanan argues that his proposed program also insulates social security from political interference and from excessive and inequitable spending on the part of Congress. Congress would not be able to manipulate the system so easily, taking some from one population group and giving more to other groups. Instead, a straight one-to-one relationship would exist on an individual basis—just as in private insurance.

Some critics of the Buchanan proposal argue, however, that it is very important for a government pension program to be able to redistribute income. Indeed, many people think that it is quite justifiable to redistribute income through a social security program.

A more fundamental concern is that the proposal calls for a radical change. The current program has strong support both from a broad segment of the population and within Congress. It is questionable whether the Buchanan proposal would have any chance of acceptance because it is so completely different and does not build on what we have at present. The tendency is for legislation to develop incrementally, and major changes that are proposed still have to embody in some way prior legislation.

Apart from the political feasibility of such a major change, it is questionable whether the resulting gains obtained in equity are worth the great cost. The new approach would still depend fundamentally on the ability of the government or private firms to fulfill the promises made "on paper." At the same time, there would be major developmental, administrative, and information costs associated with a radical shift to this or a number of other completely new programs. [11]

General Revenue Financing

Other people concerned about the financing of social security have also recommended the introduction of general government revenues to help support the costs. Like Buchanan, many of them see the blanketing-in of large groups of persons during the initial years as a burden that need not be financed by the payroll tax. Unlike Buchanan, however, most people call for general revenue financing without abandoning the basic structure of the current social security system.

General revenue financing was first suggested by the Committee on Economic Security, a presidential committee whose recommendations formed the basis of the original Social Security Act. The idea was also supported by the first Advisory Council on Social Security in 1937–1938 and the one in 1947. Later advisory councils, however, did not see an immediate need for this additional source of financing or opposed general revenue financing as destructive of the insurance principles embodied in the program.

In 1944 Congress (over presidential veto) froze the payroll tax rate and authorized an appropriation from general revenue to the trust fund for "such additional sums as may be required to finance the benefits and payment under this title." Rather than representing an enthusiastic endorsement by Congress of the concept of general revenue financing, this action, at the time, was really a by-product of a disagreement in Congress over when and how large social security reserves should grow. Ignoring the 1947 Advisory Council on Social Security's recommendation for a "government contribution," both the House Committee on Ways and Means and the Senate Finance Committee in 1950 stated that the system

---

[11] See Browning (1973) for a discussion of income distribution problems associated with the Buchanan plan and a proposed alternative.

"should be on a completely self-supporting basis," and Congress in that year repealed the general revenue provision.

Many who agree with the idea of general revenue financing favor restricting these payments to help meet the costs of "windfall benefits" (i.e., those given without contributions equal to the actuarial value of these benefits). In a working paper prepared for the U.S. Senate Special Committee on Aging, Nelson H. Cruikshank, as president of the National Council of Senior Citizens, presented such a proposal:

> *Workers already close to retirement age when the [social security] system was first started, or when coverage was extended to their employment, received full benefits even though the contributions they and their employers paid would finance only a small part of the benefit. While this was sound public policy and kept many old people off relief, it did mean that these benefits had to be financed from future contributions. There is no justification for expecting presently covered workers to pay for this "accrued liability"— estimated in the long run to amount to one-third of the total cost of the program—through a regressive payroll tax. A far fairer method would be to finance this share from general revenue sources to which all taxpayers contribute and through a more progressive tax structure. [U.S. State Special Committee on Aging, 1970]*

During the debates leading up to the 1977 social security amendments, President Carter proposed an alternative mechanism: to limit general revenue contributions to the amount of social security revenues lost as a result of an unemployment rate in excess of 6 percent. When workers lose their jobs they (and their employers) do not pay payroll taxes on their behalf, causing a shortfall in projected revenues. Through this proposed mechanism, general revenue financing would not be open-ended but would be used only when economic activity falls significantly short of full employment levels. The proposal, however, was not accepted by the Congress when it considered the 1977 amendments.

As the costs of social security increase and the burden of low earners also rises, the pressure for general revenue financing has risen. The 1979 Advisory Council on Social Security, for example, unanimously recommended "that the time has come to finance some part of social security with nonpayroll tax revenues." Their suggestion: Finance the hospital insurance program entirely through earmarked portions of the personal and corporation income taxes. Reporting soon after the Advisory Council, the National Commission on Social Security also recommended general revenue financing for half of the hospital insurance program costs.

In addition, it recommended a cap on future payroll tax rates of 18 percent (9 percent each for employees and employers), with general revenue making up the difference.

When Congress enacted major financing legislation in 1983, it did not adopt any provision to move the medical program toward what some viewed as general revenue financing. It did adopt, however, a more restrictive general revenue provision.[12] To help meet short-term funding shortfalls, it authorized an immediate and one-time transfer of about $20 billion from general revenue to cover benefits that will be paid to veterans of World War II and the Korean War. Military personnel during this period were credited with tax contributions to social security that they did not actually make. This general transfer in effect accelerates payments from general revenue to cover these costs.

A variety of arguments have been raised against general revenue financing. The major ones are:

1. It would encourage excessive increases in benefits.
2. It tends to integrate social security into the annual budget review process and makes it more "political."
3. It is contrary to the insurance and contributory principles of the program, which promote the political acceptability of social security.
4. Social security would increasingly be viewed as a welfare program, with an associated decline in congressional and public support.

Opposition to any major expansion of general revenue financing still seems to be strong in Congress.

Changing the Payroll Tax Structure

A variety of proposals have been made to change the payroll tax. The principal approach is to make the payroll tax rate progressive. One method is to provide lump-sum exemptions to the tax in the same way as exists in the current income tax law. The late union leader Walter Reuther, for example, proposed in 1967 a $600 exemption per earner. Other proposals would allow exemptions for dependents, and some propose a "standard deduction" amount equal to that in the federal income tax law.

Alternatively, it has been proposed that the payroll tax be integrated with the income tax. The present tax withholdings for

---

[12]The taxation of benefits legislated in 1983 may also be viewed as a kind of general revenue transfer (see page 184).

both social security and income taxes would continue, but at the end of the year the total amounts collected would be added together and applied to satisfy the individual or couple's income tax liability. An excess of taxes over liability would be the basis for a tax refund. To accomplish this would require higher taxes.

Arguments against the above two proposals are similar to those against general revenue financing. As we discussed in the previous chapter, the current way the issue is dealt with is the "earned income credit" provision of the federal income tax law.

Taxing Social Security Benefits

The 1979 Advisory Council on Social Security made a major recommendation designed to make social security financing more equitable. A majority of the council recommended that half of social security benefits be taxable income under the federal income tax:

> *The . . . tax treatment of social security was established at a time when both social security benefits and income tax rates were low. In 1941 the Bureau of Internal Revenue ruled that social security benefits were not taxable, most probably because they were viewed as a form of income similar to a gift or gratuity.*
>
> *The Council believes that this ruling was wrong when made and is wrong today. The right to social security benefits is derived from earnings covered employment just as is the case with private pensions.* [Advisory Council on Social Security, 1979]

When the Advisory Council's recommendation was announced, there was an immediate outpouring of criticism from Congress. In less than two months, nine bills (one with 241 co-sponsors) were introduced in the House to reaffirm the tax exemption of social security benefits, and within seven months resolutions opposing taxation were passed in both Houses.

With this history in mind, it is somewhat hard to believe that three years later Congress actually passed legislation to tax social security benefits. With a short-term financing crisis confronting it, Congress moved quickly on a group of recommendations proposed by a new commission, the National Commission on Social Security Reform, a commission that included key leaders of Congress in the social security area. Their recommendation included changes designed to deal with both short- and long-term financial problems.

The strategy developed by congressional leaders was to get Congress to vote on the changes as a package, allowing no amendments. As expressed by Ways and Means Chairman Dan Rostenkowski, "Voted on separately, very few of the controversial elements of our bill can survive. But taken together, the sacrifice they demand is fairly spread." Timothy Clark (1983) interprets what happened:

> *With a single-minded concentration rarely found on Capital Hill, leaders of Congress pushed the legislation first through the House and then through the Senate. . . . Faced with the choice between legislation that appeared to distribute its painful burden evenly and the alternative of possible failure to agree on a substitute set of reforms, Congress was quick to grasp the former.*

Beginning in 1984, a portion of social security and railroad retirement benefits has been included in taxable income. This provision applies, however, only to taxpayers whose "adjusted gross income,"[13] combined with 50 percent of their social security benefits, exceeds a base amount. The base is $25,000 for an individual, $32,000 for a married couple filing a joint return, and zero for married persons filing separate returns. The amount of benefits included in taxable income is the lesser of one-half of benefits or one-half of the excess of the taxpayers' combined income over the base amount. As specified by the 1983 law, the proceeds from the taxation of benefits are transferred by the Treasury Department to the appropriate social security trust funds.

Chapter 6 Highlights

Financing issues associated with social security are many and complex. Some of the major point we emphasized in this chapter were:

1. As social security expenditures grow, there is increased controversy over how to finance current and future benefits and the equity of various financing provisions.
2. It is important to distinguish between long-term financing problems arising from demographic factors and short-term problems resulting from a pay-as-you-go financing system confronted by cyclical instability of an unexpected magnitude.
3. Researchers do not agree on the existence or extent of

---

[13] For purposes of calculating whether income exceeds the base amount, some income normally exempt from federal taxation (e.g., interest income from tax exempt municiple bonds) is included when determining how much social security income will be subject to income taxation.

financing inequities related to younger workers, women, and/
or minorities.

4. General revenue financing of a portion of social security
continues to be looked upon unfavorably by Congress, but
the historic opposition to income taxing of benefits collapsed
in 1983 when Congress was confronted by a serious OASI
financing crisis.

Suggested Readings

AARON, HENRY J. *Economic Effects of Social Security*. Washington, D.C.: The
Brookings Institution, 1982. Chapter 6 contains a perceptive discussion of
pension equity considerations and an assessment of prior studies.

Congressional Budget Office. *Financing Social Security—Issues and Options for
the Long Run*. Washington, D.C.: CBO, 1982. A good overview of the issues.

GIBSON, MARY JO, ED. *Income Security and Long-Term Care for Women in
Midlife and Beyond*. Washington, D.C.: American Association of Retired
Persons, 1987. An extensive discussion of contemporary economic support
issues related to women in Canada and the United States.

MEYER, CHARLES W., ED., 1987. *Social Security—A Critique of Radical Reform
Proposals*. Lexington, Mass.: Lexington Books. A major focus of this book is
on proposals to phase out social security—especially on the Super-IRA
option.

MUNNELL, A., AND L. E. BLAIS. "Do We Want Large Social Security Surpluses?"
New England Economic Review (September/October, 1984): 5–21. Here is a
good place to start if you want to learn more about the social security surplus
question and the economic issues involved.

SAMMARTINO, FRANK J., AND R. A. KASTEN. "The Distributional Consequences
of Taxing Social Security Benefits: Current Law and Alternative Schemes."
In S. Danziger and K. Portnoy, eds., *Distributional Impacts of Public Policy*.
Port Washington, N.Y.: Kennicot Press, 1984. The analysis in this article
shows that the new social security taxing provisions are highly progressive,
especially in the early years.

Subcommittee on Fiscal Policy, U.S. Joint Economic Committee. "Issues in
Financing Retirement Income," Paper No. 18 in Studies in Public Welfare.
Washington, D.C.: U.S. Government Printing Office, 1974. The best available summary of the financial history of social security and the issues that
have been discussed over the years. It also contains a comprehensive
bibliography of congressional documents, monographs, and journal articles
on social security financing.

THOMPSON, LAWRENCE. "The Social Security Reform Debate." *The Journal of
Economic Literature* 21 (December 1983): 1425–67. A comprehensive review
discussing historical, institutional, and theoretical factors related to financing
social security.

U.S. Senate Special Committee on Aging. *Women and Social Security*. *Adapting to a New Era*. A working paper prepared by the Task Force on Women and Social Security. Washington, D.C.: U.S. Government Printing Office, 1975. An excellent summary of the various issues, including a discussion of various proposed changes in women's benefits.

Chapter 7

HEALTH, DISABILITY, AND SSI BENEFITS

As with pensions, the future of health care policy is being debated amid growing concern. The concern focuses on the potential financial burden of national health care. Medicare and Medicaid expenditures alone reached $74 billion in 1986 and are projected to reach about $100 billion in 1990. Many analysts now express the fear that health care costs are out of control.

On the other side are the elderly themselves, who are confronted with the prospects of paying large amounts of money out of pocket, despite existing government programs to assist them. Many health expenses (especially long-term care) still fall directly on the individual or his or her family. Thus, "fear of a long and costly final illness haunts many old people. To end one's life as a ward of the state, or to drain the resources of one's children, is an all-too-frequent prospect for old persons in America" (Brown, 1972).

In this chapter, we look at the health care system for the elderly, how it is financed, and the problems remaining to be resolved. We also discuss two other important government programs—disability and SSI.

Medicaid and Medicare

The most important legislation to help the elderly meet health care costs was passed in 1965: hospital insurance and supplementary medical insurance (collectively known as Medicare) and a means-tested medical assistance program (Medicaid). We look first at Medicaid.

Medicaid

Medicaid is a means-tested program for persons in need. Amendment of the Social Security Act in 1950 provided for federal financial participation in providing medical care to public assistance recipients. Then, in 1960 another amendment authorized additional federal matching for medical care payments resulting from the health care needs of Old Age Assistance recipients. The Medicaid program enacted in 1965 as Title XIX of the Social Security Act, however, went far beyond these prior actions. It provided, through major financial support, much better access to health care for low-income people.

Medicaid is not a program limited to aged persons. About 21 million people of all different ages were eligible for Medicaid services in 1984: about 3 million were age 65 or older. All states cover recipients of Aid to Families with Dependent Children (AFDC); about 30 percent cover all aged, blind, and disabled recipients of Supplemental Security Income (SSI); and the other states limit coverage of SSI eligibles to persons who meet restrictive medical assistance standards. In addition, about two-thirds of the states cover "medically needy" persons who are aged, blind, or disabled. Also included are members of AFDC families ineligible for cash assistance but not able to afford medical services. Needy individuals *excluded* are single people who are neither aged nor disabled, couples without children, and in many states, two-parent families with children.

General guidelines for eligibility are established by the federal government, but specific eligibility requirements are determined separately by each state. As a result, a wide measure of discretion is allowed states under the Medicaid legislation with regard to what income and asset **means tests** will be applied to various individuals. Not surprisingly, actual practice among the states varies greatly.

The provision of long-term care financing is very important. Given the high costs of nursing homes, 70 to 80 percent of the elderly today cannot afford a stay of even one year (Tell et al., 1987). In fact, 70 percent of the elderly living alone cannot finance nursing home care on their own beyond an average of 13 weeks (U.S. House Select Committee on Aging, 1987). Medicaid pays for such care when private assets are exhausted. But individuals are required to turn over all income in excess of their personal needs and the "maintenance needs" of their spouses. About half of the people covered by Medicaid's nursing home benefit became eligible due to impoverishment *after* entering the nursing home (U.S. House Select Committee on Aging, 1987).   .

Participating states are required to provide both inpatient and outpatient hospital services, skilled nursing home or home health care services, family planning services, and physicians' services. Other services—such as drug therapy, dental care, and physical therapy—are provided at the option of each state.

Medicaid provides federal funds appropriated from general revenue to states with qualified medical assistance programs. All states now participate, although Arizona obtained a waiver in 1982 to implement an alternative program. This federal cost-sharing ranges from 50 to 80 percent, based on a formula that varies the percentage in accordance with a state's per capita income. In the fiscal year 1985, expenditures were $21.7 billion from federal funds and $17.8 billion by the states.

Legislation in 1980 made three important changes in Medicaid. The Federal Council on the Aging (1985) has characterized these changes as "a significant rethinking of the Medicaid program." The following changes were made:

1. Federal financial participation was reduced.
2. Eligibility requirements for public welfare were tightened, reducing the Medicaid recipient population.
3. States were given broader discretion in program planning and granted waivers from certain federal requirements.

A substantial proportion of the 65 + Medicare population (about 15 percent) are also covered by Medicaid. For these dual enrollees, Medicare is the first payer for Medicare services, and Medicaid is responsible for the Medicare cost-sharing provisions (**deductibles** and **coinsurance**). For services not covered by Medicare, Medicaid has primary responsibility.

Medicare

The Medicare program is very different from Medicaid. According to the National Commission on Social Security (1981), it arose historically from three principal premises:

1. The cost of medical care was not something that could be budgeted in preparing for retirement, since it varied from time to time and from person to person. Therefore, insurance against this cost was necessary to retirement security.

2. For most retired people, the premium cost of adequate health insurance was too high to pay out of retirement income or savings. Therefore, a new prepayment approach and government aid were required to make health insurance in retirement feasible.

3. Adequate and affordable private-sector health insurance was generally available only through group coverage. But retired people usually could not easily be brought together into groups suitable for such coverage.

The "hospital insurance" program (often called Part A) provides benefits financed by *compulsory* payroll taxes (currently, 1.45 percent paid by both employee and employer) and covers (1) all persons age 65 or over entitled under either OASDI or the railroad retirement system and (2) most social security disability beneficiaries under age 65.[1] Hospital insurance benefits are also available to *noninsured* persons who were over age 65 in July 1966 and to other persons age 65 and over who voluntarily enroll and pay a premium rate that meets the entire cost of their protection.

"Supplementary medical insurance" (often called Part B) is a *voluntary* program for nonhospital health care financed by participant premiums ($17.90 per month in 1987)[2] and a matching but much higher contribution ($53) by the federal government out of general revenue. With certain minor exceptions, any person age 65 or over in the United States can participate.

The hospital insurance program provides a variety of hospital and posthospital benefits (with the patient subject to certain deductible and cost-sharing charges). Reimbursements for services provided are made directly to hospitals, skilled nursing facilities, and home health service agencies. With regard to hospitalization, an individual is entitled to inpatient hospital benefits for the first 90 days in a spell of illness and for an additional "lifetime reserve" of 60 days that can be used on an elective basis. In addition, 20 days of skilled nursing care are provided without cost to eligible persons for each spell of illness, and 80 days following are provided on a cost-sharing basis ($67.50 per day in 1988). Also, certain home health services can be provided under a plan established by a doctor (while the doctor is providing care to the individual). These services may include part-time or intermittent care by a visiting nurse or a physical, speech, or occupational therapist. Full-time

---

[1] Certain workers and their family members with kidney disease also receive benefits.

[2] The Health Care Financing Administration announced in 1987 an increase for 1988 to $24.80 per month. This rate does not include the increases associated with the "catastrophic illness insurance" enacted in 1988 (see page 201).

nursing is not included; nor is such care as housekeeping, meal preparation, shopping, and so forth. Finally, **hospice** services for the terminally ill are covered.

The supplementary medical insurance program covers certain nonhospital medical costs, primarily the cost of physician services. In general, the program reimburses 80 percent of "reasonable charges" after an initial deductible of $75 per calendar year. There are, however, two very different administrative procedures available for reimbursing covered services. The doctor who accepts "assignment" and thereby agrees to bill for no more than "reasonable charges" is paid directly by the government (after taking into account any deductible and coinsurance). If the doctor does not accept assignment, the beneficiary must pay the doctor's actual charges, present an itemized bill from the doctor to the government, and be reimbursed on the basis of "reasonable charges" (which may be lower than the actual charges). A great many doctors do not accept assignment—many because they would receive lower fees, some because of strong personal views against dealing with government agencies and having fees "dictated" by them, others because it has been the American Medical Association's recommended action, and still others because of alleged delays in receiving payments. In recent years the proportion of physicians accepting assignment has fallen from an initial level of about 85 percent to below 70 percent. In 1984 incentives were introduced to counteract this problem, resulting in some increase in physicians accepting assignment.

When it was enacted, Medicare was visualized as a fairly comprehensive program, comparable to the better private health insurance plans then available for people at younger ages. But as a result of rising health costs and increases in coinsurance payments, a much larger gap has now developed between the total costs of health care (for a typical elderly person) and the protection provided by Medicare. The program pays for about 75 percent of hospital bills, 55 percent of doctors' bills, but only 2 percent of nursing home bills.

National statistics for 1984 show that Medicare accounted for about 49 percent of total health care spending by those age 65 and over. Another 19 percent was paid by Medicaid (and other public programs). The rest—32 percent—came from private health insurance and out-of-pocket payments by patients and their families.

Long-Term Care

The tragedy of old age is not the fact that each of us must grow old and die but that the process of doing so has been made unnecessarily and at times excruciatingly painful, humiliating, debilitating and isolating through insensitivity, ignorance and poverty. [Butler, 1975]

At no time are older persons more sensitive to the issue Robert Butler raises in the above quote than when they confront the issue of long-term care. Persons age 65–69 face a 43 percent risk of entering a nursing home during their remaining lifetime (Task Force on Long-Term Care Policies, 1987).

Probably one of the greatest fears of old age is what will happen at the onset of severe and chronic illness or loss of capacity. The independence of living arrangements and life-styles so cherished by most Americans is threatened (and often lost) when physical and/or mental capacities diminish. In addition, as we explain below, the financial burden of dealing with this issue falls heavily upon the individual and his or her family. The costs of long-term care can wipe out the resources of all but the rich. And finally, but certainly not least in importance, is the emotional strain placed on individuals and their families in making decisions on how to meet the new medical, service, and financial demands.

Summarizing the current state of affairs, Callahan (1981) observes:

In long-term care we have the answer—a coordinated, comprehensive system of services which is case-managed and cost-effective. Now what is the question? There are a number of candidates. How can the cost of long-term care services be controlled? How can families be helped so that they do not give up caring for a disabled older person? How can an older person's functional abilities be maintained and/or enhanced? How can this country care for a growing population of very old women?

As Callahan also observes, there is one fact that seems relatively clear. The majority (but not all) of older persons with severe health and physical limitations prefer to remain out of an institutional care facility if at all possible. Hence, the major effort over the past decade or so has been to develop alternatives to institutionalization.

Yet the fact is that at present our programs and policies are still, despite improvements, heavily biased toward institutional care. Most public money for long-term care currently goes for institutional care. And the inadequate availability of community care services (and restrictions under public programs in the use of those available) encourages overutilization of institutional options.

In addition to the problem of institutional bias, it is generally recognized that the following major long-term care problems exist (Callahan and Wallack, 1981):

1. The general quality of care is typically poor.
2. Services and financing are fragmented.
3. There remain large amounts of unmet needs and a geographic maldistribution of available benefits.
4. Costs are rising rapidly, and public expenditures are not under acceptable control.
5. There is an absence of adequate case management (i.e., no centralized mechanisms for information, referral, prescription, allocating resources, and so forth).
6. The current situation places heavy burdens on individuals and families.

As yet no consensus has emerged in the United States as to what action is appropriate to deal with these issues.

Long-Term Care Providers

Hospitals still provide a significant amount of long-term care to the aged. While most hospitals are designed for short-term stays, many (especially city and county hospitals) treat patients requiring more than 60 days of care. Also, while the numbers have declined significantly, many elderly still receive care in psychiatric hospitals and residential treatment centers.

The trend has been to move the elderly from hospitals and mental institutions into other care facilities. The most common option is use of nursing homes. Over the past few decades there has been phenomenal growth in the number of such facilities, most being occupied predominantly by older people. Currently, about 1.5 million persons reside in over 20,000 of these homes.

The growth of nursing homes is not the result of satisfaction with the services provided. The quality of care provided in many of these homes has been notoriously poor. For example, a 1978 government report cited the overuse of medications, the administration of drugs by untrained staff, the rarity of physician visits, and poor quality staffing with high turnover (U.S. HEW, 1978).

The growth of nursing homes arises from a number of factors. A growing elderly population, and an even faster growing *very old* population, increases demand. More recently, federal payment procedures to hospitals (see page 197) encourage these institutions to discharge patients as soon as their health condition permits—often to a nursing home.

The cost of care in a nursing home with skilled staff is $25,000 to $60,000 per year. Medicaid pays for about 44 percent of all nursing home costs in the United States today. In order for individuals to become eligible for this financial help, however, they must first impoverish themselves and usually their spouse. And all those who qualify must then give up all future income (except a small personal allowance) in order to help meet the costs of care.

Two alternatives to nursing homes for some people are day care programs and home care. Day care is designed for people who do not require 24-hour institutional care and provides a protective environment and treatment as needed during the day as a supplement to spouse or family care at night.

However, in many ways it is home care that is the most attractive option to institutionalization. Ideally, support for the elderly is provided in these programs by making available a wide range of community services to allow elderly persons to remain in their homes. Unfortunately, the various publicly funded programs that cover community care provide only fragments of the full range of services needed. Although Medicaid coverage of home care services has improved in recent years,[3] both home care and nursing home benefit regulations require individuals to "spend down" almost all of their wealth in order to achieve eligibility for the services. Increasingly, however, private profit and nonprofit organizations are offering these services to people who can pay for them.

Finally, it is important to emphasize that over the years—and still today—it is the families of the chronically ill elderly who provide the largest amount of care. Currently, over 3 million families provide major assistance to the impaired elderly living outside institutions; this includes physical, personal, and financial help. It has been estimated that "70 percent of the elderly rely mainly on relatives to meet their personal and physical care needs in case of disability rather than on agencies" (Morris and Youket, 1981).

Covering the Costs of Long-Term Care

"Any particular individual faces a relatively small probability of needing a large, costly amount of long-term care, but for the few it can be very expensive indeed" (Ball, 1987a). At age 65, the probability of needing nursing home care before one dies is 40

---

[3] Under Section 2176 of the Omnibus Budget Reconciliation Act of 1981, states may institute a variety of home and community based services for individuals who, "but for" the services, would be in long-term care institutions.

percent, but only 10 percent of those elderly using these services remain over a year. As a result, roughly 13 percent of all elderly use 90 percent of all nursing home resources (Tell et al., 1987).

Currently, about 70 private insurance companies (EBPR, 1987a) offer policies to cover the costs of certain long-term care expenses (up from only 16 companies in 1984). Still experimental in nature, these private plans are very limited in the benefits offered and restrict eligibility through a variety of health-screening mechanisms and exclusion provisions.

Increased attention is being given to the possibility of expanding Medicare to cover long-term care costs. Policymakers are in part responding to a growing concern in the electorate over this issue. A 1987 survey sponsored by the American Association of Retired Persons and carried out by R. L. Associates found that 86 percent of those persons interviewed thought the government should be taking more responsibility for the long-term care problem. And about 70 percent were willing to tax themselves $10 to $60 per month (depending on their income) to pay for long-term care coverage (AARP, 1987). One major issue, however, dominates these discussions: how to adequately meet the needs of care recipients without generating politically unacceptable program costs and without undermining the historically important role of the family in this area.

Financing Health Care

Health costs and, consequently, program costs have risen rapidly over the years. Health care expenditures for all Americans reached $425 billion in 1985, over $1 billion each day of the year or $1,721 annually per American. Current expenditures for Medicare and Medicaid exceed $200 million per day.

By 1986 the percent of the United States' **gross national product** (GNP) devoted to health care services had risen to almost 11 percent ($462 billion), compared to 6 percent in 1965.[4] In 1950 the typical stay in a hospital was eight days at an average cost to the hospital for the entire period of $127. In 1984 the average stay had declined slightly, but the hospital cost had soared to $2,995! And the cost for some illnesses can be a great deal higher. For example, Roger Evans of the Battelle Human Affairs Research Centers estimates that in 1983 it cost about $80,000 to care for a person

---

[4]This compares, for example, to 4 percent of GNP in Great Britain.

with end-stage cardiac disease (*Newsweek,* 29 August 1983). Today, it would cost much more.

Not surprisingly, a disproportionate share of health care services go to the elderly. The personal health care costs of older persons are between two and three times higher than what one would expect from aggregate statistics for people of all ages (Zook and Moore, 1980). Here again, however, differences among the elderly are important. Many of the aged are healthy and rarely use health care services, while others require extensive services. In fact, only 9 percent of the elderly account for 70 percent of all Medicare payments (for the aged), and 40 percent of the aged receive no Medicare reimbursed services in any particular year (Davis, 1982).

Medicare is financed by a payroll tax (currently 1.45 percent) for Part A expenses. Payments by the federal government from general revenues help finance Part B (and some transitional expenses connected with Part A). Coinsurance payments by eligible individuals are used to help finance both Part A and Part B.

The rising costs of the Medicare program are a result of three principal factors:

1. General **inflation** and especially inflation in health care costs, with health costs rising much faster than the consumer price index (CPI).
2. An increased number of persons receiving services.
3. Expanding (and expensive) medical technology and increased utilization of expanding services.

Prospective Payment

In an attempt to deal with rising costs, Congress passed important legislation in 1983. Social security amendments in that year specified a major change in the way the government pays claims for inpatient hospital services. Medicare now pays a fixed amount (determined in advance) for various expense categories. Hospitals must consider these reimbursements as payments in full and are prohibited from charging beneficiaries any additional amount, apart from the statutory deductible and coinsurance amounts.

Under the new prospective payment system (called DRG), payment amounts are determined by *the average cost of providing the treatment for a particular illness diagnosis*. However, this payment amount is adjusted to reflect the wage level in the local community, the higher costs of "teaching" hospitals, whether the hospital has an exceptionally large number of low-income, Medicaid patients, and whether the hospital is in an urban or rural area.

This payment system provides an incentive to hospitals to minimize tests, treatment procedures, and overall hospital stays. If these three aspects of care can be provided by the hospital at lower cost than the DRG payment, the hospital is permitted to pocket the difference. If the hospital's costs are more, the hospital cannot make up the difference (as in prior years) by charging the government for the total costs of the care provided. Thus, the DRG payment system is designed to discourage overtreatment. It also seeks to reduce administrative costs by eliminating the processing and review of numerous treatment/test charges involved in any hospital admission. While a relatively simple concept, the DRG payment system in practice is very complicated and raises many issues.

Designed to encourage improvement in hospital management, the system may cause hospitals to give too much weight to financial matters in the provision of health care. For example, since length of stay is a critical factor in determining payments, providers may seek to keep their costs down by making discharge decisions that are in accord with the average length of stays assumed in the DRG payment schedule. Concern has been voiced that as a result of this process, some patients are being discharged prematurely from hospitals. Alternatively, the DRG payment system may affect patient care before the patients even enter the hospital—influencing hospital admissions policies. Some private hospitals have been charged with "creaming" the ill population—sending the more difficult (more expensive) cases to public hospitals.

The DRG procedure was instituted in an attempt to reduce the costs of the hospital insurance program. Estimates in 1983 projected a saving of about $34 billion over the 1983 to 1999 period. Experts currently disagree, however, about whether significant cost savings will actually be realized—especially if one looks at total rather than just inpatient hospital health care costs. Moreover, many physicians have still not accepted the change—spending over $4 million in the 1986 elections lobbying against people in the Congress who voted for the new payment system (*The Economist*, 1987). Most policymakers in the health area do agree that additional changes in health care financing will have to be made if health care costs are to be kept within reasonable limits.

One other approach currently being encouraged and tested by the government relates to **health maintenance organizations** (HMOs). For a flat monthly fee, HMOs provide a wide range of medical services both in and outside the hospital—departing from the traditional fee-for-service payment system. There are currently more than 650 HMOs with 28 million members throughout the

United States—with very high participation rates in certain states (e.g., Florida, Massachusetts, and Minnesota). The government is encouraging the enrollment in HMOs of persons covered by the Medicare program. Under contract with the government, HMOs can receive 95 percent of the average amount paid out for fee-for-service beneficiaries in the same local area. In 1986 about one million Medicare recipients were enrolled in this option.

Rising Costs to Consumers

With the federal government running large deficits in recent years, Medicare has been one of the prime targets for government cutbacks in the 1980s. To keep up with inflation, the deductible for Part A has risen from the original $40 to $540 (in 1988). Hospital coinsurance has been increased from $10 to $135 per day for days 61 through 90 in the hospital and from $20 to $270 per day for the 60 hospital "reserve days."

It is Part B costs, however, where the government has shifted more of the total cost to the aged. The Part B premium has been increased substantially. The annual Part B *deductible* has increased from $50 to $75. And a two-premium payment system has recently been initiated for catastrophic and drug coverage (page 201).

Out-of-pocket expenditures, averaging $300 in 1966, have increased to $1,850 in 1986—rising, on average, to 16 percent of elderly income. "Many experts suspect that Medicare's new prospective payment system for reimbursing hospitals, with its incentives to discharge patients 'sooner and sicker' from the hospital, may be a major force behind the shift in spending from inpatient to outpatient services" (Kosterlitz, 1986). The result is that less of the cost is paid for by Medicare.

Private Supplementation

Even before the elderly were confronted by these cutbacks, many sought additional insurance protection from private plans. These "medigap" policies are designed to cover many of the medical expenses not covered by the government program and are currently purchased by nearly 70 percent of the elderly population. Robert Ball, former Commissioner of Social Security, evaluates these programs as follows:

> *The so-called Medigap policies of private insurance are very expensive for the protection furnished. A considerable portion of premium income goes for administration—15 to 35 percent—partly because*

*the individual claims, on average, are small in amount. . . . They
seldom fill [all] the gaps in coverage (such as prescription drugs)
and do not deal at all with the cost of long-term care where the need
is primarily for personal services, such as feeding, dressing, toilet-
ting, or helping the patient move about. [Ball, 1987a]*

Another type of private insurance available is from plans sponsored by employers for their *retired* employees. In 1983, 4.3
million (one out of six) aged persons were covered by employer-
sponsored health insurance plans. The plans fall into two main
categories: (1) "Medicare Supplement Plans" that pay claims according to a schedule of payments for specified services and (2)
"Carve-out Plans" that pay the amount that is paid by the company's insurance for active workers, reduced by Medicare payments.

A recent Brandeis University study (Leavitt et al., 1987) looks at
retirees in three large companies providing some supplemental
insurance protection. It found, as would be expected, much lower
personal health insurance purchases by those retirees electing this
coverage.[5] Yet no matter how comprehensive their coverage, almost all covered retirees (even those who personally bought additional private insurance) had *noninsured* medical expenses for a
wide variety of uncovered services. For many of the retirees
surveyed in the study, these expenses were substantial. In addition, the study found that retirees with company-sponsored plans
are confronted with difficult decisions with regard to buying additional gap insurance on their own. The gap plans currently available do not "mesh" well with the company plans, *forcing retirees to
buy coverage they don't need in order to get the protection they
want.*

The costs of these corporate-sponsored plans are now a major
concern to employers. Their apprehension arises from a number
of factors. Retiree populations in many companies, particularly in
the slow growth or declining sectors of the economy, are growing
dramatically relative to employees still working. Discussions surrounding the Medicare cutbacks of recent years have also alerted
employers to the possibility that their future liabilities may rise,
even if health care costs in general are kept under control—given
the coordination through integrated payment rules that exists
between public and private programs. Finally, unlike pension
plans, virtually no prefunding by employers of retiree health
benefits has occurred, and consequently, projected employer ex-

---

[5] Retirees must often contribute financially to the costs of such insurance, and therefore
some do not elect it.

penditures in the future (if nothing changes) will be extraordinarily large.

In response to rising costs and increased uncertainties about the future, some companies have attempted to cut back on their health programs for retirees by amending or even eliminating these benefits. Retirees and unions have vigorously challenged these actions, often in the courts. Decisions in a number of court cases to date seem to limit severely the ability of employers to change or eliminate promised benefits made in the past. Still, it is clear that many companies will continue to seek ways to deal with the escalating costs of these benefits in the years to come.

Catastrophic Illness Insurance

In 1986, Secretary of Health and Human Services Otis R. Bowen proposed that government programs be modified to help Americans meet the costs of "catastrophic illnesses" requiring long hospital or nursing home stays. The Bowen plan called for expanded Medicare Part B to cover the elderly, and a combination of state and private initiatives to cover the rest of the population. A major debate over a number of alternative approaches to the problem followed.

Congress passed new legislation in 1988[6] putting a cost cap on out-of-pocket costs for Medicare covered services (for 1988, about $1,800) and requiring only one deductible ($544 in 1988). The new provisions also expand *short-term* nursing home and home health care benefits. And for the first time, coverage for prescription drugs was made available, with Medicare paying 80 percent of the costs after an initial deductible is met.

"For the first time in history, Congress is asking the elderly to pay the entire cost of a Medicare benefit. Critics of the financing scheme claim the bill is a fundamental redistribution of the income of America's senior citizens" (*Perspectives*, 1987). To finance the new provisions, the monthly premium for Part B of Medicare was raised $4 in 1988, and an additional premium charge for the drug benefit is being phased in. The basic premium increase is supplemented by an additional premium charged only to those beneficiaries who pay federal income taxes (estimated to be about 40 percent of beneficiaries in 1988). Some critics have labeled this premium as an "indirect means test."

---

[6]Congress had still not worked out the final provisions when this book went to press. Details presented here are based on the identical provisions in the House and Senate bills.

Other Social Security Programs: Disability and SSI

In previous chapters we have referred to a number of programs other than health and retirement pensions that have an important impact on the economic welfare of the aged. It is appropriate at this point to discuss two of them, since they are important complements to health and pension programs.[7]

Disability Insurance Programs

Over 16 million noninstitutionalized Americans between the ages of 20 and 64 *have limited ability to work* because of chronic health conditions and impairments. And more than three times that number suffer from one or more chronic health conditions. Approximately half the disabled (8 million) are unable either to work altogether or to work regularly (Krute and Burdette, 1978).

In general, whatever the degree of impairment, the chance of disability increases with age (see Figure 7–1). Figure 7–1 also shows how the prevalence of *total* disability rises sharply with age.

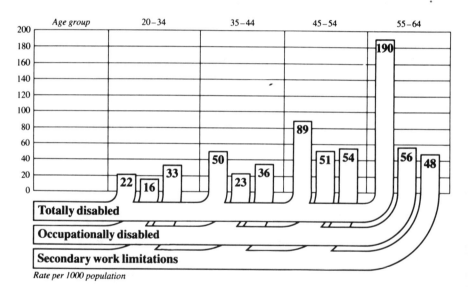

Figure 7-1   Disability by Age, 1972. Source: *Work Disability in the United States—A Chartbook* (Washington, D.C.: U.S. Government Printing Office, 1977).

[7]Not discussed are unemployment insurance, the food stamp program, and special veterans' benefits.

Among persons age 20–34, total disability occurs at a rate of 22 per 1,000 population. The rate approximately doubles for each succeeding 10-year age group—reaching 190 per 1,000 for those 55–64.

The social security disability programs discussed here are only two of many disability programs; currently, more than 85 types of public and private programs in the United States deal with disability (Berkowitz et al., 1976). Table 7–1 lists some of the major programs and shows the growth of expenditures for each. Coordination problems among these various programs create a number of difficult adequacy and equity issues related to attempts to help physically impaired individuals.

Social security's Disability Insurance (DI) program and the Supplemental Security Income (SSI) program[8] provide benefits to people who have severe long-term disabilities. Disability protec-

Table 7–1   Expenditures of Major Disability Programs: 1955, 1965, 1975, 1980 (in millions of dollars)

Program	1955	1965	1975	1980
Disability Insurance (DI)	0	1,573	8,414	14,899
Supplemental Security Income				
State	0	0	70	100[a]
Federal	135	417	3,072	4,912
Workers' compensation				
Disabled and dependents'	521	1,074	3,205	na[b]
Survivor	70	140	360	na
Hospital and medical care	325	600	2,030	na
Black lung				
Social Security Administration	0	0	948	1,032
Department of Labor	0	0	9	808[a]
Veterans' programs	1,982	3,026	5,583	8,100[a]
Railroad disability programs	155	190	451	650[a]
Government employee disability programs	355	751	2,702	5,000[a]
Vocational rehabilitation	42	211	1,036	99
Rehabilitation services (DI)	0	0	91	na
Medicaid	0	0	14,177	na
Medicare	0	0	14,781	na
Total	3,654	7,982	56,927	na

Source: Based on Richard V. Burkhauser and Robert H. Haveman, *Disability and Work: The Economics of American Policy* (Baltimore: The Johns Hopkins University Press, 1982), Table 3.1. Used by permission of Johns Hopkins University Press.
[a]Estimated by Burkhauser and Haveman from incomplete data.
[b]Not available.

---

[8] SSI is discussed in the last section of this chapter.

tion under the DI program is currently provided to (1) disabled insured workers and their dependents, (2) disabled widows and widowers of insured workers, and (3) adult (age 18 or older) sons and daughters who become disabled before age 22 of insured disabled, retired, or deceased workers.

Disability protection as part of social security was not legislated until 1956. Early social security advisory groups disagreed about the predictability of disability program costs and about whether one could administratively determine eligibility for this type of benefit (i.e., distinguish legitimate disability from malingering). Although it was proposed repeatedly in the early years of social security, major groups effectively fought against its introduction.

When the first major legislation for disability protection was debated in 1949 and 1950, strong criticism and opposition were voiced by the American Medical Association, the United States Chamber of Commerce, the National Manufacturers Association, and representatives of private insurance organizations. After the defeat of the 1949/1950 bill, strong opposition continued in succeeding years to the various new proposals that were introduced— including the disability freeze amendment of 1954.[9] All the disability proposals were attacked as potentially costly, difficult to administer, and the beginning of "socialized medicine." Given this strong opposition over the years, the ultimate passage of disability legislation in 1956 is viewed by many as a major development in the legislative history of social security in the United States.

A Restrictive Program

Many people today wonder why it is so difficult to become eligible for the DI program. Some historical perspective is important in understanding the problems and criticisms of inadequacy surrounding the current DI program. The strong opposition of major groups to the program and fears about administering the program (discussed above) influenced Congress to severely restrict the scope of the program passed in 1956. Key features of the *original* program that reflected these concerns were:

1. Establishment of not one but three different tests of insured status.
2. A very narrow and severe definition of disability.

---

[9]This was a provision that prevented periods of disability from reducing or eliminating retirement and survivors' benefits by "freezing" the individual's rights at the time of disablement. For a good discussion of the legislative history of this and other disability provisions, see Cohen (1957, Chapter 4).

3. The denial of benefits to anyone under age 50 or to any dependents.
4. Creation of a separate trust fund to help monitor program costs.
5. Establishment of vocational rehabilitation programs to move people off the disability rolls.

Thus, multiple tests of insured status were built into the disability laws. To be eligible for social security disability payments a worker must be screened on three levels: (1) determination of insured status, (2) assessment of physical condition and level of functional impairment, and (3) determination of ability to work. To achieve insured status, the worker must have one quarter of work coverage credit for each year since 1950 (or since age 21, if later) and 20 quarters of coverage during the 40-quarter period prior to disability. Disability, for purposes of benefit entitlement, is defined as the "inability to engage in any substantial gainful activity by reason of any medically determinable physical or mental impairment which can be expected to result in death or which has lasted or can be expected to last for a continuous period of not less than 12 months."

This strict disability definition excludes many people with relatively severe incapacities. *Surveys find that two-thirds of the self-described severely disabled do not receive social security disability payments* (Van De Water, 1979).

Do disability benefits at current levels discourage many people from working? A study by Haveman et al. (1984) says no. Their research indicates that rising disability benefit levels in the past have had a relatively small effect on the work effort choices of older workers.

A Joint Federal-State Program

The DI program is administered under a federal-state partnership; program administration is carried out by each state and is paid for by the federal government under negotiated agreements. The determination of an applicant's disability is by a state agency whose primary function is to develop medical, vocational, and other necessary evidence. This information is evaluated, and a determination is made based upon it.

The principal reason for establishing the federal-state relationship was that it was deemed essential that the disability program be linked with an effective vocational rehabilitation program in each state. But because of the extremely small number of workers rehabilitated (only 20,000 over the 1967–1976 period), some now argue that the principle reason for having the federal-state arrangement is not as valid and that the relationship should be modified. Thus, after a thorough review of the disability program, the U.S. General Accounting Office recommended that the disability determination process be brought under complete federal management (Ahart, 1978). Congress, instead, passed legislation in 1980 requiring the Secretary of Health and Human Services to enter into new agreements with each state. Each agreement requires states to follow performance standards and administrative requirements issued by the Secretary.

DI Benefits

Like retirement benefits, the disability pension is based on average indexed earnings (excluding the disablement period) and is calculated using the same formula and the same minimum benefit provisions as the retirement program. Initially, the social security disability benefit was reduced dollar for dollar by any **workmen's compensation** benefits received by the worker. Then in 1958 this deduction was removed, creating considerable controversy. Turnbull et al. (1967) report that with the deduction removed, "it became possible in some states for a seriously injured worker to receive combined benefits that would exceed his wages prior to his disability." Faced with the criticisms of those who feared the encroachment and possible supplantation of federal disability insurance for state and private programs, Congress reintroduced an offset provision in 1965. However, controversy continued to arise over the issue of program coordination and how to "cap" the benefit level.

The most recent action related to this issue occurred in 1981 when Congress passed a disability "Megacap." The new provision specified that a person's disability benefits (including any benefits for the spouse or children) were to be reduced (if necessary) so that the sum of all benefits payable under certain federal, state, and local public programs did not exceed 80 percent of the person's "average current earnings" (a concept defined in the law). The intent of Congress in passing this new provision was to reduce the overlapping and duplication of public disability programs and to avoid work disincentives arising out of the old law.

Controversy over Administration

The costs of the initial program in the early 1960s proved to be much lower than had been anticipated, encouraging an immediate liberalization of the program by Congress. Almost immediately, however, expenditures began to grow faster than revenues. In response, Congress tightened the definition of disability. Even under the revised definition, however, claims mushroomed, with the number of disability beneficiaries tripling between 1965 and 1978 to a total of about 5 million disabled workers and their eligible dependents.

During the same period, the costs of the program grew from $1.5 billion in 1965 to $11 billion in 1977. If not for a 1977 legislative reallocation of OASDHI payroll tax revenues—less to the retirement (OASI) and health (HI) programs and more to disability (DI)—the disability program would have exhausted its reserves and been faced with a financial crisis. While some part of the increased costs resulted from program maturation (i.e., more workers meeting the years-of-coverage requirements), much of the increase came from unanticipated increases in claims (Cardwell, 1976).

DI's financial problems in the 1970s caused policymakers to take a long, hard look at the program. The result was "belt-tightening" legislation passed in three different years (1977, 1980, and 1981). These amendments were designed to address the financial problems of the program and, at the same time, sought to improve its operation.

As a result of increased scrutiny of the disability program's operations, a major disability controversy arose in the 1980s. The federal disability program and its administrative procedures came under criticism when a 1980 General Accounting Office report estimated that over a half million people on the disability roles were capable of working. Congress responded by directing the Social Security Administration to review the eligibility of benefit recipients every three years.

Reagan administration officials, newly in office, responded enthusiastically to the directive—hastily setting into place a review process. Over 30,000 cases a month were sent out to state officials who were unprepared to review them. Between 1981 and 1984, about 1.2 million cases were reviewed; 491,000 benefits were terminated as a consequence of these reviews; however, over 215,000 terminations were reversed upon appeal. In one reversal, federal district court Judge Joseph S. Lord III wrote, "If the purpose of the U.S. Department of Health and Human Services is to crush defenseless human beings, as it seems to be, it would succeed unless . . . courts interposed a protective arm" (*Newsweek*, 1984).

Faced with an almost unprecedented refusal by Reagan administration officials to institute more humane policies, the courts, state governors, and members of Congress joined the fight. Some governors directed their disability agencies not to cooperate with federal officials. Court actions were initiated. Not until new legislation was passed by Congress in 1986 did the situation ease.

Financial Status

Currently, the financial condition of the disability program is satisfactory. The number of disabled-worker beneficiaries *peaked* in 1978 at 4.9 million, fell to a low of 3.8 million in 1983, and began slowly increasing in the years after 1983—reaching about 4 million by the beginning of 1987. Estimates by the program's actuaries in 1987 caused the trustees of the program to state that future financing would need to be carefully watched. Projections showed that the program could easily move out of financial balance, creating another period of financial concern.

The Supplemental Security Income Program

A new cash-assistance program for the needy aged, blind, and disabled went into operation at the beginning of 1974. This Supplemental Security Income (SSI) program replaced federal grants to three programs: the state-administered programs of (1) old age assistance, (2) aid to the blind, and (3) aid to the permanently and totally disabled. The SSI program is administered by the federal government and financed from general revenues. It establishes uniform eligibility requirements and benefit levels for the whole nation. In addition, states are encouraged (and some are required) to supplement the federal benefits with their own payments. In cases where they do, the states have the option of administering the supplementary payments themselves or contracting with the federal government.

Eligibility for this program requires meeting both an income and an asset test. Nonexcluded assets were set by the most recent legislation not to exceed $1,700 for an individual and $2,550 for a couple.[10] The major assets excluded from the test are (1) the value of one's home, (2) the value of household goods and personal effects up to $2,000, (3) an automobile (up to $4,500), and (4) life insurance (face value up to $1,500).

---

[10] Over the 1987–89 period, the limit increases by $100 each year for individuals and $150 for couples. Thus, the limit for 1989 and after is $2,000 and $3,000, respectively.

SSI benefits are reduced dollar for dollar (100 percent) by all *unearned* income and by 50 percent of any *earned* income above a $65 per month **disregard.** Unearned income up to $20 per month is also disregarded.

Congress increased real SSI benefits in 1983, in part as a way of offsetting the six-month delay in OASDI cost-of-living increases legislated at the same time. As of 1987, SSI guaranteed recipients (before any state supplementation) a monthly income of $340 ($4,080 per year) if single and $510 ($6,120 per year) if a couple. These benefits continue to be adjusted annually for inflation by the consumer price index.

States have the option to supplement the SSI floor for all or selected categories of persons. States *are required to supplement* the federal level if that level does not equal or exceed the benefits provided under the state OAA programs in December 1973 (just before SSI started), plus, in general the amount of federal benefits increases after 1979. In 1987 there were only two states (Texas and West Virginia) without either a mandatory or optional supplementation program.

About 4.3 million people (1987) now receive SSI payments. Surprisingly, more than half of these recipients are disabled persons—not aged. The number of aged in the program has declined over time—down from 2.4 million in 1976 to 2.0 million in 1986. Total expenditures totaled a little over $12 billion in 1987.

The Historical Origins of SSI

To better understand the issues related to SSI today, it is important to look back in history at our earlier collective actions taken in response to the poverty of various groups in the American population.

Initial efforts to deal with the needs of the poor in early America were influenced a great deal by the poor laws in England. Three principles of welfare became established early in America's history and continued to dominate policies down through the years (Schottland, 1970):

1. Principal responsibility for providing and administering welfare programs was to reside with state governments and local communities.
2. Aid was to be available primarily to persons who were established residents of a community.
3. Relatives were to be held responsible for support of their needy kinsmen.

Over the years, however, one other major principle has dominated the development of welfare polices in the United States: Those in need who were unable to work were to be viewed much more favorably than those able to work—whether or not the latter had a job and irrespective of whether they could earn a living wage. In America, children, the disabled, and the aged have always received more favorable welfare treatment than the working poor. Just before passage of the Social Security Act in 1935, for example, over half the states had an old age assistance law, and all but two had programs for needy widowed mothers. While the benefits available under these programs were small, their very existence contrasted sharply with the lack of assistance provided by governments in the United States to the unemployed and their families.

The Great Depression changed the way the nation viewed many issues. Francis E. Townsend—a 60-year-old physician who had lost his job as assistant medical officer in Long Beach, California—was one of those galvanized into action by frustration and anger. His reform .idea was presented initially in a letter to the *Long Beach Press-Telegram* on September 20, 1933. When Townsend proposed a universal pension plan for the aged, the idea spread rapidly and grew dramatically into a nationwide movement of 2 million people organized in 7,000 clubs. Although the Townsend movement never achieved its objective of a flat pension for all Americans age 60 or over, the movement itself had a major political impact—paving the way for the more moderate proposals encompassed in the Social Security Act.

The new social security law provided, among other things, grants to the states for assistance to the *needy* aged, blind, and dependent children. But the act did not mandate participation by the states. Rather, it established minimal federal standards for receipt of the funds, keeping the responsibility for "welfare assistance" within the states and allowing them wide discretion in dealing with these issues. By 1938 all but one state (Virginia) had a qualified plan, and over 22 percent of Americans age 65 and over (2 million) were receiving "old age assistance."

The Social Security Act required that an individual's income and assets be considered in determining need (except for certain special exceptions) but did not specify a standard of living to be used by the states in establishing benefit levels. Consequently, each state developed its own definition of both the amount of resources to be used in determining eligibility and the levels of assistance to be provided to those meeting the eligibility requirements.

States generally defined assistance levels in terms of the number, kinds, and cost of certain specified consumption items included in various "assistance budgets." All states took food, clothing, shelter, fuel, and utility needs into account. Most states included items for personal care, nonprescription medicines, and household supplies. And many, but not all, states recognized "special needs," such as special dietary requirements or requirements for special transportation. One of the largest variations among (and within) states was the availability and cost of rental living units for assistance recipients.

Once a state established its full standards of need, financing considerations often played an important role. In some states, actual money payments to recipients were below the amount of determined need. This was a result of limits placed on state funds made available to meet these needs. Table 7–2 shows the differences among states in the largest and smallest monthly payments. In 1970s, the largest payments were more than twice the levels in the poorest paying states.

But differences in payment levels were only the beginning. Big differences in eligibility requirements, estate recovery, and relatives' financial responsibility also existed. Seventeen states required grown children, if they had the means, to help support needy parents. Some of these states held an applicant ineligible when a child was able to contribute to his support even though the child did not and would not do so (Schorr, 1960). More than one-half the states permitted the state or local public assistance agency to obtain unsecured or secured claims against the real or personal property of recipients. In extreme cases, claims on real estate might be exercised, even though a surviving spouse or dependent was still occupying the premises.

Perhaps the most complex and widespread differences in state practices related to eligibility requirements:

Table 7–2 Monthly Old Age Assistance Benefits in Various States, 1972

High Payment States	Monthly Benefit	Low Payment States	Monthly Benefit
Michigan	$224	Mississippi	$75
Kansas	203	South Carolina	80
Wisconsin	201	Missouri	85
Vermont	196	Georgia	91
Massachusetts	189	Kentucky	96
Minnesota	183	Maryland	96

Source: U.S. Department of Health, Education, and Welfare. *Public Assistance Programs: Standards for Basic Needs* (Washington, D.C.: HEW, July 1972).

> *Under the old system [of assistance to the aged, blind, and disabled],*
> *however, one State required an aged person to use up his last dollar*
> *before receiving relief; another allowed a cash reserve equal to 1*
> *month's cost of living; six limited cash reserves to $300 or $350. Even*
> *"liberal" New York denied relief to an old person with liquid*
> *resources greater than $500 and specified that this counted the face*
> *value of life insurance "for burial." One State barred relief to*
> *anyone whose house had a value more than $750 above that of*
> *"modest homes in the community," and the rules of some states*
> *required applicants to sell their car before obtaining help. [Burke*
> *and Burke, 1974]*

In addition to the above, there were also differences in residence and citizenship requirements and differences in the treatment of residents in institutions.

It would be wrong, however, to think that the new SSI program originated primarily as a federal response to the inadequacies of these state programs and dissatisfaction with the variation among them. The establishment of a federal program guaranteeing a minimum income to the aged, blind, and disabled came about in a much more indirect way. As we indicated above, Congress and presidents over the years have been sensitive to the problems of the "deserving poor." And they were concerned about the elderly, especially given the perception that old age politics had been a significant factor in past elections and could be important in future elections.

The federal response, however, was not to focus on public assistance programs to help the needy. Quite the opposite. Congress and the presidents turned to the social security programs that were not means-tested. By liberalizing these programs and thereby raising the living standards of all the elderly, they sought to reduce the role of the less popular "welfare" programs in the various states but help the poorest aged at the same time.

OASI became the cornerstone of those efforts. But over the years, as OASI was liberalized, a serious dilemma became apparent to increasing numbers of people. The problem with a strategy of combining in OASI the objectives of both social adequacy and individual equity was that neither could be satisfactorily carried out because of the inherent contradiction between the goals. As understanding and sensitivity to this dilemma grew, authoritative calls for dealing with welfare problems outside of OASI were voiced.

According to Vincent and Vee Burke (1974), in their book on welfare reform, SSI:

> . . . *solved a problem for key politicians—the defense of the social security wage-related "insurance" system against encroachments by welfare. . . . Social Security Commissioner Ball told the congressional tax writers [House Committee on Ways and Means] that there were limits as to how far "they could go in making the social security system itself a complete replacement for an income-determined or means-tested welfare benefit" without imperiling the wage-related and contributory nature of the system.*

When President Nixon initially proposed his welfare reform legislation in 1969, SSI as we know it today was not part of the package. Instead, Nixon recommended a new "national minimum standard" to determine the amount of aid for the aged, blind, and disabled needy. But the standard was to operate under the existing state programs and under the hodgepodge of state rules on eligibility and administration.

It was not until 1971, when the House Ways and Means Committee redrafted the Nixon proposal, that SSI was created. Although hailed by a few as a revolutionary development in income maintenance policy, SSI won congressional acceptance in 1972 with hardly any discussion and no floor debate. At the time, most of the attention of Congress was on welfare reform proposals for the nonaged—proposals that were hotly debated but never passed. Also, at the time, congressional attention was given to major changes on OASDI—that is, benefit liberalization and indexation (see pp. 140-141).

SSI in Practice

When SSI was legislated, its supporters argued that it would reduce many of the traditional problems associated with other programs to help the poor—that it would produce more efficient program administration, less stigma to recipients, and more adequate benefits using a national standard. During the first years of the program, the Social Security Administration had difficulty coping with the responsibilities and the additional workload suddenly thrust upon it as the chief administrator of the new federal program. In 1977, three years after its operations began, the SSI program was described by the U.S. Senate Committee on Finance staff as follows: "The early months of the program were characterized by near total administrative breakdown, primarily as a result of insufficient and inaccurate planning and inadequate resources. The crisis stage has passed, and steady improvements in administrative capabilities are taking place."

An analysis (Schieber, 1978) of the first year of program operations indicated that comparatively few people were moved out of poverty by SSI; but most of the individuals transferred onto SSI from the old state programs did experience an increase in real income levels. As intended, the greatest income increases accrued to persons who had been the poorest before SSI was implemented and people in certain states with very low old age assistance benefit levels.

A major concern arose almost immediately with regard to the low participation level of persons eligible for the SSI program. *Studies indicated that about 40 percent of the aged eligible for SSI do not participate in the program.* Research (e.g., Drazaga et al., 1982) investigating nonparticipation indicates that the two key reasons why many aged do not participate are lack of knowledge about it and stigma. The Drazaga study found that 45 percent of nonparticipants had not even heard of the SSI program. But large numbers of those who knew of SSI still did not participate, indicating a reluctance to become involved in a means-tested program.

That some people are reluctant to participate in a means-tested program is illustrated by a surprising occurrence arising out of a recent Social Security Administration (SSA) study of nonparticipation. After the study was completed, SSA sent a letter to about 300 of the nonparticipants in the study. The letter stated that the individuals might be eligible for SSI payments and encourged them to contact their local SSA office. But even personal letters from SSA did not substantially increase participation. Only about 10 out of the 300 individuals contacted by SSA subsequently applied for and received payments! Thus, while an early study by Tissue (1978) indicates that most SSI *participants* do not find SSI stigmatizing, there seems to be a significant minority of nonparticipants who do and, as a result, never apply.

Another major issue associated with SSI is the asset test. Studies show that most low-income elderly have few assets. Yet the asset test for SSI is so stringent that some people with inadequate incomes are denied assistance because of small amounts of savings and other resources. The National Commission on Social Security (1981) reported that in 1977 approximately 58 percent of applicants were denied SSI payments due to excess resources but had savings averaging only $2,834. This average slightly exceeded the asset test, but as the commission points out, a savings account of that amount "would earn annual interest of less than $250."

A recent study (Leavitt and Schulz, 1988) of the low-income elderly found that in 1984, about one-third of those eligible for SSI *based on income* were ineligible for benefits because they had *assets* exceeding SSI eligibility maximums. But the study then went on to show that many of these ineligible older persons and couples had minimal amounts of financial assets—leaving them economically impoverished. Over half had "money income producing assets" of less than $5,000 and nearly two-thirds had less than $10,000 worth of these assets.

The National Commission on Social Security recommended in its final report that the asset test be eliminated. It argued that this action would simplify program administration, while providing SSI to many more needy persons. Various other groups studying the program have made a number of other recommendations for improving SSI, but thus far Congress has not changed the program significantly from the original provisions legislated in 1972.

Chapter 7 Highlights

The programs discussed in this chapter complement the retirement pension programs providing the bulk of income for older persons no longer working. Some important points to remember:

1. The cost of health care services for the elderly is now a major item in the federal budget and is growing rapidly—many say too rapidly.
2. Medicare finances about 75 percent of the costs of hospitalization and 55 percent of doctors' bills for persons age 65 and older. Private insurance sponsored by previous employers or through individual purchases are used by many to meet growing out-of-pocket health care expenditures.
3. Families in the United States remain the major providers of long-term care to chronically ill elderly persons, providing about 70 percent of personal and physical care needs.
4. Because of strong opposition (in the past and currently) to government disability programs, the disability programs under social security determine participant eligibility using a very narrow and severe definition of disability that excludes many people with relatively severe incapacities.
5. SSI is a means-tested program designed to provide needy aged, blind, and disabled persons throughout the 50 states with a more adequate level of minimum income.

Suggested Readings

BURKHAUSER, RICHARD V., AND ROBERT H. HAVEMAN. *Disability and Work. The Economics of American Policy*. Baltimore: The Johns Hopkins University Press, 1982. A comprehensive discussion of disability issues.

CALLAHAN, JAMES J., AND STANLEY S. WALLACK. *Reforming the Long-Term Care System*. Lexington, Mass.: Lexington Books, 1981. This study explores major options for financing and organizing long-term care: block grants, national long-term care insurance, disability allowances, case management, and the social/health maintenance organization.

EASTAUGH, STEVEN R. *Financing Health Care*. Dover, Mass.: Auburn House, 1987. An up-to-date, comprehensive, but somewhat technical discussion of financing issues.

GRIMALDI, PAUL L. *Supplemental Security Income*. Washington, D.C.: American Enterprise Institute, 1980. A careful review and analysis of SSI issues.

SCHULZ, JAMES H. 1985. "To Old Folks with Love: Aged Income Maintenance in America." *The Gerontologist* 25 (October): 464–471. A discussion of evolving American income maintenance policies toward the aged and the debate over means-test versus universal programs.

SHANAS, ETHEL, AND G. L. MADDOX. "Health, Health Resources, and the Utilization of Care" and Karen Davis. "Health Policies and the Aged: Observations from the United States." In R. Binstock and E. Shanas, eds., *Handbook of Aging and the Social Sciences*, 2d. ed. New York: Van Nostrand Reinhold, 1984. Two articles that review research in the health and the aged area.

U.S. Senate Special Committee on Aging. *The Supplemental Security Income Program: A 10-Year Overview*. Washington, D.C.: U.S. Government Printing Office, 1984. A collection of papers reviewing past and current SSI operations, policies, and issues.

Chapter 8

WHAT ROLE FOR EMPLOYER-SPONSORED PENSIONS?

Pension plans set up by private employer or employee groups did not appear in the United States until the end of the 19th century. The first company pension plan was established by the American Express Company in 1875 but provided benefits only to permanently incapacitated workers over age 60 who had at least 20 years of service. Thereafter, plans were established in the railroad industry and by a few firms in other industries. However, a congressional study reports that such pension schemes "were by and large slow in developing and [that] there were probably fewer than ten plans in operation by the end of the 19th century" (U.S. House Committee on Education and Labor, 1972).

The Civil Service Retirement Act, enacted in 1920, provided pension coverage for the first time to federal civilian employees. A year later the implementation of private plans was encouraged by the Revenue Act of 1921[1]—legislation that exempted from income taxation both the income of pension and profit-sharing trusts and the employer contributions to these plans.

Although between 3 and 4 million workers were participating in private pension plans prior to the establishment of social security, coverage was concentrated in only a few older, big businesses; benefits were very limited; less than 15 percent of the work force was covered; and payments were made only if certain very stringent age and service requirements were met. Not until the 1940s and 1950s did private pensions mushroom. Private employer cov-

---

[1] Actually, "pensions" were not mentioned in the Internal Revenue Codes until 1926, but plans were treated like profit-sharing and stock bonus plans.

217

erage rose from about 4 million employees in the late 1930s to roughly 10 million in 1950, 20 million in 1960, 35 million in 1979, and 40 million in 1984.

Various factors have been cited as responsible for this rather dramatic increase in private pension coverage:

1. Continued industrialization of the American economy, together with a movement of workers out of agriculture, which stimulated increasing interest in alternatives other than the family for providing retirement security.
2. The introduction of private pensions by some employers as a way of creating employee loyalty and discouraging job shifting, since most early plans called for workers to lose their rights to the pension if they left the firm.
3. Wage freezes during World War II and the Korean War that encouraged fringe benefit growth in lieu of wages.
4. A series of favorable tax inducements offered by the federal government, beginning with the Revenue Acts of 1921, 1926, 1928, and 1942.[2]
5. A favorable decision by the Supreme Court in 1949 supporting the National Labor Relations Board's decision that pensions were a proper issue for collective bargaining.
6. The report of the Steel Industry Fact-Finding Committee in 1949, which included a recommendation that the industry had a social obligation to provide workers with pensions.
7. Growing recognition, especially by unions, of the inadequacy for most workers of social security benefits and the consequent need for supplementation.
8. The development of multiemployer pension plans—particularly in the construction, transportation, trade, and service industries.

In years past there have been numerous serious problems related to worker protection under private pensions. Workers lost benefit rights as a result of unemployment, company mergers, plant closures, or firm bankruptcies—often after long years of service. Many workers did not know about, or understand, the sometimes very stringent age and service requirements that had to be met to actually receive benefits. Pension reserve funds, supposedly put aside to guarantee benefits to workers, were some-

---

[2]Coming at a time of sharp personal and corporate federal income tax increases, the Revenue Act of 1942 (a) treated employer contributions to qualified pension plans as tax deductible, (b) excluded plan investment income from taxation, and (c) deferred taxes on participant beneficiaries until actually received in retirement. The net effect was to discourage plan formation but to encourage worker participation in existing plans.

times mismanaged, misused, or insufficient. Benefits, when actually paid, were often inadequate.

But plans have improved over the years—in part in reaction to new government regulations. This chapter focuses on the progress that has been made in developing private pensions into a viable institution for providing income in old age. The role that private pensions will ultimately play in the economics of aging depends on the resolution of a number of remaining issues: coverage, benefit protection, and the impact of inflation on pensions.

Who Is Covered?[3]

The total number of workers covered under private pension plans has increased from about 12 percent of the *private* wage and salary labor force in 1940 to 49 percent in 1984 (U.S. Bureau of the Census, 1987).[4] The major increases occurred in the 1940s and the 1950s, averaging about 12 percent and 7 percent a year, respectively. The growth rate slowed in the 1960s and 1970s to a little over 3 percent a year. In the early 1980s the pension coverage rate actually declined as a result of poor economic conditions and employment declines in industries with high rates of pension coverage.

In 1979, almost 50 million workers did *not* participate in a pension plan on their current job. Table 8–1 shows who these uncovered workers were. Some were younger, part-time, low-wage workers and/or individuals working for small businesses. Many others, however, were full-time workers with moderate or average earnings.[5]

Sixty percent of those employees not covered by pensions work in two industries: trade and service. *But the two key factors in understanding coverage are union status and the size of the employing firm.* Almost all workers without pension coverage are nonunion and work for firms with a relatively small number of employees.

---

[3] Some analysts use the term "pension covered" to refer to all workers in a company with a pension plan, whether or not all workers actually *participate* in the plan (see Andrews, 1985). In fact, many are not eligible to participate (e.g., part-time workers are often excluded). We use the term "pension-covered" to refer to workers participating in a pension plan.

[4] When employees in government-sponsored plans are added to the total, the coverage rate rises to 55 percent of the total wage and salary labor force in 1984.

[5] The most recent data on coverage (U.S. Bureau of the Census, 1987) do not use our coverage definition in the detailed tables published. We would not expect the conclusions of Table 8–1 to change, however, if more detailed tables were available.

Table 8–1   Which Workers Were Not Covered by Pension Plans in 1979?

In 1979, 49.4 million workers were not covered by a pension plan:

Sex:	54% of these were *men;* 46% were *women*
Hours Worked:	71% of these worked *full time;* 29% *part time*
Age:	68% were *over age 25* and 51% of noncovered were over 25 and had one or more years of service with their employer
Sector:	8.2 million were employed in the *public sector*
	38.1 million were wage and salary workers in the *private sector*

Of private sector noncovered wage and salary workers:

Industry:	78% *worked in three main industries:*
	• 32% in trade
	• 28% in service
	• 18% in manufacturing
Earnings:	30% earned less than $5,000 in 1978
	36% earned between $5,000 and $10,000 in 1978
	19% earned between $10,000 and $15,000 in 1978
	15% earned over $15,000 in 1978
Firm Size:	79% were in firms with fewer than 100 employees
	8% were in firms with 500 or more employees
Union Status:	About 90% were not members of unions

Source: Based on President's Commission on Pension Policy. *Coming of Age: Toward a National Retirement Income Policy.* Report of The Commission (Washington, D.C.: The Commission, 1981), Chart 6.

It has been especially difficult to extend private pension coverage to employees in small firms. Among the factors that have been cited for this difficulty are:

1. The high costs per employee of establishing and maintaining a private plan.
2. The lack of pressure in these companies from employees or unions.
3. The fact that small business firms are often relatively young and, on average, short-lived.
4. The fact that small employers tend to view pensions as personal costs.
5. The personality of the small business owner who tends to emphasize individual self-reliance in financial matters.
6. The often unstable and insecure financial status of many small businesses and competitive pressures for cost-cutting.

As a result of these and other factors, a sizable proportion of the American work force in small firms is not likely to be covered by traditional types of private pensions. There has been increasing interest, therefore, in a wider variety of employer-sponsored mechanisms to provide retirement income. Let us look more closely at these developments.

Alternative Types of Coverage

Private pension plans vary greatly. In fact, experts disagree over just what type of arrangement should be called a pension. In this section we look at three such controversial arrangements.

Profit-Sharing Plans

Most estimates of pension coverage include workers who are covered only by a **deferred profit-sharing plan.** Yet profit-sharing plans are very different from the more traditional private plans (described beginning on page 226). Contributions into profit-sharing plans vary with the amount of a particular company's profits and, consequently, are more directly tied to the vicissitudes of the economy. Hence, profit-sharing plans—less certain with regard to ultimate payout—are a more debatable way of providing retirement benefits for the millions of workers with *only* this type of coverage. In contrast, most pension plans make a pension promise that is generally independent of fluctuations in the economy or the prosperity of a particular business enterprise (as long as it stays in business).

The pension history at the Sears and Roebuck Company is a good example of the problems that can arise. In the 1970s, over 20 percent of Sears' common stock was owned by Sears employees through the company's profit-sharing plan. In the high company profit years of the 1960s and early 1970s, employees experienced huge investment gains through this plan. But later, when business conditions became poor, the price of Sears' stock fell dramatically, the potential gains from the plan declined dramatically, and workers reacted with anger. Sears responded by creating a regular pension plan to complement the profit-sharing plan, thereby giving more security to workers approaching retirement.

Today, millions of workers covered only by profit-sharing plans still face the issue raised by the Sears example: How secure is their retirement income promise? A study (Profit Sharing Research Foundation, 1978) of the largest profit-sharing plans reported, for example, that only 58 percent of the companies surveyed also had a regular private pension plan for their employees' retirement security.

Individual Retirement Accounts

One of the newer mechanisms created to deal with the need to extend private pension coverage is the **individual retirement account** (IRA). In a message to Congress on December 8, 1971, President Nixon first proposed that pension legislation be enacted that would contain saving incentives. The legislation was ultimately enacted as part of the private pension reform legislation (**ERISA**) that became law in September 1974.

President Nixon's proposal, and the subsequent law, permitted wage and salary earners to set up their own individual retirement plans (IRAs) *if they are not covered by any qualified pension plan.* In addition, the 1974 pension reform legislation liberalized existing limitations on contributions to retirement plans for the self-employed (called Keogh plans).

In 1981 Congress legislated a major liberalization of the IRA program. Originally, IRA participation was limited to employees without pension plan coverage. The legislation passed in 1981 allowed every worker to invest up to $2,000 yearly—even if covered by a group plan. The Tax Reform Act of 1986, however, rolled back the 1981 liberalization. Only workers in families without pensions and pension-covered workers with "adjusted gross income" below $25,000 (for individuals) and $40,000 (for families) retain the full tax deductibility of IRA contributions up to $2,000 per year. However, all IRA accounts, even those for individuals not eligible for IRA tax deductibility at time of pay-in, will continue to accumulate tax-deferred investment earnings on these accounts. As of June 30, 1987, there were about $302 billion worth of financial assets held in IRA accounts (EBRI, 1987).

When President Nixon proposed the original IRA legislation, he argued that it would encourage people to save and that public policy should reward and reinforce this type of activity. In transmitting the legislation, he said:

> *Self-reliance, prudence, and independence are qualities which our government should work to encourage among our people. These are also the qualities which are involved when a person chooses to invest in a retirement savings plan, setting aside money today so that he will have greater security tomorrow. In this respect pension plans are a direct expression of some of the best elements in the American character. Public policy should be designed to reward and reinforce these qualities.*

The President also argued that this legislation would be responsive to the inequity that existed between those people who were covered by private pensions and those who were not. People covered by private pensions receive favorable tax treatment because contributions made by the employer on their behalf are not taxable. These private pension contributions are only taxable at the time they are paid out, usually at much lower tax rates because retirement income levels are lower than those of work periods.

These were the President's two principal arguments in favor of such legislation. Other people have argued that by encouraging people to save for retirement individually, one allows them greater control over their investments; they can decide what they want to invest in and the amount of risk they want to take. In contrast, if you are a member of a private pension plan, you usually have nothing to say about the investment policy of the plan. Often, the gains of good investment accrue only to the employer. But if you are sophisticated about financial matters and economics, you might be able to do better on your own, especially if you are willing to take more risks.

And, finally, it has been argued that this approach is an alternative to social security and other social welfare programs that currently exist to help older people. Such tax incentives, it is argued, give people the option to build on their social security base and give them the freedom to choose how to do it. Attorney Peter J. Ferrara, a harsh critic of the current OASDI program, proposes (1986) a "super IRA" scheme. He would allow individuals to redirect a major part of the payments going into social security into private retirement accounts.[6]

Research to date shows that under the current IRA program, the proportion of lower-paid workers who take advantage of this opportunity for tax-sheltered saving is much smaller than that of more highly paid persons. The fear that such tax-exemption proposals would turn into tax loopholes for higher-income people was the principal argument voiced in Congress against the legislation when it was proposed and continues to be an argument made today, based on the actual experience.

Thrift Plans

Another mechanism that helps workers prepare for retirement is the company thrift or savings plan. The most common and most important of these plans are designed to take advantage of the special tax advantages available under various sections of the Internal Revenue Code. Although there have been a number of

---

[6] For a critique of the "super IRA" approach, see Meyer (1987).

changes over recent years in the tax law in this area, perhaps the most important was the Revenue Act of 1978, which added section 401(k) to the tax codes.[7] Section 401(k) permits employees to make *tax-deferred* contributions to an employer-sponsored plan. Prior to this provision, such contributions could only be made by workers using money upon which federal income taxes had been paid. Section 401(k) stimulated a major expansion of these types of plans.

While some plans under section 401(k) are profit sharing or are voluntary employee contribution plans with no employer contribution, the vast majority are "savings plans." In savings plans the company *matches* some proportion of the employee's contribution.

A 1986 Bankers Trust study (1987) of 242 plans in *large* companies reported the following characteristics of such plans:

1. The maximum contribution rate is typically 5 to 6 percent of earnings.
2. Companies generally match between 50 and 100 percent of employee contributions, but employees can usually contribute additional amounts over and above the matched amount.
3. All employees usually have access, while employed, to some portion of their account accumulation through loan provisions, "hardship" withdrawal options, or conditional withdrawal provisions.

Thrift plans (and also profit-sharing plans) are not necessarily alternatives to a regular pension plan. Most companies with such plans also provide a pension plan for employees. Some companies, however, just have thrift plans.[8]

Future Coverage

Probably the most important legislation affecting the availability of private pension benefits was the Employee Retirement Income Security Act of 1974 (ERISA). ERISA extensively regulated the provision of many types of private pension benefits in an attempt to make sure promised benefits were actually paid (see pages 235–236). ERISA did not obligate, however, any employer without a pension plan to establish one. Thus, ERISA contained no provision beyond the tax incentives provided in the federal tax laws to

---

[7] Plans under Section 401(k) originated many years before 1978 were "frozen" in 1974, and "unfrozen" in 1978.

[8] Not discussed are Tax Reduction Act Stock Ownership Plans (TRASOPs) that allow companies to make contributions for employees, primarily in the company's stock.

encourage the expansion of existing private plan coverage. Rather, the principal focus of ERISA was on expanding the supervision and regulation of private plans by the federal government and creating tax-exempt IRAs.

The expansion of regulation costs money. In addition to the costs to taxpayers for the federal supervisory agencies and their staffs, considerable regulatory costs are imposed on the businesses with pension funds. These costs arise from the necessity of providing information to the government in order for it to carry out its various supervisory roles. Because of the complexity of the regulations, businesses must often either develop staff or hire outside consultants to provide them with the expertise necessary to ensure compliance with ERISA and other pension-related laws. Pension management has become big business in the United States.

Businesses have complained strongly before congressional committees about both the high costs of reporting required information to the government and the costs of simply understanding the law. Some companies have terminated their plans because of the increased administrative burdens and costs. Some pension experts say that employers today without plans are increasingly reluctant to start new ones, especially plans regulated by ERISA.

Thus, when we look at the coverage trend over the last couple of decades, we see a slowing down in coverage beginning prior to ERISA. This slowdown results primarily from the fact that almost all the workers in large, relatively affluent corporations have become covered. Noncoverage is now concentrated among nonunion, small employer groups (see Table 8–1). A profile of these small employers would include the business proprietors found on any typical small town main street or any large city neighborhood shopping center: the small retailer, the local restaurant, the service station, repair services, the barber and beauty shop, the doctor and dentist, the auto dealer, and many, many more small employers of wage and salary workers. The profile would likewise include partnership operations such as law firms, consulting engineers, accounting firms, real estate firms, and small manufacturing plants operated as corporations or by self-employed owners.

As our discussion below on **vesting** emphasizes, workers covered by a plan do not always receive a benefit. Some employees do not work long enough to achieve vesting. Others receive only a lump-sum payout when they leave their job. And still others who are eligible for very small benefits (less than $3,500 per year in 1984) may also receive a cashed-out lump sum. ERISA permits employers to do this in order to eliminate the administrative costs arising from keeping track of these small benefits and their recipients.

Currently, about 25 percent of the elderly population receive some income from private or government employee pensions (using the broadest definition of this income source); among recent retirees, however, the proportion is much higher—over half (Snyder, 1986).

Legislation passed by Congress in recent years has encouraged the development of a variety of options: "simplified pension plans" (the Revenue Act of 1978), employee stock option plans (ESOPS), and IRAs. We will have to wait and see what impact this new legislation has on the coverage problem. In the meantime, large numbers of workers without private coverage will continue to rely primarily on their social security benefits for retirement protection.

Private Plan Characteristics[9]

It is difficult to generalize about the provisions of private pension plans because of the large number of different plans with widely varying characteristics. There are close to one million corporate pension plans in the United States. These can be generally divided into *single employer* and *multiemployer* plans. Multiemployer plans usually require employers to make contributions into a central fund (typically a specified percent of payroll or cents-per-hour-worked), and employees can qualify for benefits from the fund by meeting eligibility requirements through employment in the various firms participating in the program. Reciprocity agreements among some of these multiemployer plans (and a few single employer plans) allow workers to move between plans and still accumulate pension credits. Another important difference between the two types of plans is in their administration. Single employer plans are generally managed by the employer alone; multiemployer plans are almost invariably administered by a group of trustees, with equal representation from labor and management (in accordance with terms of the federal Taft-Hartley Act).

Another common way of classifying private plans is to distinguish between *contributory* and *noncontributory* plans. Contributory plans require that the employee pay part of the cost, whereas noncontributory plans (typically government-sponsored) are financed solely by the employer. In the United States, most covered

---

[9]A highly technical but important aspect of private plans is pension plan integration, the coordination of employer-sponsored benefits with social security. We mention these plan provisions only briefly below. Interested readers are encouraged to read Schulz and Leavitt (1983) for more information.

workers (80 percent) participate in noncontributory plans—in part because employers' contributions are tax free under current laws, while employees' contributions (unless sheltered by special arrangements) are not. Also, noncontributory plans do not require the employer to put aside money for each worker at the time benefit rights accrue. This means that employers have more flexibility in funding and administration. For example, they can use actuarial assumptions that take into account employee turnover (reducing current pension expenses) and provide for funding of the plan over an extended period of years (see page 74).

Multiemployer plans cover 17 percent of all private sector workers with private pension coverage (U.S. Senate Special Committee on Aging, 1987). These plans are usually the result of bargaining between unions and management. They are concentrated in particular industries such as mining, construction, trade, transportation, and service; in these industries they affect more than 50 percent of all pension-covered workers, primarily in unionized industries.

In surveying the specific provisions of various pension plans, four key characteristics are generally considered most important: the benefit formulas, vesting and portability requirements, the availability of survivors' benefits, and early retirement options.

Benefit Determination

While there is a great deal of variation among private plans in the way benefits are calculated, three major types can be identified:

Defined benefit plans:

1. *Dollar amount times service*—benefits are determined by multiplying a specified dollar amount by the number of years of employed service credited under the plan.
2. *Combined service/earnings formulas*—benefits are based on (a) the employee's earnings over a specified period of employment (e.g., career, high five of the last ten, or last ten years of earnings) and (b) years of service.

Defined contribution plans:[10]

3. Money-purchase arrangements—periodic *contributions* are set aside according to a predetermined, or agreed upon, formula (usually a percent of earnings). Pensions are paid out

---

[10] Deferred profit-sharing plans are often listed as defined contribution plans. For the reasons given previously, we exclude them.

based on the accumulated funds (contributions plus investment income) in individual employee accounts.

The overwhelming proportion of workers covered by single employer plans belong to plans that use defined benefit formulas that
base benefits on earnings. In contrast, only a small proportion of
workers under multiemployer plans participate in plans using
earnings-based formulas. Instead, most multiemployer plans use
the "dollar amount times service" formula. Defined contribution
plans are most common in small businesses and nonprofit organizations and as *supplements* to defined benefit plans.

In recent years, however, an increasing number of new pension
plans have used the defined contribution approach. Since defined
contribution plans have been more popular with small employers,
and since most new plans are small, this is not a surprising
development. Some benefit experts have speculated, however, that
rising regulatory and financing issues associated with defined
benefit plans are causing some employers to rethink pension
design and causing them to view defined contribution more favorably. However, a 1983 decision by the Supreme Court, ruling
invalid the practice in certain defined contribution plans of providing women (who on average have longer life expectancies) with
lower benefits, may discourage some adoptions. A divided Court
held that this practice by some employers violated the law against
sex discrimination.

Another important trend has been a shift to basing benefits on
earnings just prior to retirement. The major advantage of this type
of formula is a built-in adjustment for inflation prior to retirement,
since earnings over time are usually adjusted upward for cost-of-
living increases.

An important feature of many plans is the type of mechanism
used to integrate private pensions with social security. Some plans
deduct (typically) 50 percent of the social security benefit from the
amount computed according to the private plan formula. Other
plans use a formula that provides higher benefits on earnings above
a certain specified amount, often the social security maximum
earnings ceiling.

Benefit Levels

A study (Schulz et al., 1982) of pension benefit levels in 1979
estimated the pensions received by long-service employees retiring in various industries. **Median** private pension **replacement
rates** for workers with 30 years of service and average earnings

were 27 percent for men and 34 percent for women. The rates varied from a low of 23 percent for men and women in the service industry to a high of 35 percent for women in manufacturing (Table 8–2).

More recent estimates by the Bureau of Labor Statistics are available for 1983 (Bell and Marcloy, 1987). Replacement rates were estimated in this study for 187 private plans in medium and large companies. Replacement rates were similar to the earlier Schulz study, ranging from 26 to 32 percent. Industry differences were not published, but differences by earnings level and category of worker (professional, clerical, or production) were provided. Replacement rates, for example, were found to be lower for production workers (relative to other categories) at the higher earnings levels.

Vesting and Portability Requirements

Vesting and **portability** are related pension concepts but are not identical. Vesting refers to the provision in pension plans that guarantees that those covered by the plan will receive all or part of the benefit that they have earned (i.e., accrued), whether or not they are working under the plan at the time of their retirement. Through vesting, the pension rights of otherwise qualified workers are protected—whether they are discharged, are furloughed, or quit voluntarily. Prior to ERISA, vesting provisions were common but required typically 20 to 30 years of service. Sometimes vesting

Table 8–2 1979 Median Private Pension Benefit and Relacement Rates[a] for a Hypothetical Worker with 30 Years of Service, by Sex and Industry

	Women		Men	
Industry[b]	Benefit	Replacement Rate	Benefit	Replacement Rate
Manufacturing	$3,284	35%	$4,999	27%
Transportation, Communications, and Utilities	4,432	34	6,935	34
Trade	1,794	26	4,097	24
Finance, Insurance, and Real Estate	2,647	26	5,605	30
Service	1,792	23	3,609	23

Source: James H. Schulz, T. D. Leavitt, L. Kelly, and J. Strate, *Private Pension Benefits in the 1970s* (Bryn Mawr, Pa.: McCahan Foundation for Research in Economic Security, 1982), Table 7.
[a]Rates of estimated median benefit to average earnings in the year before retirement.
[b]The mining and construction industries are omitted because of small sample size.

was nonexistent. Where vesting was available, eligibility conditions varied greatly, and many workers lost their pension rights—sometimes after long years of service and sometimes just prior to retirement. ERISA requires all plans covered by the law to provide minimum vested benefits meeting one of three alternative standards. In fact, most companies adopted the same option: vesting of 100 percent of accrued benefits after 10 years of service. Hence, those workers who changed jobs before accumulating 10 years of service received no pension credits.

The Tax Reform Act of 1986 mandated more rapid vesting. *Full vesting now begins at the end of five years of employment for most workers.* Companies, however, have the option of using an alternative vesting schedule—vesting 20 percent of the benefit after three years and increasing the vested amount to reach 100 percent at the end of seven years.[11] Thus the new law goes a long way toward eliminating the loss of pension credits as a result of job change.

A very serious problem remains, however, in connection with vesting. Vested benefits left in a pension plan after a worker voluntarily or involuntarily leaves the firm are not adjusted upward if the pension plan's formula for continuing workers is changed either to compensate for inflation or to provide a higher level of real benefits.[12]

"Portability" of pension rights permits employees to transfer the money value of these rights into another plan. Unfortunately, although portability has received a lot of public attention over the years (and is often confused with vesting), the administrative, financial, and actuarial complexities of setting up such arrangements have discouraged any significant action in this area. The multiemployer plan, however, reduces the problems associated with job change by introducing limited portability (i.e., within the boundaries of the plan) through a centralized pension fund.

The 1974 pension reform law (ERISA) permits a separated employee to transfer tax free the value of a vested benefit into an IRA permitted by the plan, or to another plan, if permitted by both plans. In fact, an employer with a noncontributory plan has a positive financial incentive not to agree to this transfer, since he can earn interest or dividends on any "funded" money he keeps and need not pass on any of these earnings to the former employee.

---

[11] Multiemployer plans are still allowed to use 10-year vesting.

[12] Also, vested benefits left in plans with earnings-related formulas do not reflect the rise in earnings that would occur if the worker remained employed by the firm. See the additional discussion of this problem in Chapter 9, page 258.

Survivors' Benefits

The survivor benefits of private plans are of four types:

1. *Joint and survivor annuity.* Regular payments are made during the combined lifetimes of retiree and spouse. It is typically calculated by reducing (15 to 20 percent) the worker's benefit to pay for the additional costs of survivor protection. Survivor benefits are typically 50 to 75 percent of the worker's benefit amount.
2. *Early survivor annuity.* This is a regular payment for survivors of workers who die before retirement, elected by the employee while working and paid for through reduced benefits.
3. *Preretirement automatic death benefit.* This benefit (like number 2 above) is provided by the employer to the survivors of those workers who die before retirement. The key difference is that the protection is provided automatically by the employer, with no elective reduction in the worker's accrued retirement benefits.
4. *Postretirement automatic death benefit.* This benefit is also automatic but is typically a small lump-sum amount, provided to help meet immediate burial expenses.

There is great variation in the provisions various private companies have made for dealing with problems arising from the death of an employee; private pensions are just one of a number of mechanisms. Some employers also provide financial assistance to employees' survivors through group life insurance and profit-sharing plans.

Death protection through private pensions was not a high priority item in the early years of pension planning. Consequently, until recently, some pension plans made little or no provision for the survivors of workers. In 1974, before ERISA became effective, for example, about 20 percent of the workers covered by defined benefit plans were in plans with no survivor provisions of any kind. The most common type of survivor benefit in those private plans that did have provisions was the joint and survivor annuity.

Federal pension law now mandates that all pension plans subject to ERISA provide any worker with vested benefits, at a minimum, an opportunity to elect a joint and survivor option. Originally under ERISA, only participants eligible for early retirement or age 55 (whichever was later) could elect such coverage. Now this option must be offered at *all* ages. The cost of this option, however, may be imposed on the worker through reduced pension benefits.

Even though ERISA requires employers to *offer* survivor benefits, the decision to provide these benefits legally rests with the worker alone. In prior years some workers, without the knowledge of their spouse, did not elect the extra protection; in other cases, the worker and spouse together decided to opt for the bigger retirement benefit, gambling (for that is what it is) that the survivor benefit won't be needed. A study done for the U.S. Department of Labor, for example, found that in 1978 only 38 percent of married workers (both men and women) elected one of the survivor benefit options available from their private plan (Myers, 1982).

The Retirement Equity Act of 1984 sought to deal more effectively with this issue. Under the provisions of this law, it is necessary (regarding the survivor option) to secure *a spouse's consent in writing*—notarized or witnessed by a representative of the plan—to the worker's rejection of the survivor option.

The existing data indicate that the most important means of providing survivor protection through private pensions continues to be the joint and survivor option, typically at the cost of a lower benefit paid to the retiring worker (which discourages its election). Survivor benefits provided over and above the joint and survivor option are not widespread, are of generally limited duration, and are often of small magnitude. Some firms do provide life insurance and/or supplemental plans which add to the level of benefits provided, but, nevertheless, current benefits often do not reflect the needs of employees and their survivors.

Early Retirement Options

During the past two decades we have witnessed a tremendous push toward early retirement. Increasing numbers of workers are retiring early under social security. Federal employees can retire on full benefits at age 55 with 30 years of service; in fact, the President's Commission on Pension Policy reported that 59 percent of retiring male civil service employees (fiscal 1978) were age 60 or younger. Most state and local government employee plans also have very liberal retirement provisions; early retirement is usually possible after 20 to 30 years of service—often as early as age 50 or 55.

Less well known are the retirement options provided under private pension plans. The generous provisions of the big plans—for example, in the auto industry—are well known. In the rubber and metal industries, special "early retirement benefits" supplement regular pension benefits until the plan's normal retirement age or until age 65, when the retiree becomes eligible for unreduced social security benefits.

Few data are published on the hundreds of thousands of plans in other industries. A study of pension plans by the U.S. Bureau of Labor Statistics (1980), however, found that more than half of covered workers were eligible to receive normal retirement benefits before age 65. And almost a third were eligible for normal benefits at age 60 or earlier!

Another study of defined benefit plans covering about 23 million workers in 1974 (Schulz et al., 1980) shows that 70 percent of these workers were eligible for early retirement benefits at age 60 (provided service requirements, if any, were met). Over half could retire as early as age 55, and 15 percent were in plans with even earlier eligibility ages (or no age requirement at all).

But these numbers do not tell the whole story. More than 90 percent of all workers covered by private pensions are in plans having early retirement options. When a worker retires early—that is, before the "normal" retirement age—the benefit is usually reduced. A large number of employers, however, encourage their employees to retire early by absorbing some of the costs of paying pensions over a longer period of time. Thus, while some plans reduce benefits by the full **actuarial** discount, many plans, in effect, give actuarial bonuses to workers who retire early.

The study of defined benefit plans in 1974 indicated that powerful economic incentives are provided in many plans. For example, about 7 million workers in 1974 were covered by plans permitting their retirement at age 60 with less than a full actuarial reduction in benefits.

More recently, Kotlikoff and Wise (1985), using data describing plans in 1979, found that many contained substantial incentives designed to encourage retirement at certain early ages. If a worker delayed retirement beyond these earlier ages, it was "not unusual for the reduction in pension benefit accrual after these retirement ages to equal the equivalent of a 30 percent reduction in wage earnings."

Thus, we see that social security today is probably not the principal pension force pushing workers into retirement. Certainly, social security income, when it becomes available, encourages workers to retire. But for many workers it is military, federal, state/local, or private plans that make it attractive to retire at increasingly early ages.

Inflation Protection[13]

What happens to the value of a private pension when inflation occurs? It is appropriate to divide the answer to that question into

---

[13] See also the discussion in Chapter 9, page 258.

two parts: the postretirement versus the preretirement period. Almost no employer-sponsored plan in the private sector *automatically* adjusts the pensions being paid in retirement for increases in the cost of living. Of course, social security pensions and federal military and civilian pensions are automatically adjusted. And most state/local government employee plans adjust automatically but with "caps" on the adjustment process (see page 248).

Many private companies adjust benefits going to retirees on an ad hoc basis. A study by Donald Schmitt (1984), using data from the Bureau of Labor Statistics on medium and large-size firms, found that 40 percent of *active* workers were in pension plans that provided some sort of increase *to retirees in these plans* during the 1978 to 1981 period. However, the study found that the increases were usually less than half the rise in the consumer price index over the same period.

If we look at the preretirement years, the situation is very different. Most defined benefit plans deliberately base benefits on some measure of average earnings in *the final years of employment*. These earnings are generally higher, not only because of seniority but because earnings tend to change over time in response to inflation. Thus, plans with "final earnings" measures have a built-in automatic mechanism to adjust for inflation, to the extent that a worker's wage adjustments keep up with inflation.

The situation is different for employees covered by defined contribution plans. Benefits from these plans are based on contributions, not earnings. Employee protection from inflation depends on the investment performance of the funds in the individual's account and are thus, in part, dependent on the investment options provided by the plan and the financial knowledge of the person (usually the employee) selecting the type of investment fund into which the monies will go. Historically, few types of financial securities have closely tracked the pattern of inflation. The result is significant inflation risk for those covered by defined contribution plans.

Another major problem that we discussed earlier is the fact that the vested benefits of employees who change jobs are not protected from inflation. The result is that many workers find their vested pensions worth very little (in real dollar terms) when they reach retirement.

Private Pension Regulation

Benefit formulas, vesting, survivors' provisions, and early retirement options are four of the most important aspects of private pensions. Another area of major concern is the danger of lost pension rights as a result of inadequate pension funding, misuse of pension funds, or the termination of plans because of plant closures, bankruptcy, or other reasons.

In August 1978 the Professional Drivers Council, a dissident Teamsters union group, charged that millions of dollars were being drained from the union's pension funds because of mismanagement and corrupt practices. The dissident group claimed that, among other abuses, multimillion-dollar loans had been made to individuals and groups with questionable backgrounds or to entities running deficits when the loans were made (BNA, 21 August 1978). That same month a U.S. district court ruled that a $20 million loan by pension trustees of Teamsters' Local 281 violated ERISA regulations; the money was loaned to finance a thousand-plus room hotel and gambling casino in Las Vegas. Earlier, a reform group called Miners for Democracy acted to displace the United Mine Workers' leadership—charged with illegal financial transactions and the use of union pension funds for personal gain. In 1985 a jury awarded $1.2 million to the Iron Workers Local 272 in Florida. The award was based on charges of fraud and negligence brought against the former trustees of the pension fund and the insurance consultant they used. In the trial it was brought out that the former trustees had purchased whole life insurance policies recommended by a consultant who had been convicted of grand larceny and stock manipulation and whose insurance license had been suspended (BNA, 20 January 1986).

A great deal of attention has been given to problems related to managing pension funds safely and wisely. Over the years there have been a number of investigating groups and legislative committees concerned about the adequacy of our laws in this area. Congressional concern for the protection of employee benefit funds resulted in the enactment of the Welfare and Pension Plan Disclosure Act in 1959 but placed primary responsibility for policing the plans on the participants themselves. As the problems grew, Congress saw that much more comprehensive and stronger regulatory supervision was needed. The Employee Retirement Income Security Act (ERISA), passed in 1974, set up a much more comprehensive set of safeguards—establishing participation, vesting, funding standards, plan termination insurance, and extensive reporting and disclosure requirements.

The following are the major provisions of ERISA:

1. Minimum vesting standards were established.
2. Plan termination insurance was established.

3. Funding standards were established, and **fiduciary standards** were strengthened.
4. Certain employees were permitted to establish "individual retirement accounts" (with contributions and returns tax-deferred).
5. Disclosure regulations were established, permitting participants to request once each year a statement from the plan administrator of total accrued benefits, both vested and non-vested, and the earliest date on which nonvested benefits will become nonforfeitable.
6. The Social Security Administration was directed to receive reports from employers (through the Treasury Department) of vested benefits due separated workers; Social Security notifies employees of all vested pension rights at the time they apply for social security.
7. Conditional on the consent and cooperation of their employers, employees were permitted to transfer, upon job separation, their vested pension rights on a tax-free basis from one plan to another; or the employee may transfer the funds to an individual retirement account.

Passed by both houses of Congress by wide vote margins, ERISA is an attempt to provide greater certainty that private pension promises will be fulfilled. But the legislation does not deal with all private pension problems. Critics were quick to cite the limitation of the legislation (as they saw them):

1. Coverage was not mandated.
2. State and local government pension plans were excluded from the law.
3. The lack of strong "portability" provisions was criticized as reducing labor mobility, and for those who move, there is a reduction in the value of pension rights relative to what the value would be if they did not change jobs.
4. Survivors' provisions were weak.
5. No provision was made for **indexing** pensions.

While the drafters of the 1974 private pension legislation admitted in debate that the legislation did not deal with all problems, they argued that it was a major step forward. The legislation itself called for further study of many of the unresolved issues. And in the years that followed, the law has been modified in a number of important ways. [14]

---

[14] Four major changes are discussed elsewhere in the chapter. They include: (a) mandated earlier vesting, (b) changes in survivor provisions and coverage requirements, (c) revised procedures for plan termination insurance, and (d) IRA liberalization and then cutbacks in these liberalization provisions.

Financing Private Pensions

In 1963 the Studebaker Corporation, a small producer of automobiles, closed its operations in the United States. The company had established a pension plan 14 years before that ultimately covered about 11,000 employees. When the company closed its South Bend, Indiana, plant, the pension fund contained assets worth $24 million. But these assets were insufficient to meet all the pension rights that had been accumulated. The result: About 4,500 workers received an average of only $600 apiece, or 15 percent of the value of their rights. And those workers who had accumulated years of service but had not achieved pension-vesting status got nothing.

Because of the number of workers affected and the prominence of the auto industry, the Studebaker case immediately became a favorite example in the days before ERISA, cited by those persons calling for private pension reform. Studebaker and numerous other defaults illustrate the major goal—but also the major hazard—of private pension financing: to ensure that there are adequate funds so that promised benefits are, in fact, paid.

Prior to ERISA, most private plans financed pensions on a reserve basis, with a few operating on a partial or full pay-as-you-go basis. Now all plans covered by the 1974 act are required to meet minimum funding standards.

In reviewing financing practices it is useful to group plans into three categories: (1) noninsured or trusteed plans, (2) insured plans, and (3) multiemployer plans. The majority of plans are noninsured or trusteed plans whose reserves are either self-administered by the individual company or administered by a trustee, in most cases commercial banks. Significantly, the great bulk of these reserves are administered by only about 25 banks. Insured plans are administered by various insurance companies. Multiemployer funds, the result of union collective bargaining, are run jointly by the union and employer trustees.

Almost all private plans are financed entirely by the employer. A major reason for the prevalence of noncontributory plans is that employee contributions from earnings are subject, with certain exceptions, to federal income taxes. In contrast, the money employers put into a **qualified pension** fund is deductible for tax purposes when made, and taxation on plan earnings is deferred until drawn as benefits. In addition, employee contributions greatly complicate the administration of a plan—requiring the establishment of a pension account for each worker and policies regulating these accounts. And, as we indicated earlier, noncontributory plans usually reduce employer pension costs during the early years (see page 227).

Although most firms have established reserve funds to be built up over the years as their pension liabilities grow, many of the pension promises made under the plans remain in jeopardy as a result of "past service credits." When new plans are established or old plans liberalized, the usual practice is to give workers full pension credits for their years of work prior to the plan's establishment or liberalization. While the pension liabilities for these past service credits accrue immediately, employers usually adopt a payment schedule for funding these liabilities that in the past extended over a 10- to 40-year period (and sometimes longer). As long as unfunded liability remains, a plan that terminates will be unable to pay all of its promised future pension benefits. This is what happened in the Studebaker case. And, in fact, many plans have terminated over the years—with a resultant loss of pension benefits to thousands of workers.

The 1981 funding status of large firms in the United States has been studied by the pension consulting firm of Johnson and Higgins (1981). The analysis covered 386 of the Fortune 500 industrial corporations and 168 of the largest 200 corporations in banking, retailing, transportation, and utilities. There was wide variation in funding status among companies, but overall assets covered about 90 percent of plan liabilities. Some particular plans, however, still had sizable unfunded liabilities. Munnell (1982b) screened Standard and Poor's 1980 data on 6,000 companies in order to isolate those companies with unfunded pension liabilities in excess of 30 percent of their net worth. Munnell identified 86 firms, with Chrysler Corporation at the top of the list with unfunded liabilities of $1.2 billion and International Harvester with $1.1 billion.

In recent years, we have witnessed a dramatic increase in pension plan terminations by large companies. These terminations have been motivated by two very different sets of circumstances: on the one hand, there were the *problems* of plans in economically distressed companies and, on the other, there were the opportunities arising out of overfunded plans in some companies—which sought to use this unexpected pension wealth for other corporate purposes. Falling into the first category, for example, were the January 1987 terminations of three LTV Corporation steelworker plans with unfunded liabilities exceeding $2.1 billion![15] In contrast,

---

[15] As of December 1987, the LTV Corporations and the PBGC were locked in a legal battle over who should assume responsibility for the plans' liabilities.

there were nearly 500 overfunded terminations in 1985 alone and excess plan liabilities in termination between 1980 and October 1986 of over $33 billion (Leavitt, 1986).

What happens to workers when a plan terminates without adequate funds or excess funds?

Terminations with Inadequate Funding

Number 10 on Munnell's list of 86 companies was Braniff Airlines. In the spring of 1982 Braniff shut down. Even before Braniff filed for bankruptcy, there were dramatic reductions in the number of employees working for the company. A few years before the shutdown about 15,000 employees were working for Braniff (in its heyday). Just before filing for bankruptcy, only 9,500 employees were left. Thus, a significant number of people had left Braniff—were forced to leave Braniff—in most cases prior to the bankruptcy. What happened to the pension rights of these particular employees? And after Braniff filed for bankruptcy and terminated its pension plans, what happened to the workers still employed who were covered by the plan and had expected to receive benefits?

One thing is certain. Those people who had fewer than 10 years of service working for Braniff Airlines—whether they had left before the bankruptcy or whether they were working at the point of bankruptcy filing—got nothing. However, ERISA, at the time, required that employees with more than 10 years of service, which was the most popular alternative of the three vesting options available at the time, receive benefits when they retire.

Those former Braniff employees retired and receiving pensions and those eligible for vested benefits were protected by the Pension Benefit Guarantee Corporation (PBGC). This government organization, part of the Labor Department, was set up under ERISA to guarantee (within limits[16]) the continued payment of benefits to retired workers and the future payment of benefits to vested workers. When a plan terminates without sufficient funds to meet these obligations, the PBGC takes over the plan and assumes responsibility for paying the benefits up to the guarantee limit. Each company or union with a plan covered by ERISA must make contributions (insurance premiums) to the PBGC to cover the costs of providing this insurance protection.

Terminations by Overfunded Plans

In recent years there has been a dramatic increase in the number of **overfunded** defined benefit plans terminating voluntarily. Upon

---

[16]The maximum monthly benefit guaranteed by the PBGC was $1,909.09 in 1988.

termination there has been a reversion of large sums of money to the sponsoring company. Getting these funds to use for other purposes has often been the primary motivation for these plan terminations. In recent years, these companies have been able to capture, on average, nearly 50 percent of the assets in these terminated plans through this termination/asset reversion process.

A major contributing factor to this situation was the existence of high interest rates in the early 1980s, followed by a sharply rising stock market before mid-1987. Investment performance widely exceeded the conservative assumptions of pension plan actuaries, resulting in the claimed overfunding of many plans (using standard actuarial evaluation practices).

A study at the Brandeis University Policy Center on Aging (Leavitt, 1986) found that overfunded terminations up to 1986 had not resulted in immediate harm to plan participants. However, the study argued that in the longer run, many employees are likely to be adversely affected by (1) some terminated plans not being replaced by another plan, (2) replacement by less generous or more risky (e.g., profit-sharing) plans, and (3) the weakened funding situation of some new plans.

Some critics have also argued that any excess assets belong to plan participants and beneficiaries, based on the idea that pension contributions by employers are deferred compensation. Employers usually respond that since they are meeting their legal obligations in providing promised benefits, there is no reason for them not to recover these assets.

What is clear in this debate is that current law does not prohibit employer terminations for any purpose; however, in an attempt to reduce this practice, the Tax Reform Act of 1986 did institute a 10 percent excise tax on these reversions.

The Pension Benefit Guaranty Corporation[17]

As we discussed above, Congress created the Pension Benefit Guaranty Corporation (PBGC) to protect workers if inadequately funded plans terminate. PBGC was there to step in when the poor economic conditions of the late 1970s and the 1980s caused plan terminations to increase. In fiscal 1986, for example, there were 6,829 plan terminations. Most terminating plans can meet their obligations; some cannot. By 1986, the PBGC had become the

---

[17] Because of space and the complexity of the issues, we do not discuss in this section a number of major problems that have also arisen in connection with insuring *multiemployer* plans.

trustee of over 1,300 plans with benefits owed to over 91,000 workers.

In 1983, PBGC told Congress that the agency would run out of funds unless Congress increased the premium on single-employer plans from its then current level of $2.60 per participant. Its chairman stated that due to underfunded terminating plans, PBGC liabilities were far higher than had ever been anticipated. This statement shocked both the Congress and the business community paying the premiums, since this was the first time the agency had publicly revealed its severe financial problems.

"A major cause of the PBGC's problems was the ease with which economically viable companies could terminate underfunded plans and dump their pension liabilities on the termination insurance program" (U.S. Senate Special Committee on Aging, 1987). By 1987, the PBGC had a deficit of nearly $4 billion, representing the difference between its assets and the value of its future liabilities.

The possibility of rapidly escalating premiums caused many employers to call for changes in the reinsurance program. They argued that companies with fully funded plans are, in effect, subsidizing unfunded plans as a result of legal loopholes that allow companies to dump their unfunded pension liabilities on the PBGC.

A major debate over these issues took place for several years, primarily in committees of the Congress. In April of 1986, legislation was finally passed that made it more difficult for employers to pass on unfunded plan liabilities to the PBGC.[18] The key feature of the new law is to distinguish between *standard* and *distress* terminations. When a standard termination occurs—where the employer is *not* in financial distress—employers must pay all benefit commitments under the plan. Only when a company has filed for bankruptcy, would clearly go out of business unless the plan was terminated, or where the cost has become unreasonably burdensome—does the financial support of the PBGC come into play. However, in such cases, the new law substantially increases the PBGC's claims on the distressed company's assets and seeks to prevent the practice of "dumping" unfunded liabilities on the PBGC. The 1986 law also addressed the financial problems of the PBGC by increasing the premium for single-employer termination insurance from $2.60 to $8.50 per participant.

No sooner was the new legislation passed in 1986 than the PBGC was confronted with distressed terminations of unprecedented proportions. PBGC's deficit nearly tripled. Congress immediately

---

[18] The Single-Employer Pension Plan Amendment Act of 1986.

began consideration of a higher premium, including consideration of variable-rate premium proposals to replace the single premium policy currently in effect. And a report by the U.S. General Accounting Office suggested, among several options, that PBGC benefit level guarantees might need to be reduced.

Reacting to a deteriorating situation, Congress again acted in late 1987. A "variable rate premium" was established. Starting January 1, 1988, a base rate of $16 per participant was levied on all plans. Then an additional charge of $6 per $1,000 of unfunded vested benefits was levied on "underfunded" plans. This additional premium, however, is not to exceed $34 per plan participant. Thus, the total premium varies from $16 to $50 per participant, depending on the funding status of the pension plan. Reacting to the new legislation, Secretary of Labor Ann McLaughlin praised the action of Congress that she thought would "stem the tide of red ink which threatens to bankrupt the pension insurance system."

Women and Private Pensions

Women are not as likely as men to receive private pension benefits. A federal Task Force on Sex Discrimination (U.S. Department of Justice, n.d.) pointed out that women, because of their home and family responsibilities, are likely to accumulate far fewer total years of service with any one employer. Aspects of ERISA that the task force thought created problems were:

1. Workers under 25 could be excluded from coverage by employers, although the 20–24 age group has the highest female labor force participation rate.
2. Coverage was not required for employees who worked less than 1,000 hours per year. This affects the high proportion of women who work part-time or part-year.
3. "**Breaks in service**" by women were likely to exceed current allowable limits.
4. Vesting requirements were too long, and survivor protection was inadequate.
5. In defined benefit plans, even vested rights, if acquired through service early in an employee's working life, might be worth little at retirement (see page 230).

With regard to spouses, the Task Force observed:

The retirement income protection provided for most women as wives of workers covered under private pension plans is generally both insecure and inadequate. . . . [ERISA] has done little to change the fact that most women, as housewives, are only one man away from poverty. [U.S. Department of Justice, n.d.]

Legislation to address these issues was passed by the Congress in 1984 and 1986. The following are major provisions of the Retirement Equity Act of 1984 and the 1986 Tax Reform Act:

1. The age before which years of service can be excluded for vesting purposes was changed from age 22 to 18.
2. The minimum age for plan participation for most workers was set at age 21 (with one year of service) instead of age 25.
3. Break-in-service rules were liberalized.
4. One hundred percent vesting after five years of service was specified (along with three other vesting alternatives).
5. Pension plans were required to provide automatic joint and survivor protection to participants with vested benefits (including terminated employees)—unless both spouses agreed to "formally" reject this benefit.
6. Pension beneficiary decisions and changes to them must be carried out with the direct consent of spouses.

Government Employee Pension Plans

Our discussion of employer-sponsored pension plans would not be complete without mentioning one other category: federal, state, and local plans for government employees. These plans have many characteristics similar to the private plans discussed above but are unique in some respects.

Federal Civil Service Plans

Most civilians working for the federal government have been covered by the civil service retirement pension system (CSRS). In 1986 an alternative system was also established (described below). In 1984 1.4 million beneficiaries were receiving about $22 billion in pension, survivor, and disability benefits under this program.

Benefits under the original CSRS program are quite generous. A worker employed for 35 years with a final salary over $30,000 will generally receive enough *from his federal pension alone* to maintain his or her standard of living in retirement (Hartman, 1983). In fact, Robert Hartman argued in his book, *Pay and Pensions for Federal Workers* (1983) that up to now federal pensions have been much better than those in the private sector and, as a result, too costly to taxpayers. Moreover, he argues that many aspects of the system were inequitable, favoring highly paid and long-term workers and those people who return to government service late in their career. Over the years, Hartman and many others (e.g., the Universal Social Security Coverage Study Group, 1980) had called for major changes in this pension program.

One of the activities receiving the most criticism was the "double-dipping" of civil servants who receive both a good federal pension and social security. Until 1984 federal civilian employees were *not* covered by social security. However, the relatively low number of quarters needed to qualify for social security in the past often permitted (and encouraged) them to obtain coverage through employment in nongovernment jobs. Many federal employees worked part-time while employed by the government. Others, after retirement (often early retirement) from government employment, took a new job to obtain social security eligibility and eventually obtained a minimum (or better) social security benefit. In fact, among those age 62 or older, the proportion of civil service pensioners eligible to receive social security retirement benefits was 63 percent in 1979 (Social Security Administration, 1982). Over the years, the cost and inequity of providing social security benefits to federal pensioners (who already had good federal pensions) was condemned by many, and recommendations were frequently made to cover all government employees. It was not until 1984, however, that all *new* federal employees were mandatorily covered.

Pension eligibility requirements, financing, and benefits were significantly revised under provisions of the Federal Employees' Retirement System Act of 1986. The new system (FERS), effective January 1987, covers all federal civilian employees hired on or after that date and virtually all earlier hires with fewer than five years of nonmilitary service on December 31, 1986.

Older employees covered by the original federal pension plan (CSRS) will remain under that system unless they opt to shift to the FERS. To be eligible for unreduced benefits under CSRS, an employee must be age 62 with five years of service; age 60 with 20 years; or age 55 with 30 years. Retirement benefits under CSRS continue to be based on the employee's average annual earnings during the three highest consecutive years of employment. The formula used is: 1.5 percent of average annual earnings during the first five years of service, plus 1.75 percent for each of the next five years of service, plus 2 percent for each year of service in excess of 10. For 30 years of service, the result is a benefit equal to 56.25 percent of average annual earnings.

The *new* civil service retirement program (FERS) consists of three benefits: social security, CSRS, and a thrift savings plan. Under social security, employees will pay a reduced OASDI tax of 5.7 percent (6.2 percent in 1990), in addition to the Medicare tax that all federal employees pay. They will receive regular benefits under the program and be subject to all the provisions.

The second benefit is the new CSRS, to which employees will contribute 1.3 percent of their annual earnings. The contribution drops to 0.94 percent in 1988 and to 0.8 percent in 1990. Age and length-of-service requirements to obtain benefits are as described above for employees under the old CSRS, but the benefit formula is different. The annual benefit will be calculated at 1.0 percent of a retiring employee's average annual earnings for the three highest consecutive years, multiplied by the number of years of service. If the employee is age 62 or older at retirement, the calculation factor will be 1.1 percent. If younger, the employee will receive a supplement equal to the estimated social security benefit that would be payable based on current federal service under social security, calculated as if the employee were age 62. The supplement, which is subject to reduction if outside earnings exceed certain limits, ceases at age 62, when the retiree is eligible to begin drawing actual social security benefits.

The third benefit is from a thrift savings plan. It offers three types of tax-deferred investment options: special government securities, fixed income securities, or a stock index fund. The government contributes an amount equal to 1 percent of each employee's pay to the plan, even if the employee does not participate. In addition, the government contributes a dollar for each employee dollar contributed up to 3 percent of pay, and 50 cents for each employee dollar up to the next 2 percent of pay. The employee can contribute beyond 5 percent (without a government match) up to a maximum of 10 percent of pay.

Old employees who remain in the original CSRS program may invest up to 5 percent of their pay in the special government securities fund, but the government will not contribute matching funds.

The Federal Employees' Retirement System Act (FERS) limits automatic cost-of-living adjustments payable from the CSRS fund. Annual adjustments will be: (1) the actual 12-month rise in the consumer price index, if it is less than 2 percent, (2) 2 percent if the rise is 2 to 3 percent, and (3) the rise minus 1 percentage point if the rise is 3 percent or more. These adjustments apply to all retirees (both old and new programs), beginning at age 62. Previously, the formula provided for unreduced adjustments for all retirees, regardless of age.

The new retirement system (FERS) was designed to save the government money—$42 million in 1987 and rising to $2.67 billion in 1991. Even with the less liberal cost-of-living and lower CSRS formula, many government and union officials contend that FERS, with social security, is a better system than its predecessor for many workers (for example, workers who eventually leave the government and take a job in the private sector). However, few workers covered by the old system have exercised their option to switch to FERS.

Military Pensions

"Of all pension plans, probably none is better than the military's," observed Congressman Les Aspin (1976). The generous attributes of this plan come at a high price. The current average lifetime cost of a pension for a high-ranking military officer retiring after 30 years of service is close to a million dollars.

Since 1935, over 12 advisory panels or commissions have recommended *major* changes in the military pension program, with little resulting action. Former Director of the Office of Budget and Management, David Stockman, in a highly publicized moment of candor, described the program as a "scandal" (Bickerman, 1985).

The military retirement program:

1. Vests and pays benefits after (but not before) 20 years of service (with no minimum age requirement).
2. Requires no financial contribution from military personnel.
3. Pays 40 percent of basic pay to those with 20 years of service and 75 percent after 30 years.[19]
4. Is indexed over the lifetime of the pensioner.
5. Does not subject benefits to an earnings test, allowing military personnel to retire and take other jobs while receiving a military pension.

The current median age of "retirement" for enlisted personnel is 40, with only 7 percent of all nondisabled persons leaving military service after age 50. This "early out" option has been justified over the years as necessary to maintain the youth and fighting vigor of

---

[19]These percentages are for new personnel covered by the 1986 amendments to the military pension law. Personnel covered by the old program receive 50 percent after 20 years. Benefits for new personnel are reduced (over previous levels) by 1 percentage point for each year of service less than 30.

the military forces. Critics point out, however, that the overwhelming majority of current military personnel are noncombatants and that the current pension program strips the service of experienced, highly trained personnel increasingly needed to run our modern, technologically sophisticated military programs.

Reacting more to budget issues than military manpower considerations, Congress recently made two major changes in the military pension law. In 1985 it created the Military Retirement Trust Fund, establishing mechanisms to move the program toward a funded system. Then, in 1986 Congress deliberalized the pension program for new personnel covered by the plan. In addition to lowering pensions paid to people leaving with fewer than 30 years of service (as discussed above), cost-of-living adjustments (COLA) were changed. Pensions under the new law are indexed by the consumer price index (CPI) *less 1 percent* each year. At age 62 the pension benefit level is adjusted upward to restore the "lost" COLA adjustments over the prior period. But once again in subsequent years, the new higher benefit level is adjusted for inflation by the "CPI minus one" rule. The result is significant cost savings to the government.

Military pensions still remain the best pension in the United States and the most expensive. Military personnel are also covered by social security. Many feel that this retirement package is far too generous and that military pensions should not be available at very early ages. Debate over these issues continues. The 1986 law directed the Secretary of Defense to review the program once again and recommend changes. (That's like asking the fox to review and suggest improvements to the security system for the hen house.)

State and Local Pension Plans

There are about 7,000 plans covering state and local government employees. These plans are similar in many ways to private employer plans. James A. Maxwell (1975) has summarized some of the differences:

> *Overall, the state and local government pension systems provide more generous benefits than do private systems. The normal retirement age and service requirements are more generous. . . . And they are more likely to have generous disability and survivor coverage. . . . (Most) require employee contributions, whereas most private plans do not.*

With regard to inflation protection, a study (Schulz et al., 1984) of the 76 major teacher and state-employee retirement plans found that 41 plans in 1982 had automatic adjustment mechanisms, with annual ceilings on these adjustments of 2 to 5 percent. Only two of these plans did not have ceilings: Maryland, for employees hired before 1980, and New Jersey, which adjusts pensions for 60 percent of the change in the consumer price index.

State and local governments were free to choose whether to cover their employees under social security; however, the option to *withdraw* from social security (once having joined the system) was eliminated in 1983. About 70 percent of state and local government employees are currently covered by both social security and a state or local pension plan. Again, for workers not covered by social security, dual coverage is often achieved by early retirement from state or local service followed by work for a nongovernment employer.

A study of 100 representative state and local plans found their benefits to be quite generous and, in some cases, to be excessive (The Urban Institute, 1981). The study found considerable variation, however, among the various plans studied. For workers age 65 with 30 years of service and a gross income of $10,000, the highest replacement rate in the sample of plans studied was 149 percent and the lowest was 52 percent.

Congressional interest in federal regulation of state and local plans was a major issue when ERISA was passed in 1974. These plans were formally exempted from the ERISA legislation, however, since it was not clear that Congress had the constitutional authority to regulate the states in this area. However, over the years legislation has been introduced in Congress to establish minimum reporting, disclosure, and financial responsibility standards for state and local plans. Supporters of the legislation believe it is constitutional and will improve the security of pensions for employees in the states. Strong opposition to the legislation has come from state and local government organizations. They maintain that regulation is unnecessary and argue that such action would be an undesirable invasion of states' rights.

Financing Government Employee Plans

Unfortunately, data on the actuarial status of the thousands of government plans (or even a representative sample of them) are difficult to obtain and also difficult to interpret when available. An early study of James A. Maxwell (1975) of the pension plans in the

29 largest cities showed that "many of them are in trouble." Using the ratio of current payments to assets as a rough indication of the financial strength or weakness of a fund, Maxwell identified four states where plan financing was especially weak: Delaware, Massachusetts, West Virginia, and Maine.

Another study by a Congressional Pension Task Force (U.S. House Committee on Education and Labor, 1978) surveyed plans covering 96 percent of all employees in public employee plans. The Pension Task Force reported serious deficiencies regarding the extent to which information is reported and disclosed to interested parties. They found that plans often did not operate in accordance with generally accepted financial and accounting procedures. And, most importantly, they found that "there is an incomplete assessment of pension costs at all levels of government due to the lack of adequate actuarial valuations and standards."

Tilove's assessment of the situation in 1976 was that significant improvements had occurred in the funding situation of state and local plans but that funding was in fact poorest where it is most needed:

> *The cases most in need of attention are the systems of the financially distressed urban centers and of the many similar cities and counties that have no real assurance of future ability to pay. It is their fiscal difficulties that have kept many on pay-as-you-go, and that is precisely why they should begin to fund on an actuarial basis—so that they may confront the long-term implications of their pension decisions and, by the same policy, assure the ultimate security of their employees. [Tilove, 1976]*

In many ways, state and local pension financing falls in between social security financing and private pension plans. Like the federal government, state and city governments are not likely ever to cease operations, and these pensions are protected by law and the taxing powers of the government. But, like private business, states and cities are not assured of a continually growing financing base. Some states and cities may experience a net loss of businesses or population base and/or their tax base. These shifts are difficult to predict and can cause serious problems if pension costs (based on past promises) are rising while the government's tax revenues are growing very slowly or falling.

Because pension benefits can be liberalized without any substantial increases in immediate costs, some people fear that government employee pension plans will be liberalized without due regard to the future financing implications. It is argued that the political process is particularly susceptible to this problem because the conduct of state and local politicians is often "determined by relatively short-run considerations. The impact of failing to adhere to actuarial principles will frequently fall upon a different mayor and a different city council. In these circumstances, concessions that condemn a city to future impoverishment may not seem intolerable" (Wellington and Winter, 1971). Despite the large number of state and local funds, the magnitude of fund assets, the growth of benefit levels, and the fears of many professionals regarding state and local pension financing, very little attention has been given to the impact of these plans on the economic status of the current and future aged. Individuals covered by these plans and relying on them for retirement security should be aware of this gap in our knowledge. State and local taxpayers should probably be more sensitive to the long-term costs of these pensions and support an increase in the availability of information in this area.

Chapter 8 Highlights

Private and government employee pensions play important roles in the United States. Some key points to remember are:

1. While many government employee pensions were in place relatively early in this century, the rapid development of private pensions did not begin until the 1940s and 1950s.
2. Still not covered by private plans are many people who work for small businesses; the uncovered are also more likely to be nonunion, female, part-time, lower paid, and in the trade or service industries.
3. Most pension-covered workers are in noncontributory defined benefit plans with five-year vesting, optional survivors' benefits, and nonindexed benefits based on years of service and final years of earnings.
4. The 1974 Employee Retirement Income Security Act (ERISA) set up a comprehensive set of minimum standards, financial safeguards, and disclosure requirements—seeking to ensure that benefits promised to workers would actually be realized.
5. The ERISA provisions have been strengthened by major legislation (since ERISA) in the areas of vesting, plan termination and reinsurance, survivors' protection, and pension integration provisions.
6. The major private pension issues currently being debated are (a) the adequacy of coverage, (b) how to reduce the risk of pension loss, and (c) the extent to which benefits should be protected from inflation.

Suggested Readings

Congressional Budget Office, U.S. Congress. *Federal Insurance of Private Pension Benefits*. Washington, D.C.: U.S. Government Printing Office, 1987. A review of the structure of employer-sponsored pensions in the United States, the role of the Pension Benefit Guaranty Corporation, and the controversy over reinsurance of plan benefits.

Employee Benefit Research Institute. *Economic Survival in Retirement: Which Pension Is for You?* Washington, D.C.: The Institute, 1982. A collection of conference papers focusing on the differences between defined benefit and defined contribution plans.

HANNAH, LESLIE. *Inventing Retirement—The Development of Occupational Pensions in Britain*. Cambridge: Cambridge University Press, 1986, p. 4. An excellent history of the evolution of private plans in Great Britain. (The British experience is quite relevant to the American situation.)

McGILL, DAN M. *Fundamentals of Private Pensions*, 5th ed. Homewood, Ill.: Irwin, 1982. A comprehensive and authoritative book that traces the historical development and regulation of private pensions, explains plan design, reviews funding procedures, and discusses actuarial practices.

MUNNELL, ALICIA H. *The Economics of Private Pensions*. Washington, D.C.: The Brookings Institution, 1982. Examines the interaction of private pensions and tax policy, saving, financial institutions, and corporate financing.

U.S. Subcommittee on Retirement Income and Employment, House Select Committee on Aging. *National Pension Policies: Private Pension Plans*. Hearings. Washington, D.C.: U.S. Government Printing Office, 1978. Testimony by government, academic, and business experts on the role and problems of private pensions.

Chapter 9

ECONOMIC SECURITY TODAY AND TOMORROW

Years of economic deprivation among the elderly in the United States called forth a variety of public and private programs to alleviate the resulting hardship. OASDI, private pensions, government employee pensions, Medicare, and the SSI program currently involve expenditures of over $400 billion per year.

Our nation's very positive response to the economic plight of the elderly and the problems of old age, however, has triggered great controversy. Some argue that the benefits are still insufficient, while others argue that the economic burden of providing even the benefits promised is becoming excessive.

At the heart of this controversy are two major questions: What should be the mix of public and private programs and how should these programs be financed? As OASDI, private pensions, government employee plans, and health programs grow in size and cost, it is clear that we must clarify the way we intend them to relate to each other, the level of benefits to be provided by each, and who will ultimately pay the costs. In addition, we must be clear about what responsibilities before and during retirement remain the individual's (or his or her family's).

The Pension System—Stability or Change?

Writers have frequently described the country's provisions for retirement as a three-legged stool with social security, private pensions, and individual saving comprising each leg. However, the information provided in prior chapters indicates that the legs of that stool have changed over time. The evidence is clear: The overwhelming bulk of the population does not save sufficiently for old age. Home equity accounts for the bulk of most people's wealth, but these assets are not readily or willingly converted to spendable funds when people grow old.

It is *collective* saving through various pension programs that currently makes the big difference; wealth in the form of accrued future benefits constitutes the overwhelming proportion of assets for most Americans today. Thus, the three-legged stool for retirement provision is more appropriately viewed as composed of the three basic parts of the pension system currently operating in the United States: OASDHI, private pensions, and government employee pensions. Together, these three institutions provide (and finance) most of the income (and health services) going to people who are retired.

In prior chapters we have discussed how provision for old age in the United States has evolved into a mix of multifarious collective pension structures. *For better or worse, this pension system is now in place, and its basic structure is not likely to change significantly in the years to come*. That is, we are not likely to see a shift to providing much more of our retirement income through social security (as in West Germany, Italy, and Belgium, where most comes from social security). Nor, for reasons we discuss below, are we likely to see the role of private pensions greatly increased. And despite all the pleas and advocacy of some to the contrary, it is doubtful that we will see a significant shift to self-reliance through individual saving as an important retirement provisions mechanism. Some people advocate such a shift, together with an expanded needs-tested income support program. Such a **means-tested** program would likely be a broadened and more developed version of the SSI program that is currently a part of social security. Again, there does not seem to be much political support for such a change.

The stability of the existing situation does not mean, of course, that all the major issues of providing retirement income are resolved. This is hardly the case, as anyone who has gotten this far in the book (or who, for that matter, has recently read the newspapers) knows all too well. Discussions about health and pension programs and how best to provide for old age have never been more numerous, except perhaps during the social security debates of the 1930s. It is not unusual today to hear or read clarion calls for the fundamental rethinking of how we should provide for retirement. And there is no dearth of proposals for major structural changes in our current health and pension systems, especially government programs.

Regarding pensions, most experts would agree that the present public-private pension system is in some sense a nonsystem with gaps, flaws, inequities, and inadequacies. However, it also contains the basic elements of stability that will ensure its long-term continuity. These elements (described more fully in prior chapters) are:

- An evolving retirement policy based primarily on collective financing—reducing the magnitude and complexity of individual retirement preparation.
- The institutionalization of retirement: rising retirement expectations and benefits as a matter of right, not need—eliminating social stigma from retirement income receipt.
- Individuals being subject to "forced saving" through private and public group plans, countering the tendency for individual economic myopia.
- Benefits related to preretirement earnings, which is a necessary prerequisite for developing "adequate" pension income.
- A heavy reliance on government taxes for financing social security and tax-incentive mechanisms to encourage provision through private pensions.
- Universal involvement of the population in pension programs and the development of a large number of organizations (governments, corporations, banks, insurance companies, and so forth) providing pension services—both helping to ensure broad-based political support for existing programs.

It is important to reiterate that this growing stability does not mean that our system for providing income in old age has no major problems. In prior chapters we have stressed, for example, the still precarious economic state of most people covered *only* by social security, the economic problems of many widows, the conflicting actions around encouraging early retirement while facilitating later retirement, and the plight of those workers whose private pension plans are inadequate or inequitable. Thus, although a basic retirement income provision system is in place, we will need to improve it over the years to come.

Coping with Inflation

A major challenge that continues to face many of the elderly is the need to deal with inflation. Inflation has often been very high—in the early 1980s at unprecedented levels. But what is more worrisome is the evidence indicating that high inflation rates are not an uncommon phenomenon. A number of fundamental changes that have taken place in our economy will make it difficult to return permanently to the very low inflation rates of old. Instead, we probably face recurring periods of rapidly rising prices.

The world is now going through a long-term transition with regard to energy sources and the costs of energy. Until a new cheap energy source is developed, we face the threat of continuing pressures on prices from the energy component of the goods and services we produce.

Perhaps more fundamental are the implications of our current economic structure. Large businesses, unions, and governments, together with public and private economic security provisions, have created an institutional environment that effectively insulates most industries from price and wage reductions. At the same time, this environment often encourages wage and price increases that are not justified by productivity gains.

Finally, there is no evidence that the American electorate appreciates the need for higher taxes to meet the rising need for public goods and services in an increasingly affluent and complex society. As John Kenneth Galbraith (1958) pointed out some years ago:

> *The line which divides our area of wealth from our area of poverty is roughly that which divides privately produced and marketed goods and services from publicly rendered services. Our wealth in the first is not only in startling contrast with the meagerness of the latter but our wealth in privately produced goods is, to a marked degree, the cause of crisis in the supply of public services. For we have failed to see the importance, indeed the urgent need, of maintaining a balance between the two.*

The result is a continuing tendency for the government to run deficits as social problems generate pressures by citizens through various interest groups for action while the collective polity (of these same citizens) remains stingy with its hard-earned income. The tax and spending "solutions" promoted by President Reagan to our economic problems and government deficits were but one dramatic example of our long, vacillating history with regard to the national mix of private versus public goods and services.

One recent tax reform—**indexing** federal income tax brackets for inflation—creates great uncertainty for the future. This new law, which went into effect in 1985, eliminates the increase in individuals' taxes that, in prior years, resulted from inflation increasing people's incomes and pushing many into higher tax brackets. But in turn, this loss of revenue to the government contributes to its financing problems and practically insures there will be budget deficits in the future—deficits that could be inflationary.

The Vulnerable Elderly

The promise of continuing **inflation** in the years to come demands that we think seriously of appropriate safeguards for the most economically vulnerable of our population. Two major sources of elderly income are still highly vulnerable to inflation: financial assets and private pensions. Most financial assets—bonds, checking accounts, savings accounts, and insurance policies—do not adjust when the general level of prices changes. Others, which have at times adjusted better, require considerable financial sophistication or have much higher associated risk: real estate, corporate stock, and gold. The recent development of money market funds and similar financial securities offers some help for the small saver but again does not offer complete security from inflation over any particular short-run period.

At present, the most serious problem with regard to inflation and the elderly is the vulnerability of the near-poor aged. The overwhelming proportion of elderly live on incomes above the official poverty level but below $18,000 a year. Many of these elderly families depend on their financial savings and their private pensions to provide the margin of support necessary for a modest but more comfortable life-style. How can these people be helped?

Purchasing Power Bonds

Some people have argued that saving, particularly personal saving, is discouraged by the uncertainty of not knowing future rates of inflation. Another way of saying this is that people are discouraged from saving by the certainty of knowing that inflation is bound to take place at some rate and that their savings are likely to become devalued over time. Various proposals have been made for the creation of a different type of financial asset, a constant purchasing power bond. These bonds would be sold by the government to people to protect their savings from inflation. The basic idea of constant purchasing power bonds is that people should be able to buy these bonds from the government to save for retirement or other purposes. They might or might not receive interest from them. Economist James Tobin has argued, for example, that people might even be willing to buy these bonds at a zero rate of interest—as long as there was a firm guarantee that their value would not depreciate from inflation. Having been purchased for a stated amount, the bond would be redeemable at some point in the future for that amount, adjusted for any inflation that took place over the intervening period. Thus, the value of the bond would remain constant in real terms and actually increase if there was a rate of interest associated with it.

Henry Wallich (1969), himself an advocate of the bonds, summarizes the *opposition* to them as follows:

> *The case against purchasing power bonds every good official can recite in his sleep. If you escalate government obligations, people will say that you are throwing in the towel against inflation. Investors will stop worrying about inflation if they are protected. And the government with its unlimited resources would be competing unfairly with private borrowers who could not take the risk of assuming this kind of open-ended debt.*

Milton Friedman (1971) provides an alternative viewpoint:

> *The government alone is responsible for inflation. By inflation it has expropriated the capital of persons who bought government securities. Often at the urging of high officials who eloquently proclaimed that patriotism and self-interest went hand-in-hand (the good old government savings bond). The right way to avoid this disgraceful shell game is for the government to borrow in the form of purchasing power securities. Let the Treasury promise to pay not $1,000, but a sum that will have the same purchasing power as $1,000 had when the security was issued. Let it pay as interest each year not a fixed amount of dollars but that number adjusted for any rise in prices. This would be the precise counterpart of the escalator clauses that have become so popular in wage contracts.*

The late Senator Pat McNamara from Michigan, when he was chairman of the Special Committee on Aging, introduced legislation in the early 1960s to allow the government to sell purchasing power bonds to individuals up to a certain maximum amount, on the condition that the individuals would be willing to hold the bonds until retirement (an indexed IRA). The proposed legislation specified that if the bonds were cashed in before retirement, there would not be an escalator adjustment; instead, individuals would only get back the original amount plus a stipulated amount of interest. Senator McNamara introduced the bill over a period of many years, but hearings were never held on the proposal.

The principal opposition to purchasing power bonds is centered in the U.S. Treasury Department. In addition to the reasons cited by Wallich, the Treasury worries about possible destabilizing effects on the bond markets of introducing this new type of bond and the possibility of making more difficult the government's debt financing. In this particular area—debt management and federal debt issue—the Treasury is politically very powerful. Thus far, it has been persuasive in preventing Congress from seriously considering legislation of this sort.

Private Pensions and Inflation

As we discussed in Chapter 8, there are almost no private pension plans that automatically adjust pensions during retirement for increases in the consumer price index. Some plans adjust benefits on an ad hoc basis every few years, but these adjustments usually lag far behind the rise in prices.

Some people have recommended "retiree bargaining" as a way of dealing with this problem. However, the Supreme Court ruled in 1971 *(Allied Chemical and Alkali Workers v. Pittsburgh Plate Glass)* that retirees are not "employees" within the meaning of the National Labor Relations Act and, therefore, that benefits for retirees are not mandatory subjects of union bargaining. This means that if a company does not want to discuss increases in retirees' pensions, there is no way a union can legally force it to do so. Thus, for example, a few years ago major companies in the electrical manufacturing industry refused to bargain with unions seeking to improve what they saw as the serious financial plight of many retirees (Fitzgerald, 1978).

It is not likely that many private plans will ever voluntarily adopt full indexing provisions similar to social security. The uncertainties involved in funding such provisions are extremely high, and the costs of such provisions would make private plans unattractive to both employers and workers.

But that does not mean that there are no meaningful options. Two options immediately suggest themselves. Workers could be offered benefits when they retire that are initially at a lower level than otherwise and that increase annually by some predetermined and guaranteed amount.[1] This option is not likely to be very appealing to most workers, however. Retirees have shown a strong inclination to opt for money now and to postpone worrying about the future. Such an option, however, would provide a way of

---

[1] The pension fund for most college teachers (TIAA/CREF) currently offers an option similar to this.

collectively combating this myopic tendency that most of us exhibit in greater or lesser degree.

Perhaps a more feasible response to the problem is adding automatic adjustment mechanisms to plans at employers' expense but with limits or ceilings placed on the increases.[2] Limits could be specified in terms of a maximum percentage increase, a specific dollar limitation, or a specified fraction of the movement in the consumer price index (e.g., 50 percent). Alternatively, increases could be limited to retirees of a certain age or period of years in retirement.

Many other variations or specifications of this option are possible. The important point is that private companies can respond to the inflation problem *without exposing themselves to unknown and unlimited costs*. Thus, for example, a typical plan with a postretirement adjustment every three years of 2 percent less than the increase in the consumer price index would cost a firm about 2 percent of payroll at a 7 percent inflation rate ceiling (Cooper, 1980). This does not seem like an unreasonably excessive cost, and the level of protection, while not total, is quite good.

Will We Pay the Price of Economic Adequacy?

Throughout the book we have discussed the growing costs of income support for the elderly. It is now common for people to point out the growing proportion of the federal budget that is spent on the elderly. For example, Barbara Torrey (1982), when she was at the federal Office of Management and Budget, began a paper entitled "Guns vs. Canes: The Fiscal Implications of an Aging Population":

> *The share of the federal budget devoted to the older population . . . has expanded substantially from approximately 2 percent in 1940 to 25 percent today. Over the next fifty years this older population is expected to more than double in size. . . . Even if no further responsibilities are assumed by the federal government, this population increase alone will put inexorable fiscal pressures on future federal budgets.*

More recent numbers developed by Storey (1983) for fiscal year 1981 show that $173 billion in federal outlays directly benefited

---

[2]Ultimately the increased benefits paid out by these mechanisms would be paid for (in most cases) in terms of lower wage increases, lower improvements in other fringe benefits, or higher prices.

the aged that year and represented 26 percent of all federal spending. However, social security programs financed by payroll taxes (OASDHI) accounted for 77 percent of these expenditures, or $133 billion.

Social security was included in the federal budget for the first time in 1969. This inclusion of the operations of the social security trust funds in the federal budget has been criticized by many social security experts. They argue that social security operations were put into the budget primarily for political reasons. The surpluses being generated in social security during the 1960s and early 1970s had the effect of helping to "balance the budget." In fact, when the accounting procedure was introduced in 1969, the expected social security surplus for that year permitted President Johnson to send a balanced budget to Congress, instead of one with a deficit. In recent years, when social security has often had a deficit, some government officials have tried to blame the very much larger total budget deficits on "out of control" nondiscretionary programs like social security. As shown in Table 9–1, however, the sizes of the two deficits are very different. As we discussed previously, operating on a pay-as-you-go basis, social security taxes and expenditures must be kept in close balance. Unlike the federal budget, social security is not as likely to generate large deficits over long periods of time.

Critics of the "unified budget" concept argue that these "artifi-

Table 9–1   Deficits: All Federal Programs vs. OASDHI

Fiscal Year	Total Federal Operations ($, billions)	OASDHI Only ($, billions)
1973	− 14.9	+ 5.2
1974	− 6.1	+ 4.1
1975	− 53.2	− 0.1
1976	− 73.7	− 2.3
1977	− 53.6	− 5.1
1978	− 59.2	− 3.1
1979	− 40.2	+ 0.3
1980	− 73.8	+ 3.3
1981	− 78.9	+ 3.1
1982	− 127.9	− 8.8
1983	− 207.8	+ 4.8
1984	− 185.3	+ 9.0
1985	− 212.3	+ 15.5
1986	− 220.7	+ 24.3

Sources: Social Security Administration, *Annual Statistical Supplement, 1986* (Washington, D.C.: SSA, n.d.); and *Economic Report of the President,* 1987.

cial" and sometimes manipulative accounting procedures actually hinder the budget-making process. Thus, the 1981 National Commission on Social Security recommended that the social security trust funds be removed from the unified budget. This recommendation was accepted by the Congress and a provision was put into the Social Security Amendments of 1983, scheduling social security's removal from the annual budgeting process by fiscal year 1993. Later Congressional action, as part of the Gramm-Rudman-Hollings (G-R-H) procedures to promote a balanced federal budget, accelerated the timetable to 1987 but introduced a more complicated arrangement. Under the G-R-H provisions, social security's income and outlays are excluded from budget documents, budget resolutions, and budget reconciliation legislation. However, the system's projected surpluses over the next couple of decades (or deficits, if they happen to occur) are taken into account in the calculation of the "budgeting targets" called for by the G-R-H process. The result is that social security is once again being used to serve the needs of those in Washington seeking to avoid the politically difficult decisions of budget cuts or tax increases. "Were it not for the inclusion of the large Social Security surpluses, then the [overall federal] budget deficit would have to be cut by an additional $50 to $60 billion in order to meet the targets set for the final years of . . . [G-R-H]" (U.S. Senate Special Committee on Aging, 1987).

It is not likely, given social security's current size, that officials in Washington will be willing or able to disentangle the actual economic impact of social security from the day-to-day politics of the budgetary process. It may be possible to reduce the outpouring of misinformation and scare statistics about social security that we have seen over the years, but we will still be continually reminded about the rising costs of our growing retired population, which is comprised of both older *and increasing numbers of relatively young* persons. Changing how we incorporate social security into federal budget statistics, while necessary, will not change the fact that providing adequately for the retirement period is an expensive proposition. As the retirement age continues to decline, we face the prospect of providing individuals with income and services for a 20- to 30-year period outside the labor force. Increasingly, people are developing expectations that retirement can and should be an enjoyable period of life and that economic resources should be sufficient to avoid the limitations imposed on retirement living by financial stringency. Unfortunately, if individuals only begin to worry and seriously plan for their own retirement shortly before the event, the magnitude of the financing problem becomes insuperable for most. The best and easiest way of accumulating the resources necessary for retirement is to begin very early. But historically most people have shown a reluctance to think about retirement until it is *almost* a reality or until it is a reality. The result has been a great deal of poverty among the aged.

Pension systems and, before them, families have stepped in to provide needed economic support for many of these people—often preventing destitution. The level of support has often been very low. Yet (as we discussed in the first chapter) the rising financial burden imposed on the working population, even at these low levels of support, has created political concern, and there is particular concern regarding the future burden.

There is considerable debate over what the future costs of social security will be. Despite the lack of agreement, it is clear that rather sizable amounts will be required. How willing are people to finance the required levels of support?

It seems to me that one of the best answers is provided by the individuals *now covered* by good private pensions and social security. The combined reduction in their take-home pay to provide social security and a good private pension is quite large (about 16 to 20 percent). Yet there is little complaining from this group, probably in large part because these costs are taken out before they ever get their earnings check. We can also look at the European experience, shown in Table 9–2. Other industrialized countries have payroll taxes for OASDI that average over 17 percent. Despite these high rates, there has been relatively little political opposition in these countries to this level of taxation for pension purposes. Rather, as in the United States, there has been concern in Europe about rising government deficits (and some cutbacks) caused by record high unemployment and inflation.

Survey data indicate, in fact, a willingness of American workers to pay for better benefits. A 1977 survey by the University of Michigan Survey Research Center found that a great many wage and salary workers expressed a willingness to trade increments in pay for better retirement benefits. In the survey, 54 percent of workers preferred an improvement in retirement benefits over a pay increase (Staines and Quinn, 1979). The Peter D. Hart (1979) poll for the National Commission on Social Security asked people their choice between higher social security taxes or lower future retirement benefits. Higher taxes were clearly favored by the majority (63 percent).

Some people—such as Peterson (1982) and Robertson (1981)— see social security expenditures out of control and too costly to maintain in what they foresee as a no-growth economic environ-

Table 9–2 Social Security Tax Tates in Selected Countries, 1981

Country	Combined Employee-Employer Tax	
	All Social Security Programs	OASDI Only
Austria	43.70	21.10
Belgium	37.87	15.11[b]
Canada	8.44[a]	3.60[c]
France	47.55	13.00[d]
West Germany	34.40	18.50
Italy	55.02	24.46
Japan	22.07	10.60
Netherlands	57.65	34.90[e]
Sweden	35.20	21.15
Switzerland	17.72	9.40
United Kingdom	21.45	na[f]
United States	18.00	10.70

Source: Alicia Munnell, "A Calm Look, at Social Security," *New York Review of Books* 30 (March 17, 1983). Used by permission of the author.
[a]Excludes work injury insurance.
[b]Invalidity pension financed through sickness insurance.
[c]Includes only the Canadian Pension Plan and excludes the Old-Age Security Program financed out of general revenue.
[d]Invalidity and survivors' benefits financed through sickness insurance.
[e]Disability insurance also includes work-injury compensation.
[f]Not available.

ment. If nothing is done, they predict that payroll taxes will reach unbelievably high levels and that workers will rebel at such high taxes.

Certainly, we must be sensitive to both the economic and political realities associated with retirement costs. The recent years of economic chaos are a vivid reminder of the uncertainties that lie ahead. We must constantly monitor developments and seek to anticipate problems. Some of the problems that must be dealt with—such as escalating health costs and the baby boom phenomenon—can be clearly seen. Most future developments, both negative and positive, are hidden from our view. The debate, consequently, often centers on two points of view: The pessimist sees the glass half *empty* but the optimist sees it half *full.*

Despite this dilemma, it is foolish to think we can escape the cost of providing an individual with an adequate retirement income by keeping the cost of social security down. *If we do not provide for older Americans through taxation, then we will do so by other but less visible means*—for example, by reducing a worker's take-home pay to finance private pensions or by transferring income within the family from the young to the old. Older people are no longer willing to live as paupers in their retirement. They expect to be provided for, one way or another.

Certainly, the days of cheap social security, like the days of cheap gasoline, are gone forever. We will have to do some very hard thinking and some belt-tightening. But there is no rational justification for the hysteria that is being promoted today by some people who are attacking social security.

In 1961, then Secretary of Health, Education, and Welfare Abraham Ribicoff stated that he thought the limit to public acceptance of the social security payroll tax was 10 percent. We have passed through that ceiling without difficulty. Now people worry about the high rates in the year 2010 or 2020. But as economist Martin Feldstein (1975) has pointed out:

> *An increase in the social security tax rate to 16 or 20 percent would be a substantial increase. . . . There are some who believe that such high rates would create an intolerable burden on low-income and middle-income families. This is a false argument that ignores the substantial increase in real earnings that these families will enjoy at the same time that tax rates rise. Even a tax rate increase of 10 percentage points over the next 50 years is only an increase of 0.2 percent per year. The higher tax would absorb only one-tenth of the annual real wage growth of 2 percent. Stated somewhat differently, with a 2 percent annual rate of growth, real wages would rise by 200 percent between now and 2030, and the higher social security tax would absorb no more than 10 percentage points of this 200 percentage point increase in real wages.*

Thus, it is important to remember the political acceptability of *gradual* increases in tax rates. This suggests that higher pension costs should be phased in over a period of years—similar to the way many other countries have introduced the major improvements in their programs. And it is certainly prudent to anticipate the demographic bulge and consequent sharp rise in costs beginning around the year 2010 as a result of the World War II baby boom.

Also, there is a need for a greater awareness of the intra- and intergenerational equity issues.[3] As the costs of aged retirement living increase, more attention should be given to these issues in order both to maintain public confidence in and support for the programs and to use with maximum effectiveness the money allocated.

One of the most important issues we must deal with is the trend

---

[3] See, for example, Easterlin (1987) and Kingson et al. (1986).

toward increasingly early retirement. It is certainly natural for many people to want to retire as early as possible. The evidence shows that as one gets older, the desire to continue working is clearly not as strong as it was once thought to be by many sociologists (see Chapter 3). There are many people who enjoy the new life-style retirement provides. But as society responds to the pressure for bigger pensions at earlier ages, pension costs rise at dramatic and staggering rates. For example, actuaries point out that pension costs increase by about 50 percent once the normal age of retirement is reduced from age 65 to age 60. Some private pension plans today allow people to retire below the age of 60 with no serious penalty. The cost of earlier retirement is measured not only by the costs of the pension benefits paid out, but also by the reduced economic output resulting when fewer workers remain in the work force.

Apart from the natural desire of many people to retire at an earlier age, there has also been a systematic, institutionalized pressure in this country to encourage older workers to leave the labor force. The Social Security Act itself still imposes a severe retirement test on workers. More recently, private pension systems and early retirement policies have been instrumental in encouraging, and even forcing, workers to retire at increasingly earlier ages. Unions and management have responded to chronic unemployment in this country by devising pension systems that encourage one part of the labor force, the older workers, to leave in order to make room for another part, the younger workers.

What economists call "the lump of labor fallacy" is at the heart of this kind of thinking. There are those who believe there is a fixed number of jobs in the economy; so if younger people enter the labor force, older people must leave it. We do not need to accept such reasoning, however; the number of jobs in the economy is not fixed. We can provide jobs for younger and older people if we are willing to undertake the policies necessary to promote and ensure full employment while restraining prices. Full employment policies would reverse the trend toward early retirement.

Unfortunately, however, this solution does not appear to be a politically viable one—at least not in the near future; the political record of equivocation speaks for itself. Full employment without high inflation probably requires some major changes in the structure of the American economy and the rules under which it operates. Such changes are unlikely to occur in the near future, given the "privileged position of business" and the insecure position of unions (Lindblom, 1977).

Instead, we must look at more marginal, less effective solutions.

Stopgap measures such as offering bonuses for delayed retirement, abolishing mandatory retirement policies, liberalizing the social security retirement test, and promoting full-time and part-time work among older people are being tried. But these attempts alone *will not have a major effect* on the trend toward early retirement.

We may have to do something more dramatic. In addition to raising the social security "normal" age of eligibility, we may need to regulate the early retirement pension policies of private employers. As unattractive as government action is in this area, it may be necessary in order to combat the very serious alternative of increasing early retirement. In this country the large and very prosperous corporations cover most of the workers with private pensions. When these large companies introduce an early retirement policy, competitive pressures force other less prosperous and smaller companies to follow suit.

One thing is clear about future costs. The major economic issue is not whether—in the face of other public expenditure problems such as urban blight, national defense, and pollution—we can have better pensions and services for the aged. The issue is whether we want a higher standard of living in our retirement years at the expense of a lower standard in our younger years. While trade-offs must be continually made in the short run, rising incomes in retirement are closely related over the long run to sacrifices in consumption made in the earlier years. Whether we like it or not, the "economics of aging" begins for most of us quite early in life.

Suggested Readings

BINSTOCK, ROBERT H., MARTIN A. LEVIN, AND RICHARD WEATHERLY. "Political Dilemmas of Social Intervention." In Robert H. Binstock and Ethel Shanas, eds., *Handbook of Aging and the Social Sciences*, 2d ed. New York: Van Nostrand Reinhold, 1984. An excellent discussion of the problems of implementing social policies and programs.

CRYSTAL, STEPHEN. *America's Old Age Crisis*. New York: Basic Books, 1982. A clearly written and thoughtful perspective on the aging dilemma, with an emphasis on pensions, family support, and long-term care.

ESTES, CARROLL L., AND R. J. NEWCOMER (AND ASSOCIATES). *Fiscal Austerity and Aging*. Beverly Hills: Sage Publications, 1983. Federal-state responsibilities and relationships are examined in the light of the fiscal austerity of the 1980s.

HECLO, HUGH. "Toward a New Welfare State?" In P. Flora and A. J. Heidenheimer, eds., *The Development of Welfare States in Europe and America*. New Brunswick: Transaction Books, 1982. A comparative view of political and economic developments, both past and present, as they relate to developing welfare programs and policies.

MYLES, JOHN F. *Old Age in the Welfare State: The Political Economy of Public Pensions.* Boston: Little, Brown, 1984. A penetrating discussion of old age and the role of patterns.

PETERSON, PETER G. "Social Security: The Coming Crash." *New York Review of Books* 29 (2 December 1982) and "The Salvation of Social Security." *New York Review of Books* 29 (16 December 1982), Munnell, Alicia H. "A Calm Look at-Social Security." and P. G. Peterson. "A Reply to Critics." *New York Review of Books* 30 (17 March 1983). A provocative exchange of views on social security that emphasizes the funding controversy.

SCHULZ, JAMES H. "Issues in Aged Income Maintenance: Population Aging and the Early Retirement 'Timebomb.' " In U. S. House Select Committee and U.S. Senate Special Committee on Aging. *Proceedings: Congressional Forum on a Legislative Agenda for an Aging Society—1988 and Beyond.* Washington, D.C.: U.S. Government Printing Office, 1988. This article focuses on the impact of an aging population and the potential problems arising from continued early retirement in the United States.

GLOSSARY

Accrued benefits Pension benefits are typically based on the number of years a person works with an employer or works under a particular plan sponsored by that employer. In addition, the work's level of earnings in specified years is used frequently to also determine benefits. Thus, each year worked results in accumulated pension rights to future payments, if all required conditions are met. Based on the plan rules, government regulations, the benefit formula, and actuarial assumptions, the amount accumulated can be calculated. This amount is generally called the accrued benefit.

Actuarial Cost projections that take into account (for pensions) the number of employees retiring and dying each year, labor force turnover, the benefit formula, plan expenses, and investment income.

Age Discrimination in Employment Act Originally enacted by the federal government in 1967 "to promote employment of older persons based on their ability rather than age; to prohibit arbitrary age discrimination in employment; and to help employers and workers find ways of meeting problems arising from the impact of age on employment." The original act prohibited discrimination based on age against persons age 40–65. Amendments in 1978 raised the upper age limit to 70 but eliminated all age limits for most federal employees. In October 1986, amendments prohibited job termination *at any age* on the basis of age—temporarily excluding for seven years police officers, firefighters, prison guards, and tenured academic faculty. Fully excluded are employees in small businesses (less than 12 employees).

Breaks in service Pension plans often have requirements regarding the number of years employment required to participate in, be vested, or accumulate a certain amount of benefits. One important aspect of this counting process is determining when a "break" in employment occurs, terminating the continued accumulation or counting of the service years necessary to comply with various plan provisions. ERISA contains very specific rules with regard to how years of service should be counted.

Capital The word "capital" is used in two ways. As an economic

269

concept it refers to actual buildings and equipment used to produce goods and services; as a financial concept it refers to the monetary funds used to finance business enterprises, including the acquisition of economic capital.

Coinsurance Coinsurance payments are often required by health insurance programs to keep costs down. Under such arrangements, individuals are required to pay (out-of-pocket or through other insurance) some percentage of the covered costs, with the insurer usually paying the rent. For example, under Part B of Medicare, the program pays only 80 percent of covered charges—after the deductible provision is met. (See also **deductible**.)

Deductible A common technique for reducing the costs of insurance companies is to set an initial amount that must be paid by the person being insured, before benefits begin under the insurance policy. For example, under Part B of Medicare, an individual must pay the first $75 of covered expenses *each year* before Medicare begins paying for additional expenses. (See also **coinsurance**.)

Deferred profit-sharing plan A plan in which the company's contributions are based primarily or exclusively on business profits. Profits are credited to employee accounts to be paid at retirement or other stated dates or circumstances (for example, disability or death).

Defined benefit plans Pension plans that state before retirement how much they will pay in benefits at retirement, benefits usually varying by years of service and/or earnings. These plans contrast with defined contribution plans that specify certain contributions to be made on an employee's behalf; the benefit is then determined at retirement on the basis of the total contribution accumulated.

Defined contribution plans See **defined benefit plans.**

Dependency ratios A numerical measure that compares (divides) the number of older and/or younger persons, typically, age 65 + and under age 18 with (by) persons in the middle ages (e.g., ages 18 to 64). For example, the "aged dependency ratio" is projected to increase from its current level of 19 elderly persons (per 100 persons ages 18 to 64) to 37 per 100 in the year 2030. But simultaneously, the proportion of the population under 18 will decline over the next several decades. The net result is that the *overall* dependency ratio will be lower than it was in the 1960s.

Depreciation allowance A charge against the current income of a business to reflect the using up or "wear and tear" on a certain amount of its assets, primarily buildings and equipment. This charge is not paid out to other businesses but is retained within the firm as a bookkeeping entry.

Depression The recurrent ups and downs in the level of economic activity that extend over a period of years are referred to as the "business cycle." Depression usually refers to extreme low levels of economic activity extending over a long period (not seasonally). The Great Depression of the 1930s extended over almost a decade and resulted, at one point, in about one-quarter of the work force being unemployed.

Discount rate The present price of something whose receipt is deferred for some period is sometimes known as a discounted value. The term "discounting" is suggested by the fact that, at positive rates of interest, $1 due in a year (i.e., deferred for a year) has a "present value" of less than $1. The lower present price of a future amount due is the "discounted" value of the future amount due. The interest rate used for discounting is known as the discount rate.

Disregard A term used to refer to provisions in means-tested financial support programs that exempt certain amounts of financial resources in determining benefit eligibility. For example, in the SSI program, $20 per month of unearned income is disregarded in determining whether an applicant's total income falls below the level specified for payment of benefits.

Equity (home quity) The accumulated value (less any liabilities) of a property or business. In the typical home mortgage situation, the homeowner gradually repays the loan used to purchase the house, while paying interest on the outstanding loan amount. Thus, the portion of the home value "owned" by the person gradually increases over time and is known as his or her equity in the property.

Equivalency scale An index that takes account of differences in family size, composition, health status, age, sex, and other relevant characteristics when determining the level of income necessary to achieve a given level of economic well-being. (See page 54 for discussion of some empirical estimates.)

ERISA Employee Retirement Income Security Act of 1974. Federal legislation establishing participation, vesting, funding standards, plan termination insurance, disclosure requirements, and individual retirement accounts (IRAs).

Federal Reserve A central banking system for the United States established in 1913. There are 12 district banks and a coordinating seven-member Federal Reserve Board of Governors in Washington, D.C. Appointed by the President to the Board of Governors for 14-year terms, members constitute a body that has been purposely established as an independent monetary authority.

Fertility rate The total fertility rate is the number of births that 1,000 women would have in their lifetime if, at each year of age, they experienced the birth rates occurring in the specified calendar year. The fertility rate is an annual (or percentage) measure, even though it is expressed as a hypothetical lifetime (or cohort) measure.

Fiduciary standards The expected or legally specified behavior of individuals or institutions entrusted with authority to make financial decisions on behalf of or affecting other persons or institutions. ERISA sets out a detailed body of law governing the behavior and decisions of people and institutions managing pensions funds on behalf of future beneficiaries.

Fiscal policy Action by the government to influence the economy (especially to promote employment and decrease inflation) through changing tax rates and expenditure levels.

Gross national product (GNP) The dollar value of the total annual output of final goods and services in the nation.

Health maintenance organizations (HMOs) A special kind of group medical practice operating under a prepayment plan. HMOs provide a wide range of medical services in and outside a hospital for a specified premium. Operating in a more competitive environment, providers of medical services under these plans are encouraged to keep costs down and to emphasize preventive health care, since their monetary gains depend on keeping costs under the prepaid fees received from the covered group (or their employers).

Hospice Programs specializing in social and health care services to the terminally ill, usually emphasizing care provided in the home. To be eligible for hospice benefits under Medicare, a person's physician must verify the person has less than six months to live.

Income For every dollar of goods or services produced and sold there is a dollar of income created. Thus, we speak about both the national product and the national income of a country. People, as workers or owners of capital or natural resources, receive income in return for the services provided by factors of production (land, labor, and capital) in the production process.

Index(ing) The use of mathematical ratios to make comparisons between two different periods of time (or comparisons between different locations, industries, nationalities, etc.). The consumer price index is probably the most well-known index, comparing "average" prices in a given year with those in a predetermined base year.

Individual retirement account (IRA) Originally, workers not covered by a retirement plan where they were employed could make tax-deferrable contributions of 15 percent of earned income up to $1,500 per year to an individual account or annuity. Beginning in 1977, if there was a nonemployed spouse, the maximum was increased to $1,750. Funds in IRAs may be placed in a life insurance company, a bank, a mutual fund, or in certain special government bonds. There are penalties and immediate tax liability if funds are withdrawn prematurely. (See text for recent changes.)

Inflation A general and widely diffused increase in the level of prices for various goods and services. The result is a loss in the purchasing power of money, customarily measured by various price indexes (e.g., the consumer price index). Inflation hurts those whose incomes do not rise as fast as prices increase: people with fixed or slowly rising income and savers who lend money. A rise in the index of prices means that it will take more money to buy the same amount of goods and services.

Investment Economic investment is an activity (usually by businesses) that uses the resources of a nation to maintain or add to its stock of physical capital (i.e., buildings and equipment). The main source of investment expenditure is the retained earnings and depreciation allowances of business. Expenditures, however, are also made possible by savings from households (1) by direct borrowing or by sale of new stock issues or (2) indirectly via financial institutions.

Life expectancy A statistical measure of the average number of years persons born in a given year can be expected to live under the conditions prevailing in that year. Life expectancy is measured both at birth and at other years (or stages) of life.

Lifetime rate of return The interest rate that equalizes the compounded value of total taxes paid over a lifetime and the "present value" of the expected stream of benefits. A less technical definition is the rate at which the total value of accumulated payroll taxes (increased for interest) is equated to the value of benefits (decreased for interest). The present value of a sum of money due at a future date is the amount which, put at compound interest at a given rate, will amount to the sum specified at the stated date. The present value of, say, $1,000 six years hence at 5 percent is $746.30, since that sum compounded at 5 percent equals $1,000.

Means test A regulation stipulating that eligibility for aid and the amount of aid provided depend not, for example, on past employment or earnings but on specified amounts of income and/or assets of the persons (family) requesting assistance.

Median A statistical measure that is often used instead of the mean (or average) to describe the center, middle, or "average" of a set of data. It is the value of the middle data item when the items are arranged in an increasing or decreasing order of magnitude. For example, the median of the data set 13 16 18 20 40 is 18.

Monetary policy Action by the government to influence the economy by changing the demand for, and supply of, money.

Money income Income before payment of federal, state, local, or social security (FICA) taxes and before any other deductions, such as union dues or Medicare premiums. Major components of money income are wages and salaries, self-employment income, social security and SSI, public assistance, interest, dividends, rents, unemployment and workers' compensation, other pension income, and alimony/child support. Excluded in almost all reported statistics are capital gains (or losses), lump-sum or one-time payments, and in-kind income (as discussed on pages 42–43).

National income accounting   A generally accepted methodology developed by economists to assist in describing and analyzing a nation's economy. Productive activity and income generated by that activity are measured and organized in a set of standardized tables called "the national accounts." Information from these accounts is used to derive specific economic measures, such as gross national product, national income, and personal income. The tables, and statistics based on them, are usually published by the governments concerned or international agencies such as the Statistics Division of the United Nations.

Negative income tax   A type of benefit proposed to deal with the problem of poverty. As the name implies, a negative income tax is an "income tax in reverse." Income tax programs collect revenues from individuals who have taxable incomes in excess of certain deductions, exemptions, and credits. In contrast, a negative income tax would require the government to make payments to individuals with income below some specified poverty level. Thus, such plans subsidize people with low incomes.

Net worth   An accounting measure of the value of assets minus the value of liabilities.

Overfunded pension plans   Pension plans (either by law or, in a few cases, by convention) maintain assets to meet future liabilities. When plan assets exceed liabilities, this is commonly referred to as overfunding. ERISA requires that only liabilities accrued to termination be covered. Since many plan benefits are based on employee earnings (which generally increase over time), termination liabilities are typically lower than liabilities calculated on an ongoing basis. Hence, the term "overfunding" is not free from ambiguity and measurement issues.

Pension   A fixed dollar amount that is paid regularly over time by a former employer or the government to a retired, disabled, or deserving person (or his or her dependents). The amount may be increased partially or fully in later years to compensate for inflation.

Pension replacement rate   The ratio of retirement income to preretirement income. The definition (or measure) of both numerator and denominator varies. One of the most important measures is the ratio of *pension* income to preretirement earnings. Pension income is typically measured at the "normal retirement age" or at the time of initial start-up of the pension. Earnings are typically an average of the years just before retirement—last three years, high five of the last ten, etc.

Portability A type of vesting (defined below) mechanism that allows employees to take their pension credits with them when they change jobs. For credits to be portable, they must be vested—that is, nonforfeitable. ERISA permits portability but only if both employees and the involved employers mutually agree.

Private pensions Pensions obtained through employment in the nongovernment sector of the economy. (See also **pension**.)

Productivity An economic concept defined as the total output of a good or service divided by the total number of man-hours expended in producing the goods. Productivity is influenced by the level of technology, changes in capital plant and equipment, and the quality of the labor force.

Profit-sharing plan See **deferred profit-sharing plan**.

Progressive tax A tax that takes a larger proportion of income in taxes, the higher the income. The key to whether a tax is progressive or not lies in the increasing percentage of income paid in taxes, not in the increasing amount paid. Thus, the payroll tax is "proportional" up to the taxable earnings ceiling, but the federal income tax is progressive.

Qualified pension plan After a pension plan is initially set up, formal legal documents are usually prepared for submission to the Internal Revenue Service, since few employers are willing to operate a plan whose costs are not deductable for tax purposes. The usual practice is for the employer to submit these documents and ask for a "determination letter" that indicates whether or not the plan "qualifies" under the relevant laws for special tax treatment.

Recession A "mild" depression. (See **depression** defined above.)

Replacement rate See **pension replacement rate**.

Retained earnings Business income after expenses that is not paid out in dividends or government taxes.

Transfer income Income that results from government disbursements for which no products or services are received. Most government welfare expenditures fall into this classification—social security payments, unemployment compensation, etc. Transfer payments, in a sense, rechannel tax revenues of the public sector back into the hands of individuals and groups in the private sector.

Unemployment rate A measure of the number unemployed as a percent of the (usually) civilian labor force. The percent is determined by surveying a sample of the population. Those persons who did not work during the survey week, but were available for work (except for temporary illness) and had looked for jobs within the preceding four weeks.

Vesting The pension rights of a terminating employee depend on the plan provisions. Vesting refers to the provision that gives a participant the right to receive an accrued benefit at a designated age, regardless of whether the employee is still employed at that time. Thus, vesting removes the obligation of the participant to remain in the pension plan until the date of early or normal retirement.

Wage index A measure of the change in general wage levels. Such an index is used in the social security program to adjust recorded wages of workers before calculating benefits. Thus, if a worker earned $3,000 in 1956, retired at age 65 in 1985, and wage levels were, say, two and one half times higher than in 1956, the indexing factor of two and one half would be applied to the $3,000 and the index earnings would be $7,500. (See also **indexing**.)

Workmen's Compensation Various state laws have created programs—some elective and some compulsory—that provide financial compensation to workers injured in work-related activities. Benefits are financed by contributions from employers, and, in return, these employers are relieved of liability from common-law suits. (That is, injured workers agree to accept the benefits under the law on a no-fault basis.) Benefits usually include cash payments, medical services, and rehabilitation opportunities.

REFERENCES

AARON, HENRY J. 1977. "Demographic Effects on the Equity of Social Security Benefits." In M. S. Feldstein and R. P. Inman, eds., *The Economics of Public Service*. New York: Macmillan, pp. 151–173.

———. 1981. "Salvaging Social Security." *The Brookings Bulletin* 17 (Spring): 13–16.

———. 1982. *Economic Effects of Social Security*. Washington, D.C.: The Brookings Institution.

ABBOTT, JULIAN. 1977. "Socioeconomic Characteristics of the Elderly: Some Black-White Differences." *Social Security* 40 (July): 16–42.

Ad Hoc Advisory Committee. 1975. "Social Security: A Sound and Durable Institution of Great Value." In U.S. Senate Special Committee on Aging. *Future Directions in Social Security—Unresolved Issues: An Interim Staff Report*. Washington, D.C.: U.S. Government Printing Office.

ADAMCHAK, DONALD J., AND EUGENE A. FRIEDMAN. 1983. "Societal Aging and Generational Dependency Relationships: Problems of Measurement and Conceptualization." *Research on Aging* 5 (September): 319–338.

Advisory Council on Social Security. 1979. *Social Security Financing and Benefits*. Reports. Washington, D.C.: mimeo.

Advisory Council on Social Security. 1975. Reports. Washington, D.C.: mimeo.

AHART, GREGORY J. 1978. Testimony. In Subcommittee on Social Security, U.S. House Committee on Ways and Means, *Disability Insurance Program: 1978*. Washington, D.C.: U.S. Government Printing Office, pp. 2–9.

American Association of Retired Persons (AARP). 1987. "Older Workers Are Bearing Brunt of Most Downsizing Programs." *AARP News Bulletin* 28 (December): 1, 4–5.

———. 1987. "AARP Leads Drive to Put 'Care' Issues in '88 Race." *AARP News Bulletin* 28 (November): 1, 4–5.

ANDREWS, EMILY S. 1985. *The Changing Profile of Pensions in America*. Washington. D. C.: Employee Benefit Research Institute.

ANDRISANI, PAUL J. 1977. "Effects of Health Problems on the Work Experience of Middle-aged Men." *Industrial Gerontology* 4 (Spring): 97–112.

ARENSON, KAREN W. 1981. "The Low U.S. Rate of Savings." *The New York Times* (22 December): D1 and D7.

ASPIN, LES. 1976. "The Burden of Generosity." *Harper's* 253 (December): 22–24.

ATCHLEY, ROBERT. 1971. "Retirement and Leisure Participation: Continuity or Crisis?" *The Gerontologist* 11 (Spring, Part 1): 13–17.

———. 1976. *The Sociology of Retirement*. New York: Wiley/Schenkman.

ATCHLEY, ROBERT C., AND JUDITH L. ROBINSON. 1982. "Attitudes Toward Retirement and Distance from the Event." *Research on Aging* 4 (September): 299–313.

BALL, ROBERT. 1978. *Social Security Today and Tomorrow*. New York: Columbia University Press.

———. 1987a. "Gaps in Health Care Insurance Coverage of the Elderly." Testimony before the Senate Labor and Human Resources Committee (January 12).

———. 1987b. "Don't Drain the Social Security Fund." *The Washington Post* (August 30): C7.

Bankers Trust Co. 1987. *Corporate Defined Contribution Plans*. N.Y.: Bankers Trust.

BARFIELD, RICHARD E., AND JAMES N. MORGAN. "Trends in Satisfaction with Retirement." *The Gerontologist* 18 (February): 19–23.

BARNES, ROBERTA, AND SHEILA ZEDLEWSKI. 1981. *The Impact of Inflation on the Income and Expenditures of Elderly Families*. Final Report to the Administration on Aging. Washington, D.C.: mimeo.

BARRO, ROBERT J. 1978. *The Impact of Social Security on Private Saving— Evidence from the U.S. Time Series*. Washington, D.C.: American Enterprise Institute.

BASSETT, PRESTON C. 1978. "Future Pension Policy and the President's Commission." *Employee Benefit Plan Review* 33 (December): 28, 30, 91.

BATTEN, MICHAEL D. 1973. "Application of a Unique Industrial Health System." *Industrial Gerontology* (Fall): 38–48.

BECK, S. H. 1984. "Retirement Preparation Programs: Differentials in Opportunity and Use." *Journal of Gerontology* 39: 596–602.

BECKER, GARY S. 1986. "What Really Hurts the Job Market for Older Workers." *Business Week* (October 6): 15.

BELL, DONALD, AND W. MARCLOY. 1987. "Trends in Retirement Eligibility and Pension Benefits, 1974–83." *Monthly Labor Review* 110 (April): 18–25.

BERKOWITZ, MONROE; WILLIAM G. JOHNSON; AND EDWARD H. MURPHY. 1976. *Public Policy Toward Disability*. New York: Praeger.

BICKERMAN, JOHN. 1985. "Stockman Is Right: Military Pensions Are a Scandal." *The Washington Post National Weekly* (April 1): 24–25.

BINSTOCK, ROBERT H. 1983. "The Aged as Scapegoat." *The Gerontologist* 23 (April): 136–143.

BNA. 1978. *Pension Reporter* 202 (August 21): A-9.

———. 1986. *Pension Reporter* 13 (January 20): 114.

———. 1987. *Pension Reporter* 15 (January 11): 92.

BORZILLERI, THOMAS C. 1978. "The Need for a Separate Consumer Index for Older Persons." *The Gerontologist* 18 (June): 230–236.

BOSKIN, MICHAEL J. 1986. *Too Many Promises: The Uncertain Future of Social Security*. Homewood, Ill.: Dow Jones-Irwin

BOSKIN, MICHAEL, AND M. HURD. 1982. "Are Inflation Rates Different for the Elderly?" Mimeo.

BOSKIN, MICHAEL J.; L. J. KOTLIKOFF; D. J. PUFFERT; AND J. B. SHOVEN. 1986. "Social Security: A Financial Appraisal across and within Generations." Working Paper No. 1891. Cambridge Mass.: National Bureau of Economic Research.

BOULDING, KENNETH. 1958. *Principles of Economic Policy*. Englewood Cliffs, N.J.: Prentice-Hall.

BRADFORD, KENNETH. 1979. "Can You Survive Your Retirement?" *Harvard Business Review* (November/December): 103–107.

BRIDGES, B., AND M. PACKARD. 1981. "Prices and Income Changes for the Elderly." *Social Security Bulletin* 44 (January): 3–15.

BRITTAIN, JOHN A. 1972. *The Payroll Tax for Social Security*. Washington, D.C.: The Brookings Institution.

BRODER, DAVID S. 1973. "Budget Funds for Elderly Grow Rapidly." *The Washington Post* (January 30): A-16.

BROWN, J. DOUGLAS. 1972. *An American Philosophy of Social Security*. Princeton, N.J.: Princeton University Press.

———. 1973. Memorandum. In U.S. Senate Special Committee on Aging, *Future Directions in Social Security*. Part 3. Washington, D.C.: U.S. Government Printing Office, pp. 220–221.

BROWNING, EDGAR K. 1973. "Social Insurance and Intergenerational Transfers." *Journal of Law and Economics* (October): 215–237.

BUCHANAN, JAMES M. 1968. "Social Insurance in a Growing Economy: A Proposal for Radical Reform." *National Tax Journal* (December): 386–395.

BURKE, VINCENT J., AND VEE BURKE. 1974. *Nixon's Good Deed. Welfare Reform*. N.Y.: Columbia University Press.

BURKHAUSER, RICHARD V., AND J. P. QUINN. 1985. "Planned and Actual Retirement: An Emperical Analysis." In Z. S. Blau. *Current Perspectives on Aging and the Life Cycle*, Vol 1. Greenwich, Conn.: JAI Press.

BURTLESS, GARY. 1987. "Occupational Effects on the Health and Work Capacity of Older Men." In Gary Burtless, ed., *Work, Health, and Income among the Elderly*. Washington, D.C.: The Brookings Institution, pp. 103–141.

BUTLER, ROBERT N. 1975. *Why Survive? Being Old in America*. New York: Harper & Row.

CALIFANO, JOSEPH A., JR. 1979. Testimony. In U.S. Senate Special Committee on Aging, *Retirement, Work, and Lifelong Learning*. Washington, D.C.: U.S. Government Printing Office.

CALLAHAN, JAMES. 1981. "How Much, For What, and For Whom?" *American Journal of Public Health* 71 (September): 987–988.

CALLAHAN, JAMES, AND STANLEY S. WALLACK, eds. 1981. *Reforming the Long-Term Care System*. Lexington, Mass.: Lexington Books, D. C. Heath.

CAMPBELL, COLIN D., AND ROSEMARY G. CAMPBELL. 1976. "Conflicting Views on the Effect of Old-Age and Survivors Insurance on Retirement." *Economic Inquiry* 14 (September): 369–388.

CAMPBELL, RITA RICARDO. 1975. Supplementary Statement. In *Reports of the Quadrennial Advisory Council on Social Security*. Washington, D.C.: U.S. Government Printing Office.

CARDWELL, JAMES B. 1976. Testimony. In Subcommittee on Social Security, U.S. House Committee on Ways and Means, *Disability Insurance Program*. Washington, D.C.: U.S. Government Printing Office, pp. 273–281.

CHEN, YUNG-PING. 1984. "Economic Status of the Aged." In Robert H. Binstock and Ethel Shanas, eds., *Handbook of Aging and the Social Sciences*, 2nd ed. New York: Van Nostrand Reinhold.

CHEN, YUNG-PING, AND KWANG-WEN CHU. 1974. "Tax-benefit Ratios and Rates of Return Under OASI: 1974 Retirees and Entrants." *The Journal of Risk and Insurance* 41 (June): 189–206.

CLARK, ROBERT, L.; D. T. BARKER; AND R. S. CANTRELL. 1979. *Outlawing Age Discrimination: Economic and Institutional Response to the Elimination of Mandatory Retirement.* Final Report to the Administration on Aging. Mimeo.

CLARK, ROBERT, AND JOSEPH SPENGLER. 1978. "The Implications of Future Dependency Ratios and Their Composition." In Barbara Pieman Herzog, ed., *Aging and Income*, New York: Human Sciences Press, pp. 55–89.

CLARK, TIMOTHY B. 1983. "Congress Avoiding Political Abyss by Approving Social Security Changes." *National Journal* (19 March): 611–615.

———. 1985. "Too Much. Too Soon?" *National Journal* (September 21): 2172.

COHEN, WILBUR J. 1957. *Retirement Policies Under Social Security*. Berkeley: University of California Press.

COHEN, WILBUR J., AND MILTON FRIEDMAN. 1972. *Social Security: Universal or Selective?* Rational Debate Seminars. Washington, D.C.: American Enterprise Institute for Public Policy Research.

COLBERG, MARSHALL R. 1978. *The Social Security Retirement Test—Right or Wrong?* Washington, D.C.: American Enterprise Institute for Public Policy Research.

Congressional Budget Office. 1986. *Earnings Sharing Options for the Social Security System*. Washington, D.C.: CBO.

COOPER, KEITH H. 1980. "Pensions, Inflation and Benefit Indexing." In Aspen Institute, *The Quiet Crisis of Public Pensions*. Conference Report. New York: The Institute.

COTTRELL, FRED, AND ROBERT C. ATCHLEY. 1969. *Women in Retirement. A Preliminary Report*. Oxford, Ohio: Scripps Foundation.

COWGILL, DONALD O. 1981. "Can We Afford Our Aging Populations?" Paper prepared for Conference on Economics of Aging, Kansas City, Missouri, April 1981. Mimeo

COWGILL, DONALD O., AND LOWELL D. HOLMES. 1970. "The Demography of Aging." In A. M. Hoffman, ed., *The Daily Needs and Interests of Older People*. Springfield, Ill.: C. C. Thomas, pp. 27–69.

CROWN, WILLIAM H., AND J. H. SCHULZ. 1987. *Private Expenditures Related to the Support of Younger and Older Persons Not in the Labor Force*. Washington, D.C.: American Association of Retired Persons.

CUTLER, NEAL E., AND ROBERT A. HAROOTYAN. 1975. "Demography of the Aged." In Diana S. Woodruff and James E. Birren, eds., *Aging*. New York: Van Nostrand, pp. 31–69.

DALE, EDWIN L., JR. 1973. "The Young Pay for the Old." *New York Times Magazine* (14 January): 8ff.

DANZIGER, S.; J. VAN DER GAAG; E.SMOLENSKY; AND M. K. TAUSSIG. 1982–83. "The Life-Cycle Hypothesis and the Consumption Behavior of the Elderly." *Journal of Post Keynesian Economics* 5 (Winter): 208–227.

———. "Implications of the Relative Economic Status of the Elderly for Transfer

Policy." In H.J. Aaron and G. Burtless, eds. *Retirement and Economic Behavior*. Washington, D.C.: The Brookings Institution.

DAVIS, KAREN. 1982. "Medicare Reconsidered." Paper prepared for the Duke University Medical Center Seventh Private Sector Conference on Financial Support of Health Care for the Elderly and Indigent. Durham, N.C.: mimeo.

DAYMONT, T. N., AND P. J. ANDRISANI. 1983. "The Health and Economic Status of Very Early Retirees." *Aging and Work* 6: 117–135.

DEVITA, CAROL J. 1981. "Measuring Dependency in the U.S. and in Canada." Paper presented at the 34th Annual Meeting of the Gerontological Society of America, Toronto.

DIAMOND, P. A. 1977. "A Framework for Social Security Analysis." *Journal of Public Economics* 8 (December): 275–298.

DOCTORS, S. I.; Y. M. SHKOP; K. C. DENNING; AND V. T. DOCTORS. 1980. "Older Worker Employment Services." *Aging and Work* 3 (Fall): 229–237.

DONAHUE, WILMA; HAROLD L. ORBACH; AND OTTO POLLAK. 1960. "Retirement: The Emerging Social Pattern." In Clark Tibbitts, ed., *Handbook of Social Gerontology*. Chicago: University of Chicago Press, pp. 330–406.

DOWD, JAMES J., AND VERN BENGTSON. 1978. "Aging in Minority Populations." *Journal of Gerontology* 33 (May): 427–436.

DRAZAGA, LINDA; M. UPP; AND V. RENO. 1982. "Low Income Aged; Eligibility and Participation in SSI." *Social Security Bulletin* 45 (May): 28–35.

DRI (Data Resources, Inc.). 1980. *Inflation and the Elderly*. Report to NRTA/AARP. Lexington, Mass. mimeo.

EASTERLIN, RICHARD A. 1987. "The New Age Structure of Poverty in America: Permanent or Transient?" *Population and Development Review* 13 (June): 195–208.

EBPR *(Employee Benefit Plan Review)*. 1987a. "HIAA Spokesman Urges Help for Long-Term Care." 42 (October): 78, 80.

———. 1987b. "Preretirement Planning Eases the Transition." 42 (December): 122–125.

EBRI (Employee Benefit Research Institute). 1987. *Employee Benefit Notes*. (December 11): 1.

The Economist. 1987. "Health Care—The Battle to Contain Costs." October 31: 34, 36.

EKERDT, DAVID J. 1987. "Why the Notion Persists that Retirement Harms Health." *The Gerontologist* 27 (August): 454–457.

EPSTEIN, LENORE A., AND JANET H. MURRAY. 1967. *The Aged Population of the United States*. Office of Research and Statistics, Social Security Administration. Report No. 19. Washington, D.C.: U.S. Government Printing Office.

ESPOSITO, LOUIS; L. B. MALLAN; AND D. PODOFF. 1980. "Distribution of Increased Benefits under Alternative Earnings Tests." *Social Security Bulletin* 43 (September): 3–9.

FAIRHOLM, GILBERT W. 1978. *Property Tax Relief Programs for the Elderly. A Review of Current Literature and Policy Implications for Virginia*. Richmond: Virginia Center on Aging, Virginia Commonwealth University, mimeo.

Federal Council on Aging. 1975. *Study of Interrelationships of Benefit Programs for the Elderly*. Appendix I: "Handbook of Federal Programs Benefiting Older Americans." Prepared for the Federal Council on Aging by the Human Resources and Income Security Project, The Urban Institute. Washington, D.C.: mimeo.

————. 1985. *Health Care Study for Older Americans*. Washington, D.C.: Office of Human Development Services. DHHS.

FELDSTEIN, MARTIN S. 1972. "The Incidence of the Social Security Payroll Tax: Comment." *The American Economic Review* 42 (September): 735–742.

————. 1975. "Toward a Reform of Social Security." *The Public Interest* 40 (Summer): 80–81.

————. 1977. "Facing the Social Security Crisis." *The Public Interest* 47 (Spring): 88–100.

FERRARA, PETER J. 1986. "Intergenerational Transfers and Super IRA's." *Cato Journal* 6 (Spring/Summer): 195–228.

FITZGERALD, ALBERT J. 1978. Testimony. In Subcommittee on Retirement Income and Employment, U.S. House Select Committee on Aging, *National Pension Policies: Private Pension Plans*. Washington, D.C.: U.S. Government Printing Office, pp. 486–494.

FLINT, JERRY. 1977. "Early Retirement Is Growing in U.S." *New York Times* (10 July): 1.

————. 1980. "The Old Folks." *Forbes* (18 February): 51–56.

FLOWERS, MARILYN R. 1977. *Women and Social Security: An Institutional Dilemma*. Washington, D.C.: American Enterprise Institute for Public Policy Research.

FONER, ANNE, AND KAREN SCHWAB. 1983. "Work and Retirement in a Changing Society." In Matilda White Riley, Beth B. Hess, and K. Bond, eds., *Aging in Society: Selected Reviews of Recent Research*. Hillsdale, N.J.: Lawrence Erlbaum Associates.

FORMAN, MAXINE. 1987. "Consumer Perspectives on Impact of Retirement Income Systems on Women in the United States." In Mary Jo Gibson, ed., *Income Security and Long Term Care for Women in Midlife and Beyond*. Washington, D.C.: American Association of Retired Persons.

————. 1982. "Earnings Replacement Rates and Total Income: Findings from the Retirement History Study." *Social Security Bulletin* 45 (October): 3–24.

FRIEDEN, ALAN; DEAN LEIMER; AND RONALD HOFFMAN. 1976. *Internal Rates of Return to Retired Worker-Only Beneficiaries Under Social Security, 1967–70*. Studies in Income Distribution No. 5. Washington, D.C.: Office of Research and Statistics, Social Security Administration.

FRIEDMAN, EUGENE A., AND HAROLD L. ORBACH. "Adjustment to Retirement." In Silvano Arieti, ed., *The Foundation of Psychiatry*. Vol. 1, *American Handbook of Psychiatry*, 2nd ed. New York: Basic Books, pp. 609–645.

FRIEDMAN, MILTON. 1971. "Purchasing Power Bonds." *Newsweek* (12 April): 86.

————. 1972. "Second Lecture." In Wilbur J. Cohen and Milton Friedman, *Social Security: Universal or Selective?* Rational Debate Seminars. Washington, D.C.: American Enterprise Institute.

FULLERTON, HOWARD N., JR. 1987. "Labor Force Projections: 1986–2000." *Monthly Labor Review* 110 (September): 19–29.

GALBRAITH, JOHN KENNETH. 1958. *The Affluent Society*. Boston: Houghton Mifflin.

GIBSON, MARY JO, ed. 1987. *Income Security and Long Term Care for Women in*

Midlife and Beyond: U.S. and Canadian Perspectives. Washington, D.C.: American Association of Retired Persons.

GORDON, ROBERT J. 1981. "The Consumer Price Index: Measuring Inflation and Causing It." *The Public Interest* (Spring): 112–134.

GOUDY, WILLIS J. 1981. "Changing Work Expectations: Findings from the Retirement History Study." *The Gerontologist* 21 (December): 644–649.

GRAD, SUSAN. 1985. *Income of the Population 55 and Over, 1984*. Washington. D.C.: U.S. Social Security Administration.

GUTTENTAG, JACK M. n.d. "Home Equity Conversion: A New Factor in Retirement Planning." In Philip Cagan, ed., *Saving for Retirement*. Washington, D.C.: American Council of Life Insurance.

GWIRTZMAN, MILTON. 1985. "Social Security into Terra Incognita." *The Journal of the Institute for Socioeconomic Studies* 10 (Autumn): 11.

HARTMAN, ROBERT. 1983. *Pay and Pensions for Federal Workers*. Washington, D.C.: The Brookings Institution.

HAVEMAN, ROBERT H.; B. L. WOLFE; AND J. T. WARLICK. 1984. "Disability Transfers, Early Retirement, and Retrenchment." In H. J. Aaron and G. T. Burtless, eds., *Retirement and Economic Behavior*. Washington, D.C.: The Brookings Institution, pp. 65–96.

HEIDBREDER, E. M., AND M. D. BATTEN. 1974. "ESAR II—A Comparative View of Services to Age Groups." *Facts and Trends* No. 4. Washington, D.C.: National Council on Aging.

HEW Task Force (on the Treatment of Women Under Social Security). 1978 *Report*. Washington, D.C.: U.S. Department of Health, Education and Welfare.

HEWITT, EDWIN S. 1970. Testimony. In U.S. Senate Special Committee on Aging, *Economics of Aging: Toward a Full Share in Abundance*, Part 10B. Washington, D.C.: U.S. Government Printing Office.

HOLDEN, KAREN C. 1982. "Supplemental OASI Benefits to Homemakers through Current Spouse Benefits, a Homemaker Credit, and Child-Care Drop-Out Years." In R. V. Burkhauser and K. C. Holden, *A Challenge to Social Security*. N.Y.: Academic Press.

HOLDEN, KAREN C.; R. V. BURKHAUSER; AND D. J. FEASTER. 1987. "The Timing of Falls into Poverty after Retirement and Widowhood." Paper presented at the 1987 meeting of the Gerontological Society of America (reproduced).

HOLLISTER, ROBINSON G., AND JOHN L. PALMER. 1972. "The Impact of Inflation on the Poor." In Kenneth Boulding and M. Pfaff, eds., *Redistribution to the Rich and Poor: The Grants Economics of Income Distribution*. Belmont, Calif.: Wadsworth, pp. 240–270.

HUDSON, ROBERT. 1978. "The 'Graying' of the Federal Budget and Its Consequences for Old-Age Policy." *The Gerontologist* 18 (October): 428–440.

Institute on Poverty, University of Wisconsin. 1983. "The Relative Economic Status of the Aged." *IRP Focus* 6 (Spring): 1–4, 11–14.

IRELAN, LOLA M., AND K. BOND. 1976. "Retirees of the 1970's." In Gary S. Kart and Barbara B. Manard, *Aging in America—Readings in Social Gerontology*. Sherman Oaks, Calif.: Alfred, pp. 231–251.

JACKSON, J. J. 1970. "Aged Negroes: Their Cultural Departures from Statistical

Stereotypes of Rural-Urban Differences." *The Gerontologist* 10 (Summer): 140–145.

JOHNSON AND HIGGINS, INC. 1979. *1979 Study of American Attitudes toward Pensions and Retirement*. New York: Johnson and Higgins.

———. 1981. *Funding Costs and Liabilities of Large Corporate Pension Plans*. New York: Johnson and Higgins.

JUSTER, F. THOMAS. n.d. "Current and Prospective Financial Status of the Elderly Population." In Phillip Cagan, ed., *Saving Retirement*. Washington, D.C.: American Council of Life Insurance.

KAHNE, HILDA. 1975. "Economic Perspectives on the Roles of Women in the American Economy." *The Journal of Economic Literature* 13 (December): 1249–1292.

KASSCHAU, PATRICIA L. 1974. "Reevaluating the Need for Retirement Preparation Programs." *Industrial Gerontology*, new series 1 (Winter): 42–59.

KING, JILL. 1976. *The Consumer Price Index*. Technical Paper V. The Measure of Poverty reports. Washington, D.C.: U.S. Department of Health, Education, and Welfare.

KINGSON, ERIC R. 1979. "Men Who Leave Work Before Age 62: A Study of Advantaged and Disadvantaged Very Early Labor Force Withdrawal." Ph.D. dissertation, Florence Heller Graduate School, Brandeis University.

KINGSON, ERIC. R., B. A. HIRSHORN, AND J. M. CORNMAN. 1986. *Ties that Bind—The Interdependence of Generations*. Cabin John, Md.: Seven Locks Press.

KOSTERLITZ, JULIE. 1986. "Protecting the Elderly," *National Journal* (May 24): 1254–1258.

KOTLIKOFF, LAURENCE J.; AVIA SPIVAK; AND LAWRENCE SUMMERS. 1982. "The Adequacy of Savings," *American Economic Review* 72 (December): 1056-1069.

KOTLIKOFF, LAWRENCE J., AND D. A. WISE. 1985. "Labor Compensation and the Structure of Private Pension Plans: Evidence for Contractural versus Spot Labor Markets." In D. A. Wise, ed., *Pensions, Labor, and Individual Choice*. Chicago, Ill.: The University of Chicago Press, pp. 55–88.

KREPS, JUANITA M. 1977. "Age, Work, and Income." *Southern Economic Journal* 43 (April): 1423–1437.

KREPS, JUANITA M., AND JOSEPH J. SPENGLER. 1966. "The Leisure Component of Economic Growth." In National Commission on Technology, Automation, and Economic Progress. *Technology and the Economy*. Appendix 2: The Employment Impact of Technological Change. Washington, D.C.: U.S. Government Printing Office.

KRUTE, AARON, AND MARY ELLEN BURDETTE. 1978. "1972 Survey of Disabled and Nondisabled Adults: Chronic Disease, Injury, and Work Disability." *Social Security Bulletin* 41 (April): 3–17.

LAPKOFF, SHELLY. 1981. "Working Women, Marriage, and Retirement." Chapter 42 in the Appendix of the President's Commission on Pension Policy. *Coming of Age: Toward a National Retirement Policy*. Washington, D.C.: The Commission.

LaROCK, SEYMOUR. 1987. "Retirement Patterns 1978–86: ADEA Protection Has Little Effect on Employee Decision." *Employee Benefit Plan Review* (April): 30–34.

LAWRENCE, JIM. 1986. "House Votes to End Mandatory Retirement." *The Boston Globe* (September 24): 5.

LEAVITT, THOMAS D. 1983. *Early Retirement Incentive Programs*. Waltham, Mass.: Policy Center on Aging, Brandeis University.

———. 1986. *The Impact of "Overfunded" Pension Terminations on Workers*. Publication 8603. Washington, D.C.: AARP Public Policy Institute.

LEAVITT, THOMAS D., AND J. H. SCHULZ. 1988. "The Role of the Asset Test In Program Eligibility and Participation: The Case of SSI." Working Paper. Waltham, MA.: Policy Center on Aging, Heller School, Brandeis University.

LEAVITT, THOMAS D; J. H. SCHULZ; S. FOURNIER; K. SOHN; AND L. DIAMOND. 1987. *Corporate Health Benefits for Medicare Eligible Retirees: An Analysis of Retiree Experience and Attitudes*. Washington, D.C.: American Association of Retired Persons.

LEIMER, DEAN R. 1979. "Projected Rates of Return to Future Social Security Retirees Under Alternative Benefit Structures." In *Proceedings of the Workshop on Policy Analysis with Social Security Record Files*. Washington, D.C.: Social Security Administration.

LEONARD, HERMAN B. 1986. *Checks Unbalanced: The Quiet Side of Public Spending*. New York: Basic Books.

LESNOY, SELIG D., AND D. R. LEIMER. 1981. "Social Security and Private Saving: New Time Series Evidence with Alternative Specifications." Working Paper No. 22. Washington, D.C.: Office of Research and Statistics, Social Security Administration.

LEUTHOLD, JANE H. 1975. "The Incidence of the Payroll Tax in the United States." *Public Finance Quarterly* 3 (January): 3–13.

LIANG, J., AND T. J. FAIRCHILD. 1979. "Relative Deprivation and Perception of Financial Adequacy Among the Aged." *Gerontology* 34 (September): 747–760.

LINDBLOM, CHARLES E. 1977. *Politics and Markets—The World's Political-Economic Systems*. New York: Basic Books.

McCONNEL, CHARLES E., AND F. DELJAVAN. 1983. "Consumption Patterns of the Retired Household." *Journal of Gerontology* 38 (July): 480–490.

McGILL, DAN M. 1975. *Fundamentals of Private Pensions*, 3rd ed. Homewood, ILL.: Irwin.

MALLAN, LUCY B. 1975. "Young Widows and Their Children: A Comparative Report." *Social Security Bulletin* 38 (May): 3–21.

MARKIDES, KYRIAKOS S. 1981. Letter to the Editor. *Journal of Gerontology* 36 (July): 494.

———. 1983. "Minority Aging." In Matilda White Riley, B. Hess, and K. Bond, *Aging in Society: Selected Reviews of Recent Research*. Hillsdale, N.J.: Lawrence Erlbaum Associates.

MAXWELL, JAMES A. 1975. "Characteristics of State and Local Trust Funds." In David J. Ott, Attiat F. Ott, James A. Maxwell, and J. Richard Aronson, *State-Local Finances in the Last Half of the 1970's*. Washington, D.C.: The American Enterprise Institute, pp. 35–62.

MEYER, CHARLES W., ed. 1987. *Social Security—A Critique of Radical Reform Proposals*. Lexington, Mass.: Lexington Books.

MICHAEL, ROBERT T. 1979. "Variations Across Households in the Rate of Inflation." *Journal of Money, Credit and Banking* 2 (February): 32–46.

MINARIK, JOSEPH J. 1981. Testimony before the U.S. Senate Special Committee on Aging. Hearings on "Social Security Oversight: Cost-of-Living Adjustments." Part 3. Washington, D.C.: U.S. Government Printing Office.

MIRER, THAD W. 1974. "The Distributional Impact of Inflation and Anti-inflation Policy." Discussion Paper 231–74. Madison: Institute for Research on Poverty, University of Wisconsin-Madison.

―――. 1980. "The Dissaving Behavior of the Retired Aged." *Southern Economic Journal* 46 (April): 1197–1205.

MITCHELL, OLIVIA S., AND E. S. ANDREWS. 1981. "Scale Economies in Private Multi-Employer Pension Systems." *Industrial and Labor Relations Review* 34 (July): 522–530.

MITCHELL, OLIVIA S., AND G. S. FIELDS. 1982. "The Effects of Pensions and Earnings on Retirement: A Review Essay." In R. Ehrenberg, *Research in Labor Economies*, Vol. 5. Greenwich, Conn.: Jai Press.

MODIGLIANI, FRANCO. 1987. "The Key to Saving Is Growth, Not Thrift." *Challenge* 30 (May-June): 24–29.

MOELLER, CHARLES. 1972. "The Role of Private Pension Plans in the Economy." In *Financing Retirement: Public and Private*. Conference Proceedings. New York: The Tax Foundation, Inc.

MORGAN, JAMES N. 1977. "An Economic Theory of the Social Security System and Its Relation to Fiscal Policy." In G. S. Tolley and Richard V. Burkhauser, eds. *Income Support Policies for the Aged*. Cambridge, Mass.: Ballinger, pp. 107–126.

―――. 1978. "Intra-Family Transfers Revisited: The Support of Dependents Inside the Family." In G. Duncan and J. Morgan, eds., *Five Thousand American Families: Patterns of Economic Progress*, Vol. 6. Ann Arbor, Mich.: Survey Research Center, Institute of Social Research, The University of Michigan.

―――. 1980. "Retirement in Prospect and Retrospect." In Greg J. Duncan and James N. Morgan, eds., *Five Thousand American Families—Patterns of Economic Progress*, Vol. 8. Analyses of the First Eleven Years of the Panel Study of Income Dynamics, Ann Arbor, Mich.: Survey Research Center, Institute for Social Research, University of Michigan.

―――. 1983. "The Redistribution of Income by Families and Institutions and Emergency Help Patterns." In G. J. Duncan and J. N. Morgan. eds., *Five Thousand American Families—Patterns of Economic Progress*. Ann Arbor, Mich.: Institute for Social Research. The University of Michigan, pp. 1–59.

MORGAN, JAMES N.; KATHERINE DICKINSON; JONATHAN DICKINSON; JACOB BENUS; AND GREG DUNCAN. 1974. *Five Thousand American Families—Patterns of Economic Progress*. Ann Arbor, Mich.: Survey Research Center, Institute for Social Research, University of Michigan.

MORRIS, ROBERT, AND PAUL YOUKET. 1981. "The Long-Term Care Issues: Identifying the Problems and Potential Solutions." In J. J. Callahan and S. Wallack, eds., *Reforming the Long-Term Care System*. Lexington, Mass.: Lexington Books, D. C. Heath.

MORRISON, PETER A. 1982. "Demographic Links to Social Security." *Challenge* 24 (January/February): 44–48.

MOTHNER, IRA. 1985. *Children and Elders: Intergenerational Relations in an Aging Society*. New York: Carnegie Foundation.

MOTLEY, DENA K. 1978. "Availability of Retired Persons for Work: Findings from the Retirement History Study." *Social Security Bulletin* 41 (April): 18–29.

MUNNELL, ALICIA H. 1977. *The Future of Social Security*. Washington, D.C.: The Brookings Institution.

———. 1979. "Are Private Pensions Doomed?" *New England Economic Review* (March/April): 5–20.

———. 1982a. *The Economics of Private Pensions*. Washington, D.C.: The Brookings Institution.

———. 1982b. "Guaranteeing Private Pension Benefits: A Potentially Expensive Business." *New England Economic Review* (March/April): 24–47.

MUNNELL, ALICIA H., AND L. E. BLAIS. 1984. "Do We Want Large Social Security Surpluses?" *New England Economic Review* (September/October): 5–21.

MUSGRAVE, RICHARD. 1968. "The Role of Social Insurance in an Overall Program for Social Welfare." In Bowen et al., *The American System of Social Insurance*. New York: McGraw-Hill, pp. 23–45.

MYERS, GEORGE C. 1984. "Aging and World-Wide Population Change." In Robert H. Binstock and Ethel Shanas, eds., *Handbook of Aging and the Social Sciences*, 2nd ed. New York: Van Nostrand Reinhold.

MYERS, ROBERT J. 1970. "Government and Pension." In *Private Pensions and the Public Interest*. Washington, D.C.: The American Enterprise Institute.

———. 1982. "Prevalence of Elections of Joint-and-Survivor Annuities under Private Pension Plans." Memorandum No. 25 to the National Commission on Social Security Reform. Washington, D.C.: mimeo.

———. 1985. *Social Security*, 3d ed. Homewood, Ill.: Irwin.

———. 1987. "Social Security Roller Coaster." *The Washington Post* (August 20, 1987): A23.

MYERS, ROBERT J., AND B. D. SCHOBEL. 1983. "A Money's-Worth Analysis of Social Security Retirement Benefits." *Transactions* (of the Society of Actuaries): 533–561.

MYRDAL, GUNNAR. 1963. *Challenge to Affluence*. New York: Pantheon Books.

National Association of Working Women (NOW). 1987. *Social Security: The Economic Marginalization of Workers*. Washington, D.C.: NOW.

National Commission on Social Security. 1981. *Social Security in America's Future*. Report of the Commission to the President. Washington, D.C.: The Commission.

NCOA (National Council on the Aging). 1975. *The Myth and Reality of Aging in America*. Washington, D.C.: NCOA.

———. 1980. "Retirement Preparation: Growing Corporate Involvement." *Aging and Work* 3 (Winter): 1–26.

———. 1981. *Aging in the Eighties*. Washington, D.C.: NCOA.

Newsweek. 1984. "The Social Security Scandals." September 24: 32–33.

NORDHAUS, W., AND J. TOBIN. 1973. "Is Growth Obsolete?" In *The Measurement of Economic and Social Performance*. New York: National Bureau of Economic Research, pp. 509–532.

OKONKWO, UBADIGBO. 1975. "Intragenerational Equity Under Social Security." Washington, D.C.: mimeo.

OKUN, ARTHUR. 1975. *Equality and Efficiency—The Big Trade-Off*. Washington, D.C.: The Brookings Institution.

ORSHANSKY, MOLLIE. 1978. Testimony. In U.S. House Select Committee on Aging, *Poverty Among America's Aged*. Washington, D.C.: U.S. Government Printing Office.

PALMORE, ERDMAN. 1977. "Facts on Aging—A Short Quiz." *The Gerontologist* 17 (July): 315–320.

PALMORE, ERDMAN; G. G. FILLENBAUM; AND L. K. GEORGE. 1984. "Consequences of Retirement." *Journal of Gerontology* 39 (January): 109–116.

PALTIEL, FREDA L. 1982. "Women and Pensions in Canada." *International Social Security Review* 35 (No. 3): 333–334.

PARNES, HERBERT S. 1981. "From the Middle to the Later Years." *Research on Aging* 3 (December): 387–402.

PARNES, HERBERT S., AND GILBERT NESTEL. 1979. "The Retirement Experience." In H. S. Parnes, G. Nestel, T. H. Chirikos, T. N. Daymont, F. L. Mott, and D. O. Parsons. *From the Middle to Later Years*. Columbus, Ohio: Center for Human Resources, Ohio State University.

PECHMAN, JOSEPH A.; HENRY J. AARON; AND MICHAEL K. TAUSSIG. 1968. *Social Security: Perspectives for Reform*. Washington, D.C.: The Brookings Institution.

PELLECHIO, ANTHONY J., AND GORDON P. GOODFELLOW. 1983. "Individual Gains and Losses from Social Security before and after the 1983 Social Security Amendments." Paper prepared for the Cato Institute Conference on Social Security. Mimeo.

Perspectives. 1987. *Medicine and Health Perspectives Newsletter* (November 2).

PETER D. HART RESEARCH ASSOCIATES, INC. 1979. *A National Survey of Attitudes toward Social Security*. A report prepared for the National Commission on Social Security. Washington, D.C.: mimeo.

PETERSON, PETER G. 1982. "Social Security: The Coming Crash." *New York Review of Books* 29 (2 December): 34.

———. 1987. "The Morning After." *The Atlantic* 260 (October): 43–69.

Poverty Studies Task Force. 1976. *The Measure of Poverty*. A Report to Congress as Mandated by the Education Amendments of 1974. Washington, D.C.: U.S. Department of Health, Education, and Welfare.

President's Commission on Pension Policy. 1981. *Coming of Age: Toward a National Retirement Income Policy*. Report of the Commission. Washington, D.C.: The Commission.

Profit Sharing Research Foundation. 1978. *Profit Sharing in 38 Large Companies*. Evanston, Ill.

PURSELL, DONALD E., AND WILLIAM D. TORRENCE. 1979. "Age and the Jobhunting Methods of the Unemployed." *Monthly Labor Review* 102 (January): 68–69.

QUINN, JOSEPH F. 1975. "The Microeconomics of Early Retirement: A Cross-

Section View of White Married Men." *Journal of Human Resources* 12 (Summer): 329–346.

RADNER, DANIEL B. 1982. "Distribution of Family Income: Improved Estimates." *Social Security Bulletin* 45 (July): 13–21.

RAUCH, JONATHAN. 1987a. "Uncle Sam Inc." *National Journal* (September 5): 2242.

———. 1987b. "False Security." *National Journal* 19 (February 14): 362–365.

REICH, MURRAY H. 1977. "Group Preretirement Education Programs: Whither the Proliferation?" *Industrial Gerontology* 4 (Winter): 29–43.

RENO, VIRGINIA. 1971. "Why Men Stop Working At or Before Age 65: Findings from the Survey of New Beneficiaries." *Social Security Bulletin* (June): 3–11.

RICH, SPENCER. 1983. "Census Finds Elderly's After-Tax Income Higher than Average." *Washington Post,* 19 August.

RILEY, MATILDA WHITE, AND ANN FONER. 1968. *Aging and Society,* Vol. 1. New York: Russell Sage Foundation.

ROBERTSON, A. HAEWORTH. 1977. "OASDI: Fiscal Basis and Long-Range Cost Projections." *Social Security Bulletin* 40 (January): 1–9.

———. 1981. *The Coming Revolution in Social Security.* McLean, Va.: Security Press.

ROBINSON, PAULINE; SALLY COBERLY; AND C. E. PAUL. 1984. "Work and Retirement." In Robert H. Binstock and Ethel Shanas, eds. *Handbook of Aging and the Social Sciences,* 2nd ed. New York: Van Nostrand Reinhold.

RONES, PHILIP L. 1978. "Older Men—The Choice Between Work and Retirement." *Monthly Labor Review* 101 (November): 3–10.

———. 1983. "The Labor Market Problems of Older Workers." *Monthly Labor Review* 106 (May): 3–12.

ROSENBLUM, M., AND H. SHEPPARD. 1977. *Jobs for Older Workers in U.S. Industry: Possibilities and Prospects.* Report to the U.S. Department of Commerce, Economic Development Administration. Washington, D.C.: mimeo.

ROSS, C. M.; S. DANZIGER; AND E. SMOLENSKY. 1987. "Interpreting Changes in the Economic Status of the Elderly, 1949–1979." *Contemporary Policy Issues* 5: 98–112.

ROSS, JANE L. 1987. "Changing the Retirement Age in the United States: A Case Study on Research and Social Security Policy-making." *International Social Security Review* 40(3): 231–247.

ROWEN, HOBART. 1978. "Rethinking That Bite in Social Security." *Washington Post* (16 February): A-19.

RUPP, KALMAN. 1983. *Eligibility and Participation Rates of Older Americans in Employment and Training Programs.* Research Report Series, RR-83-11. Washington, D.C.: National Commission for Employment Policy.

SAMUELSON, PAUL. 1958. "An Exact Consumption-Loan Model of Interest With or Without the Social Contrivance of Money." *Journal of Political Economy* 66 (December): 467–482.

SCHIEBER, SYLVESTER J. 1978. "First Year Impact of SSI on Economic Status of 1973 Adult Assistance Populations." *Social Security Bulletin* 41 (February): 18–51.

SCHMITT, DONALD G. 1984. "Postretirement Increases under Private Pension Plans." *Monthly Labor Review* 107 (September): 3–8.

SCHMUNDT, M.; E. SMOLENSKY; AND L. STIEFEL. 1975. "The Evaluation of Recipients of In-Kind Transfers." In I. Laurie, ed., *Integrating Income Maintenance Programs*. New York: Academic Press, pp. 189–207.

SCHOLEN, KEN; AND YUNG-PING CHEN. 1980. *Unlocking Home Equity for the Elderly*. Cambridge, Mass.: Ballinger.

SCHORR, ALVIN L. 1960. *Filial Responsibility in the Modern American Family*. Washington, D.C.: U.S. Government Printing Office.

SCHOTTLAND, CHARLES I. 1970. *The Social Security Program in the United States*, 2nd ed. New York: Appleton-Century-Crofts.

SCHRAM, S. F.; AND D. F. OSTEN. 1978. "CETA and the Aging," *Aging and Work*, 1 (Summer): 163–174.

SCHULZ, JAMES H. 1977. "The Social Security Retirement Test: Time for a Change?" *The Urban and Social Change Review* 10 (Summer): 14–18.

———. 1978. "Liberalizing the Social Security Retirement Test—Who Would Receive the Increased Pension Benefits?" *Journal of Gerontology* 22 (March): 262–268.

SCHULZ, JAMES H., AND GUY CARRIN. 1972. "The Role of Savings and Pension Systems in Maintaining Living Standards in Retirement." *Journal of Human Resources* 7 (Summer): 343–365.

SCHULZ, JAMES H.; G. CARRIN; H. KRUPP; M. PESCHKE; E. SCLAR; AND J. VAN STEENBERGE. 1974. *Providing Adequate Retirement Income—Pension Reform in the United States and Abroad*. Hanover, N.H.: New England Press for Brandeis University Press.

SCHULZ, JAMES H.; A. BOROWSKI; L. KELLY; T. D. LEAVITT; AND W. SPECTOR. 1980. *Private Pension Policy Simulations*. Final report to the U.S. Department of Labor. Waltham, Mass.: mimeo.

SCHULZ, JAMES H.; T. D. LEAVITT; L. KELLY; AND J. STRATE. 1982. *Private Pension Benefits in the 1970s*. Bryn Mawr, Pa.: McCahan Foundation for Research in Economic Security.

SCHULZ, JAMES H. AND T. D. LEAVITT. 1983. *Pension Integration: Concepts, Issues and Proposals*. Washington, D.C.: Employee Benefit Research Institute.

SCHULZ, JAMES H.; T. D. LEAVITT; J. STRATE; AND M. STUBBS. 1984. *State, Local, and Teachers Pensions: Coping with Inflation Over the 1975–1982 Period*. Final report to the AARP Andrus Foundation. Waltham, Mass.: Policy Center on Aging, mimeo.

SCHWAB, KAREN. 1976. "Early Labor-Force Withdrawal of Men: Participants and Non-participants Aged 58–63." In Social Security Administration, *Almost 65: Baseline Data from the Retirement History Study*. Washington, D.C.: Office of Research and Statistics, pp. 43–56.

SCOTT, HILDA, AND JULIET F. BRUDNEY. 1987. *Forced Out*. New York: Simon & Schuster.

SHANAS, ETHEL. 1977. *National Survey of the Aged*. Final report to the U.S. Administration on Aging. Chicago: mimeo.

SHANAS, ETHEL, AND PHILIP M. HAUSER. 1974. "Zero Population Growth and the Family Life of Old People." *Journal of Social Issues* 30: 79–92.

SHANAS, ETHEL; PETER TOWNSEND; DOROTHY WEDDERBURN; HENNING FRIIS; POUL MILHOG; AND JAN STEHOUWER. 1968. *Old People in Three Industrial Societies*. New York: Atherton.

SHEPPARD, HAROLD L. 1977. "Factors Associated with Early Withdrawal from the Labor Force." In S. L. Wolfbein, *Men in the Pre-retirement Years*. Philadelphia: Temple University.

———. 1978. "The Economics of Population, Mortality, and Retirement." In *The Economics of Aging*. A National Journal Issues Book. Washington, D.C.: The Government Research Corporation, pp. 1880–1883.

SHEPPARD, HAROLD L., AND A. HARVEY BELITSKY. 1966. *The Job Hunt*. Baltimore, Md.: Johns-Hopkins Press.

SHUCHMAN, CAROL. 1983. "Family Transfers and Household Living Arrangements among the Elderly." Paper presented at the Population Association of America Meetings, April 13–16. Mimeo.

SIEGEL, JACOB S. 1976. *Demographic Aspects of Aging and the Older Population in the United States*. Current Population Reports, Special Studies. Series P-23, No. 59. Washington, D.C.: U.S. Government Printing Office.

SIEGFRIED, CHARLES A. 1970. "The Role of Private Pensions." In *Private Pensions and the Public Interest*. Washington, D.C.: The American Enterprise Institute.

SKOLNIK, ALFRED M. 1975. "Restructuring the Railroad Retirement System." *Social Security Bulletin* 38 (April): 23–29.

SLAVICK, FRED. 1966. *Compulsory and Flexible Retirement in the American Economy*. Ithaca, N.Y.: Cornell University Press.

SMEEDING, TIMOTHY M. 1982. "Alternative Methods for Valuing Selected In-Kind Transfer Benefits and Measuring Their Effect on Poverty." Technical Paper 50. Washington, D.C.: U.S. Bureau of the Census.

SNYDER, DONALD. 1986. "Pension Status of Recently Retired Workers on Their Longest Job: Findings from the New Beneficiary Survey." *Social Security Bulletin* 49 (August): 5–19.

SOBEL, IRVIN, AND RICHARD C. WILCOCK. 1963. "Job Placement Services for Older Workers in the United States." *International Labor Review* 88: 129–156.

Social Security Administration. 1976. *Almost 65: Baseline Data from the Retirement History Study*. Washington, D.C.: Office of Research and Statistics.

———. "Erroneous Public Perception of SSA Administrative Expenses." *Social Security Bulletin* 44 (September): 1.

SOLDO, BETH J. 1981. "The Living Arrangements of the Elderly in the Near Future." In S. B. Kiesler; J. N. Morgan; and V. K. Oppenheimer. *Aging: Social Change*. New York: Academic Press.

SOLOW, ROBERT M. 1975. "The Intelligent Citizen's Guide to Inflation." *The Public Interest* 38 (Winter): 30–66.

SPARROW, PAUL R. 1986. "Job Performance among Older Workers." *Ageing International* 13 (Autumn/Winter): 5–6, 22.

STAINES, GRAHAM L., AND ROBERT P. QUINN. 1979. "American Workers Evaluate the Quality of Their Jobs." *Monthly Labor Review* 102 (January): 3–12.

STEUERLE, EUGENE, AND P. WILSON. 1987. "The Earned Income Tax Credit." *Focus* 10 (Spring): 1–8.

STOREY, JAMES R. 1983. Testimony before the Health and Long-term Care Subcommittee, House Select Committee on Aging (May 5).

STREIB, GORDON F., AND CLEMENT J. SCHNEIDER. 1971. *Retirement in American Society*. Ithaca, N.Y.: Cornell University Press.

Task Force on Long-Term Care Policies. 1987. *Report to Congress and the Secretary* [of HHS]. Washington, D.C.: U.S. Government Printing Office.

Task Force on Women and Social Security. 1975. *Women and Social Security: Adapting to a New Era*. Prepared for the Special Senate Committee on Aging. Washington, D.C.: U.S. Government Printing Office.

TELL, EILEEN J.; M. A. COHEN; AND S. S. WALLACK. 1987. "Life Care at Home: A New Model for Financing and Delivering Long-term Care." *Inquiry* 24 (Fall): 245–252.

THOMPSON, LAWRENCE H. 1974. *An Analysis of the Factors Currently Determining Benefit Level Adjustments in the Social Security Program*. Technical Analysis Paper No. 1. Office of Income Security Policy, Office of the Assistant Secretary of Planning and Evaluation. Washington, D.C.: Department of Health, Education, and Welfare.

THOMPSON, LAWRENCE H., AND PAUL N. VAN DE WATER. 1975. "The Short-Run Behavior of the Social Security Trust Funds." *Technical Analysis Paper*, No. 8. Washington, D.C.: Office of Income Security Policy, Department of Health, Education, and Welfare.

THUROW, LESTER. 1976. "Tax Wealth, Not Income." *New York Times Magazine* (11 April): 32.

TIBBITTS, CLARK. 1977. "Older Americans in the Family Context." *Aging* (April–May): 6–11.

TILOVE, ROBERT. 1976. *Public Employee Pension Funds*. Twentieth Century Fund. New York: Columbia University Press.

TISSUE, THOMAS. 1978. "Response to Recipiency Under Public Assistance and SSI." *Social Security Bulletin* 41 (November): 3–15.

TORDA, THEODORE S. 1972. "The Impact of Inflation on the Elderly." *Federal Reserve Bank of Cleveland Monthly Review* (October–November): 3–19.

TORREY, BARBARA BOYLE. 1982. "Guns vs. Canes. The Fiscal Implications of an Aging Population." *American Economic Association Papers and Proceedings* (May): 309–313.

TRACY, MARTIN B. 1987. "Credit-Splitting and Private Pension Awards in Divorce." *Research on Aging* 9 (March): 148–159.

TURNBULL, JOHN G.; C. ARTHUR WILLIAMS, JR.; AND EARL F. CHEIT. 1967. *Economic and Social Security*, 3rd ed. New York: Ronald Press.

UNIVERSAL SOCIAL SECURITY COVERAGE STUDY GROUP. 1980. *The Desirability and Feasibility of Social Security Coverage for Employees of Federal, State, and Local Governments and Private Non-Profit Organizations*. Report of the Study Group. Washington, D.C.: U.S. Department of Health, Education, and Welfare.

THE URBAN INSTITUTE. 1981. *The Future of State and Local Pensions*. Final Report to Department of Housing and Urban Development. Washington, D.C.: mimeo.

U.S. Bureau of Labor Statistics. 1966. *Retired Couple's Budget for a Moderate Living Standard*. Bulletin No. 1570-4. Washington, D.C.: U.S. Government Printing Office.

———. 1980. *Employee Benefits in Industry: A Pilot Survey*, Report 615. Washington, D.C.: U.S. Department of Labor.

U.S. Bureau of the Census. 1983. *Estimating After-tax Money Income Distribu-*

tions Using Data from the March Current Population Survey. Current Population Reports, Series P-23, No. 126. Washington, D.C.: U.S. Government Printing Office.

———. 1987. *Pensions: Worker Coverage and Retirement Benefits, 1984*. Current Population Reports, Series P-70, No. 12. Washington, D.C.: U.S. Government Printing office.

U.S. Department of Health, Education, and Welfare. 1978. "Major Initiative: Long-Term Care/Community Services." Memorandum, Office of the Secretary. Washington, D.C.: mimeo, July 14.

———. 1979. *Social Security and the Changing Roles of Men and Women*. Report to Congress. Washington, D.C.: U.S. Department of Health, Education, and Welfare.

U.S. Department of Health and Human Services (HHS). 1986. "Increasing the Social Security Retirement Age: Older Workers in Physically Demanding Occupations or Ill Health." *Social Security Bulletin* 49 (October): 5–23.

U.S. Department of Justice, n.d. *The Pension Game: American System from the Viewpoint of the Average Woman*. Task Force on Sex Discrimination, Civil Rights Division. Washington, D.C.: U.S. Government Printing Office.

U.S. Department of Labor. 1965. *The Older American Worker*. Washington,. D.C.: U.S. Department of Labor.

U.S. General Accounting Office (GA0). 1987. *Pension Plans—Many Workers Don't Know When They Can Retire*. Washington, D.C.: GA0.

U.S. House Committee on Education and Labor. 1972. *Interim Staff Report of Activities of the Pension Study Task Force*. Washington, D.C.: Government Printing office.

———. 1978. *Pension Task Force Report on Public Employee Retirement Systems*. Washington, D.C.: U.S. Government Printing Office.

U.S. House Committee on Ways and Means. 1967. *President's Proposals for Revision in the Social Security System*. Hearings, Part 1. Washington, D.C.: U.S. Government Printing Office.

———. 1985. *Report on Earnings Sharing Implementation Study*. Washington, D.C.: U.S. Government Printing Office.

———. 1978. *Poverty Among America's Aged—A Staff Review*. In U.S. House Select Committee on Aging, *Poverty Among America's Aged*. Hearings. Washington, D.C.: U.S. Government Printing Office.

———. 1987. *Longterm Care and Personal Impoverishment*. Washington, D.C.: U.S. Government Printing Office.

U.S. Office of Technology and Assessment (OTA). 1985. *Technology and the Aging in America*. Washington, D.C.: OTA.

U.S. Senate Committee on Finance. 1975. *Report of the Panel on Social Security Financing*. Washington, D.C.: U.S. Government Printing Office.

U.S. Senate Special Committee on Aging. 1970. *The Stake of Today's Workers in Retirement Security*. Washington, D.C.: U.S. Government Printing Office.

———. 1987. *Developments in Aging: 1986*, Vol. 1. Washington, D.C.: U.S. Government Printing Office.

VAN DE WATER, PAUL N. 1979. "Disability Insurance." *American Economic Review* 69 (May): 275–278.

VISCUSI DE WALTER, PAUL N. 1979. *Welfare of the Elderly*. New York: Wiley-Interscience.

WALLICH, HENRY. 1969. "Adjustable Bonds: Purchasing Power Bonds." *Newsweek* (24 November).

WEAVER, WARREN, JR. 1981. "Goal of Retiring at 65 Recedes under Economic Pressure and Population Curve." *New York Times* (9 March): 21.

WELLINGTON, H. H., AND RALPH K. WINTER, JR. 1971. *The Unions and the Cities*. Washington, D.C.: The Brookings Institution.

ZOOK, C., AND F. MOORE. 1980. "High-Cost Users of Medical Care." *New England Journal of Medicine* 302 (May): 96–1002.

INDEX